Racial Capitalism and International Tax Law

Racial Capitalism and International Tax Law

The Story of Global Jim Crow

STEVEN A. DEAN, *JD*

OXFORD
UNIVERSITY PRESS

OXFORD
UNIVERSITY PRESS

Oxford University Press is a department of the University of Oxford.
It furthers the University's objective of excellence in research, scholarship, and education by publishing worldwide. Oxford is a registered trade mark of Oxford University Press in the UK and in certain other countries.

Published in the United States of America by Oxford University Press
198 Madison Avenue, New York, NY 10016, United States of America.

Library of Congress Cataloging-in-Publication Data
Names: Dean, Steven A., author.
Title: Racial Capitalism and International Tax Law : The Story of Global Jim Crow / Steven A. Dean.
Description: New York : Oxford University Press, 2025. |
Includes bibliographical references and index.
Identifiers: LCCN 2025018278 (print) | LCCN 2025018279 (ebook) |
ISBN 9780197525975 (hardback) | ISBN 9780197525982 (updf) | ISBN 9780197525999 (epub) |
ISBN 9780197526002 (online)
Subjects: LCSH: Taxation—Law and legislation—United States. | African Americans—Taxation—Law and legislation. | African Americans—Civil rights. | Race discrimination—Law and legislation—United States. | United States—Race relations—History. | Taxation—Law and legislation. | Race discrimination—Law and legislation. | Black people—Economic conditions. | Ethnicity—Economic aspects.
Classification: LCC KF6289 .D43 2025 (print) | LCC KF6289 (ebook) |
DDC 343.04—dcundefined
LC record available at https://lccn.loc.gov/2025018278
LC ebook record available at https://lccn.loc.gov/2025018279

DOI: 10.1093/9780197526002.001.0001

Printed by Marquis Book Printing, Canada

The manufacturer's authorized representative in the EU for product safety is Oxford University Press España S.A., Parque Empresarial San Fernando de Henares, Avenida de Castilla, 2 – 28830 Madrid (www.oup.es/en or product.safety@oup.com). OUP España S.A. also acts as importer into Spain of products made by the manufacturer.

Note to Readers

This publication is designed to provide accurate and authoritative information in regard to the subject matter covered. It is based upon sources believed to be accurate and reliable and is intended to be current as of the time it was written. It is sold with the understanding that the publisher is not engaged in rendering legal, accounting, or other professional services. If legal advice or other expert assistance is required, the services of a competent professional person should be sought. Also, to confirm that the information has not been affected or changed by recent developments, traditional legal research techniques should be used, including checking primary sources where appropriate.

(Based on the Declaration of Principles jointly adopted by a Committee of the American Bar Association and a Committee of Publishers and Associations.)

For Ruth Dean, who showed me what it means to be fearless

Contents

Acknowledgments ix

Introduction: Tax and the Origins of Global Inequality 1

1. The Perils of Precision 20
2. A Surprising Generosity 44
3. The Rise of Global Jim Crow 60
4. US Power and Global Jim Crow 79
5. Contesting Global Jim Crow 95
6. Global Jim Crow's Pyrrhic Victory 113
7. Beyond Global Jim Crow 142

Conclusion: Fear of a Black Planet 162

Index 173

Acknowledgments

This book has been fueled by contributions from so many people across so many institutions. Support from friends and family has been the most important. Felipe Ossa has been there for me through thick and thin. Eileen Luhr taught me a great deal and encouraged me at crucial moments. Dana Brakman Reiser's bottomless confidence in me helped me to believe in myself. Betty Peña helped keep me sane. Attiya Waris taught me about courage. John Cox generously shared his artwork for the cover. Christine Gray and Juli Zanetta have been far away, but their love and support have always felt close. My father passed away just as this project began, but, as you will see, my mother has been an integral part of the writing and research. My son's passion for birds and ecology has been a constant source of inspiration.

The roots of this book extend back three decades to my time as a research assistant at KPMG's Economic Consulting Services, where I first learned about transfer pricing. Professor Sam Thompson formally introduced me to international tax law and invited me to work with him as he advised South Africa's tax authorities on reforming their corporate tax system. Professors Owen Fiss and Sara Suleri Goodyear offered a law school class on the legacy of colonialism in Africa, sowing seeds that would find fertile ground in my growing understanding of how global tax policy operates.

The book may seem disconnected from my early international tax scholarship, but the opposite is true. Parts of the book, particularly Chapters 1, 4, and 6, are based on articles I published as a junior scholar, initially trying to make sense of the blatant injustices in a global tax system that everyone assured me was designed in good faith to maximize global economic welfare. My first article *Attractive Complexity: Tax Deregulation, the Check-the-Box Election, and the Future of Tax Simplification*, published in the Hofstra Law Review, forms a critical part of Chapter 4's exploration of US power. *Neither Rules Nor Standards*, published in the Notre Dame Law Review, is essentially Chapter 1. *More Cooperation, Less Uniformity: Tax Deharmonization and the Future of the International Tax Regime*, published in the Tulane Law Review, forms much of Chapter 6.

I am grateful for detailed feedback from Dana Brakman Reiser, Alex Cobham, Alison Lacroix, Eileen Luhr, Emmanuel Mauleón, and Linda Sydänmaanlakka. I am also thankful for helpful input received in connection with presentations at Boston University's Global Development Policy Center; the 2025 American Society of International Law International Economic Law Interest Group Biennial Conference on International Economic Law; Tax in Politics, Politics in Tax: A Dialogue on the Political Economy of Tax Laws; the 2025 Annual Meeting of the Law & Society Association; the NYC-DSA Campaign to Tax the Rich; Race and Tax: Looking Beyond the Borders and Tax Exempt Organizations at the Center for Taxpayer Rights; the 2024 National Tax Association Spring Symposium; Past & Future of Global Tax Justice at the University of Zurich; the University of Minnesota Law School Faculty Workshop; Jay Butler's International Business Transactions class at the University of Virginia; the 2024 Critical Approaches to Taxation and Society Network Conference: Taxation Without Borders; Roundtable for UN Special Mandates on the Linkages Between Tax Justice and Human Rights; Temple Law School; Aston University (UK), Institute for Forensic Linguistics; the 2024 Association of American Law Schools Annual Meeting; the 2023 National Tax Association Annual Conference; the Barbara Jordan Lecture at Boston University School of Law; Global Tax Governance at a Crossroads, Kenya School of Revenue Administration and University of Nairobi; Taxing People: The Next 100 Years Conference, Oxford University; Law, Identity, and Economic Development in the Post-Colonial Era: The Case of the Northern Atlantic and Larger Caribbean Regions, Princeton University; The Tax Committee of the International Law Association Research Seminar; The Federal Income Tax: Racially Blind But Not Racially Neutral, American Tax Policy Institute; the Amsterdam Centre for Tax Law, University of Amsterdam; the Joint Center for Political and Economic Studies: Improving Tax Policy for Black Communities; the Washington & Lee Law Faculty Workshop; and the Cambridge Tax Policy Workshop. Last but not least, it was a special privilege to present this work at the United Nations Economic and Social Council Special Meeting on International Cooperation in Tax Matters.

Throughout working on this project, I have had no shortage of excellent administrative support from Simone Clemente, David Kleinman, Anthony Pietrangelo, Beth Pollastro, Joanne Tapia, Sabine Tessono, and Krista Woods. Top-notch research assistants have included Kitwana Akindele, Temitope Banjo, Roselyn Cantu, Kalina Hannsz, Danna Lopez-Flores,

Thanaa Mahmoudi, Shivani Patel, and Erin Ryu. Support from Dean Angela Onwuachi-Willig and the exceptional students in each of my Taxation and Racial Capitalism seminars at Boston University helped make the book what it is. At Oxford, I am grateful to Getsy Deva Kirubai and the NewGen production team, as well as to Jacqueline Larabee and Brian Stone. The errors are all mine, but there would have been many more without their generous help. To all those I have forgotten to thank by name, please accept my apologies along with my gratitude.

Introduction

Tax and the Origins of Global Inequality

> When someone shows you who they are, believe them the first time. People know themselves much better than you do. That's why it's important to stop expecting them to be something other than who they are.
>
> Maya Angelou

Balloons

As a girl growing up in Fargo, my mother may have dreamed of one day chatting with a prince at a party. She would go on to do precisely that after marrying a man from a soon-to-be-independent British colony. Mom caught the attention of the future King Charles III as she collected four helium balloons—one for each of her children—at a Bahamian independence celebration in 1973.

Before independence put her on the path to a new career, mom had been a nurse. The end of colonial rule meant many things, including celebrations. It also produced significant change for her and so many others. Once free of colonial rule, Bahamians faced the daunting reality of building a country. That demanded delivering the public services long denied to Bahamians. She became a guidance counselor at one of the newly created high schools in a freshly independent Bahamas.

As in many colonies, no real public secondary education system existed before self-government arrived in the islands. Government High earned that name by being the only one of its kind serving Nassau, the British colony's bustling capital. Demands for a public education system that served all the new nation's people created an opportunity. Mom returned to school and earned a master's degree in education. Along with thousands of others from

Racial Capitalism and International Tax Law. Steven A. Dean, Oxford University Press. © Steven A. Dean 2025.
DOI: 10.1093/9780197526002.003.0001

her adopted home, she served generations of young people who would not have received an education when Britain exercised control.

Had there been a real public education system in the Bahamas when my father was young, my parents might never have met. Happily for me and my sisters, he went to high school before decolonization. He did not attend Government High but went to a school my grandfather had helped build, nestled within a Benedictine monastery called St. Augustine's. His teachers decided that he should continue his education and steered him toward a Benedictine college in Minnesota. From there, he found his way to North Dakota to study engineering, where he and mom met.

That North Dakotan transplant tended to catch the attention of her many former students. "Mrs. Dean!" became a refrain of my childhood whenever I navigated Nassau's streets with her. Although one of the more recognizable, she was far from the only educator (and education only one of many demands of a newly empowered electorate) to balloon the young nation's payroll. She may not have been paid handsomely, but over decades, her compensation and that of countless others represented a meaningful sum.

Mom's modest paycheck would, in fact, irrevocably alter the course of global tax policy. Her salary catalyzed the profound transformation documented in the following chapters. Prince Charles noticed those balloons, but he may have been thinking of the cumulative pay she and many others would soon collect as new states asserted their sovereignty. After all, the unpaid salaries of legions of teachers and doctors the British Empire never hired had helped make him unimaginably wealthy.

A Remarkable Generosity

Today, it may be hard for tax experts to imagine a global tax system that showered vulnerable countries in tax revenues. They might find the prospect of an international tax system not dominated by a club of rich countries and its handiwork impossible to picture. But the system they know today is not much older than I am, only taking shape as the last great empire collapsed.

When my father attended high school at St. Augustine's, the United Nations—succeeding the defunct League of Nations—controlled global tax policy. The quiet coup that allowed a small group of wealthy states to dominate global taxation came later.[1] Direct imperial control could no longer fend off the financial burden of his education—or my mother's paycheck—so Global Jim Crow was born.

Armed with the knowledge that the tax treaties that form the backbone of today's global tax system offer unproven benefits for—while imposing clear costs on—poor countries, experts have asked why poor countries would sign them.[2] The question has generally been framed as one of competence. President John F. Kennedy's chief tax advisor, Stanley Surrey, opined that "although the more astute negotiators from developing countries saw the problem for them in using the OECD treaty . . . developing countries . . . being new to international tax negotiations . . . lacked the experience and insight necessary to reshape [treaties] in a direction to benefit them."[3] But

[1] Mehrsa Baradaran uses the term to describe the impact of neoliberalism's adherents in the US domestic context. MEHRSA BARADARAN, THE QUIET COUP: NEOLIBERALISM AND THE LOOTING OF AMERICA (2024). Quinn Slobodian tells the story of today's unequal international economic law as a triumph of neoliberalism. QUINN SLOBODIAN, GLOBALISTS: THE END OF EMPIRE AND THE BIRTH OF NEOLIBERALISM (2018).

[2] *See* Charles R. Irish, *International Double Taxation Agreements and Income Taxation at Source*, 23 INT'L & COMP. L.Q. 292, 292 (1974) ("In a developing country, nobody would propose unrestricted grants in aid from his country to a developed one. And yet, the practical effect of the present network of double taxation agreements between developed and developing countries is to shift substantial amounts of income tax revenues to which developing countries have a strong legitimate and equitable claim from their treasuries to those of developed countries."); Kim Brooks & Richard Krever, *The Troubling Role of Tax Treaties*, in TAX DESIGN ISSUES WORLDWIDE 159, 160 (Geerten M. M. Michielse & Victor Thuronyi eds., 2015) ("The tragedy for low-income countries is that the success of the high-income states in negotiating ever more treaties has come at the expense of the tax revenue bases of low-income countries. These treaties may be a true 'poisoned chalice' for developing countries, perversely transferring tax revenue from low-income countries to high-income countries (and from low-income countries to multinationals) while yielding limited or no offsetting benefits such as increased foreign direct investment. Surprisingly, however, sceptical questioning by scholars of the need for tax treaties as a way of dividing taxing rights between nations is a relatively recent phenomenon."); other scholars have taken a more nuanced view. *See, e.g.*, Eric M. Zolt, *Tax Treaties and Developing Countries*, 72 TAX L. REV. 111, 147 (2018) ("For some, perhaps many, developing countries, it makes little economic sense to enter into tax treaties with developed countries. The game is not worth the candle. The potential tax revenues lost under either OECD or UN-type tax treaties do not justify the gains from increased foreign investment and the other treaty benefits (such as information exchanges with other countries and assistance in collection of taxes). But for many other developing countries, the decision about whether to enter into tax treaties with developed countries is more complex.").

[3] STANLEY S. SURREY, A HALF-CENTURY WITH THE INTERNAL REVENUE CODE: THE MEMOIRS OF STANLEY S. SURREY 284 (Lawrence A. Zelenak & Ajay K. Mehrotra eds., 2022) ("[S]oon the more astute negotiators from the developing countries saw the problem for them in using the OECD treaty. That treaty, in its solution to the elimination or reduction of double taxation, was based on relinquishment of jurisdiction to tax by the country of the source of the income. This was supplemented, where taxation at source remained, by provision for a foreign tax credit or exemption of foreign income in the country of residence. As between developed countries, this solution worked reasonably well for they were both countries of the source of income through investment or trade from the other countries and also countries from whence investment or trade originated. Hence no country appreciably lost tax revenues under the OECD Model—the revenue lost through relinquishment of source jurisdiction was made up either through the revenue gained by consequently lower foreign tax credits, or in exemption countries through an increase in profits of their enterprises. But developing

"poor preparation"[4] does not account for the sweeping structural changes that occurred just as those Ruth Deans stood poised to earn salaries as nurses and teachers.

Asking why the vulnerable embrace suboptimal legal arrangements can reveal important insights. But often, the explanation lies in their vulnerability.[5] Equally uninteresting would be why the wealthy and privileged would exploit those advantages to extract painful concessions from others.

This book poses a different set of questions. Why would rich countries ever do the opposite? Why would a wealthy and powerful state implement a remarkably generous approach to international taxation and embrace it for nearly half a century? And why would the allure of self-interest break the spell at the precise moment it did?[6]

countries were almost entirely countries of the source of income, and did not have enterprises engaged to a significant extent in investment or trade in other countries. The OECD Model, with its emphasis on reduction in source taxation, thus would mean for these developing countries a revenue loss without a compensating revenue gain. Many developing countries were therefore dissatisfied with the OECD Model. But, often being new to international tax negotiations, they lacked the experience and insight necessary to reshape the OECD Model in a direction to benefit them.").

[4] Martin Hearson, Imposing Standards: The North-South Dimension to Global Tax Politics 19 (2021) ("It was an admission of past mistakes by a civil servant that originally motivated this research project. While I was researching tax planning by a multinational company in Ghana, a tax policy official told me that his country had lost out in tax treaty negotiations through poor preparation and had not fully taken into account the way treaties could allow certain jurisdictions to act as conduits for tax avoidance. Empirical legal research often highlights deficits in the knowledge, capacity, and ideas of those making the decisions. As early as 1974, Charles Irish, reflecting on his experience in Zambia, bemoaned lower-income countries' 'unawareness of the adverse nature of double taxation agreements' and 'unquestioned acceptance of the status quo.'")

[5] Táíwò reexamines the fable of the Emperor's New Clothes and asks "not why the townspeople believe the emperor, but rather why they are acting as if they believe the emperor" allowing for the possibility that what "all those townspeople cheering the naked emperor were thinking might simply and plausibly be: 'If I don't play along with the emperor, something bad might happen to me.'" Olúfẹ́mi O. Táíwò, Elite Capture: How the Powerful Took Over Identity Politics (And Everything Else) 20 (2022).

[6] *See* Thomas Rixen, *From Double Tax Avoidance to Tax Competition: Explaining the Institutional Trajectory of International Tax Governance*, Rev. Int'l. Pol. Econ. 197, 207 (2011) ("[W]hile the basic principles were established by the League of Nations in the 1920s and early 1930s, the regime remained largely dormant. In 1928, 35 DTAs were in force. In the 1950s the regime was still of limited practical significance. While the bilateral treaty network grew (from 108 in 1948 to 263 in 1958), the number of DTAs in force was still low. After the Second World War, the OECD replaced the League of Nations, and briefly the United Nations, as the main multilateral policy forum for discussion of international tax issues."). Rixen insists that tax avoidance was a risk that experts creating the double tax treaty foresaw but did not intend. He also observes that double tax treaties remained dormant until the 1960s, when the negative consequences of the embrace of tax treaties—driven by the "sheer magnitude of multinational activity"—would have been obvious. *Id* at 212 ("What governments could not foresee was that the sheer magnitude of multinational activity, and the increasing importance of intangible assets would one day overburden tax administrations' capacities of effective enforcement. Thus, while policymakers did foresee that taxpayers could more easily engage in tax avoidance and evasion in an international economic environment, this problem was not given priority. It was feared that restrictive measures would harm efforts to liberalize trade and investment—the primary objective at the time of the regime's establishment.") Timing matters, and it was only upon seeing a chart

Tax and Jim Crow

This book tells the story of what happened after the celebrations ended and imperial control gave way to independence. It highlights the rise of a global tax system that quietly did for the world what racially discriminatory policies achieved in the United States for a century after slavery's end.[7] Theoretically free to pursue an education, Black Americans found themselves universally denied the opportunity to attend schools comparable to those provided to white Americans (or, in some cases, to attend school at all).

The US system of Jim Crow, like South Africa's Apartheid, embodied a complex mixture of restrictions and requirements that denied Black Americans fundamental rights and freedoms. Its brutal violence and legally sanctioned discrimination would endure until the 1960s. Jim Crow ensured that Americans lived separate lives divided by the color of their skin.

Although separate, those lives need not have been unequal. Tax laws played a key role in creating the inequality.[8] Black Americans paid taxes,

in an article by Ash and Marian tracing the evolution of the language of treaties that I understood how irrelevant the regime had been prior to the 1960s. Elliott Ash & Omri Marian, *The Making of International Tax Law: Empirical Evidence from Tax Treaties Text*, 24 Fla. Tax Rev. 151, 168 figs. 1 & 2, 171 fig. 3 (2020) (illustrating the dramatic change in the trajectory of treaties coinciding with the creation of the OECD).

[7] Jim Crow in the United States and neocolonialism both represent outgrowths of the end of the direct control of slavery and colonialism. In his seminal work, Anghie explains that just as slavery lies at the core of US racial inequality, colonialism and bias have shaped international law in ways that harm the Global South. Antony Anghie, Imperialism, Sovereignty and the Making of International Law 3 (2005) ("My broad argument is that colonialism was central to the constitution of international law in that many of the basic doctrines of international law—including, most importantly, sovereignty doctrine—were forged out of the attempt to create a legal system that could account for relations between the European and non-European worlds in the colonial confrontation. In making this argument, I focus on the colonial origins of international law; I attempt, furthermore, to show how these origins create a set of structures that continually repeat themselves at various stages in the history of international law. In so doing I seek to challenge conventional histories of the discipline which present colonialism as peripheral, an unfortunate episode that has long since been overcome by the heroic initiatives of decolonization that resulted in the emergence of colonial societies as independent, sovereign states. I examine the relationship between international law and colonialism by focusing on the civilizing mission, the grand project that has justified colonialism as a means of redeeming the backward, aberrant, violent, oppressed, undeveloped people of the non-European world by incorporating them into the universal civilization of Europe.").

[8] Segregation did not, on its own, impoverish Black Americans. A host of apparently racially neutral legal regimes accomplished that. Tax law, the country's primary tool for redistributing wealth, arguably played the most important role in sustaining the enormous racial wealth gap between white and Black Americans. *See* Dorothy A. Brown, The Whiteness of Wealth: How the Tax System Impoverishes Black Americans—And How We Can Fix It (2021); Andrew W. Kahrl, The Black Tax: 150 Years of Theft, Exploitation, and Dispossession in America (2024). Countless other legal regimes and policy choices did the same, ranging from the banking system to the creation of US highways. *See* Mehrsa Baradaran, The Color of Money: Black Banks and

but "unequal tax structures . . . deployed by all-white school boards and excise boards . . . ensure[d] that black schools received a tiny fraction of the resources due them and that in many cases African Americans were doubly taxed for the support of white schooling."[9] Armed with the *Plessy v. Ferguson* mandate of separate but equal,[10] more than a few courageously challenged those results in court during the first half of the twentieth century. Despite repeated courthouse wins challenging flagrant violations of the obligation to ensure that separate schools did not mean no schools at all, US states and cities proved endlessly resourceful in finding new ways to deny education to Black children.

For example, "a Kentucky state statute . . . designated all corporate property taxes for the benefit of white schools only."[11] In her book *Racial Taxation*,

THE RACIAL WEALTH GAP (2017); Deborah N. Archer, "*White Men's Roads Through Black Men's Homes*": *Advancing Racial Equity Through Highway Reconstruction*, 73 VAND. L. REV. 1259 (2020).

[9] CAMILLE WALSH, RACIAL TAXATION: SCHOOLS, SEGREGATION, AND TAXPAYER CITIZENSHIP, 1869–1973, at 12 (2018). Walsh documents the persistent efforts Black Americans made in demanding fair treatment as taxpayers. She notes that, ironically, their arguments would be turned against them during subsequent debates over desegregation of schools. *Id.* at 85 ("Ultimately, one of the most common refrains in the grassroots debates around judicial desegregation from 1954 to 1970 was . . . that those speaking in opposition to desegregation were the taxpayers and had a legal right as 'taxpaying citizens' to an all-white educational experience. The same argument that African American citizens had attempted to deploy before the Brown case was now put forth vehemently by segregationists as the reason Brown's ruling should not be implemented.").

[10] The famous phrase "separate but equal" does not appear in the majority opinion that provided the foundation for Jim Crow. It was used by the lone dissenting Justice John Marshall Harlan, a onetime slaveholder from Kentucky. Harlan warned that "The destinies of the two races in this country are indissolubly linked together, and the interests of both require that the common government of all shall not permit the seeds of race hate to be planted under the sanction of law." Plessy v. Ferguson, 163 U.S. 537, 560 (1896).

[11] After the discriminatory tax rule was successfully challenged, white legislators, courts, and administrators repeatedly found ways to flout the ruling. WALSH, *supra* note 9, at 52 ("In that case, the state court of appeals ruled that the law was unconstitutional, and held that corporate taxes should be distributed between white and black schools based on proportion of students. The court stated that 'a corporation cannot be said to have color; it is neither white nor black,' and that the attempt by the legislature to treat the race of a corporation's shareholders as determinative of the 'race' of the corporation, and therefore of the beneficiary of its tax payments, violated the equal protection clause. The Kentucky legislature passed a new law in 1920 that provided that certain cities should consolidate their black and white boards of education under a single board, which also meant the consolidation of the school tax fund and the end of separate black and white taxes. White school boards sought ways to escape the implications of this law and avoid consolidation, but the state court of appeals held that they had to implement the legislation. The next workaround by white taxpayers and school boards came the following year, when the City of Pineville consolidated separate schools under one board but refused to make any levies in support of black schools until John Moore, an African American 'citizen and taxpayer,' filed suit to demand they provide support for black education. After his litigation commenced, the board did finally meet and issue a levy for black schools, but in their later appeal the state court found that the levy was issued 'too late' in the year and reversed the lower-court ruling in favor of Moore. While the court did affirm generally that white taxpayers in some cases could be taxed in support of black schools after 1920, in the actual case at hand, the court nonetheless refused to provide a remedy to address the failure of the consolidated board in Pineville to support black schools. Following this, an unpublished summary judgment opinion in 1926 and a

Camille Walsh details the lengths those in power went to—even after decisive losses—to ensure that Black schools received little or no funding. A Kentucky court properly found that the Kentucky corporate property tax statute violated the Equal Protection Clause of the US Constitution's 14th Amendment, enshrined in the wake of the Civil War to prevent such discrimination. But the court's ruling changed nothing. Walsh documents fruitless lawsuits over many years by Black taxpayers—eventually with the assistance of the National Association for the Advancement of Colored People—attempting to secure support for Black schools after that hollow victory.

When the Supreme Court in *Brown v. Board of Education* concluded that "[s]eparate educational facilities are inherently unequal," it effectively conceded that laws delivering unequal funding for education would remain a fixture of the nation's landscape.[12] The Supreme Court acknowledged that not even a constitutional amendment designed for that express purpose could prevent such discrimination. Indeed, three post-Civil War amendments crafted to carve a place for Black Americans in the nation's civic life could not prevent Jim Crow tax laws from redirecting Black resources away from Black communities as the nation—and for a time, the world—looked on indifferently.

Seligman's Treaties

Settler colonialism may be universal, but Jim Crow represents an American story. In key respects, so does Global Jim Crow. Denying millions of Black Americans the right to vote produced profound inequality within the United States. Preemptively excluding Black countries from the global tax policymaking structure achieved the same for billions, making independence's promise hollow.

restatement of that opinion in a 1928 case both clarified that, in white independent school districts, white taxpayers could not be made to support black schools within the boundaries of their previously organized districts. In their holding, the court said that a 1926 statute under contention 'was never intended to burden that race with the duty to also educate the pupils therein belonging to the race not so organizing.'").

[12] Brown v. Board of Education, 347 U.S. 483, 495 (1954). Today, inequality in the resources provided to schools serving Black and white Americans remains pervasive. At the time, the Court accepted that "Negro and white schools . . . have been equalized, or are being equalized, with respect to buildings, curricula, qualifications and salaries of teachers, and other 'tangible' factors." *Id.* at 492. The Court's ruling was anchored in a conclusion that to "separate [children] from others of similar age and qualifications solely because of their race generates a feeling of inferiority as to their status in the community that may affect their hearts and minds in a way unlikely ever to be undone." *Id.* at 494.

In her influential book, *The New Jim Crow: Mass Incarceration in the Age of Colorblindness,* Michelle Alexander argues that after Jim Crow ended, racial bias in the US criminal justice system recreated it. Alexander details how mass incarceration, felon disenfranchisement, and countless other legal burdens reconstruct Jim Crow's inequality. In the Preface to the tenth-anniversary edition, she notes that immigration restrictions—with "mass deportations" serving as an echo of mass incarceration—lent her New Jim Crow an international dimension.[13]

Alexander does not attempt to trace the origins of the legal frameworks that entrench cross-border inequality. Others have detailed the rise of barriers that produced a global segregation fueled by racism. Adam Mckeown shows, for example, that "most of the basic principles of border control . . . were developed from the 1880s to the 1910s through the exclusion of Asians from white settler nations."[14] The following chapters reveal that legal technologies designed in the 1920s to strip tax sovereignty from nominally independent states only became entrenched in the 1950s and 1960s. As former imperial powers lost the authority to directly prevent spending on public services in what had become majority-Black states, the generous approach in place for nearly half a century suddenly lost its appeal.

The economic threat represented by dad's education loomed. The United Nations, transformed by an influx of sovereign states from the Global South, could not be counted on to contain it. Without a dramatic rewrite of the global tax rulebook, former colonies would be free—even encouraged—to collect taxes sufficient to fund schools and other public services. If they chose to impose tax burdens on multinational corporations doing business within their borders, no legal barriers would prevent them from doing so. Long-standing US international tax rules actually invited them to do so.

[13] Immigration restrictions create a form of segregation on a global scale. In the Preface to the tenth-anniversary edition of her influential book, *The New Jim Crow,* Alexander notes that although her work focuses on the domestic consequences of mass incarceration, immigration restrictions—"mass deportations"—form part of the New Jim Crow she describes. *See* MICHELLE ALEXANDER, THE NEW JIM CROW: MASS INCARCERATION IN THE AGE OF COLORBLINDNESS xvii–xviii (2020) ("[T]he modest criminal justice reforms that were achieved during the Obama administration coincided with the expansion of the system of mass deportation. At the same time that the administration was phasing out federal contracts for private prisons, it was making enormous investments in private detention centers for immigrants, including the granting of a $1 billion contract to Corrections Corporation of America, the nation's largest prison company (recently renamed Core Civic), to build a massive detention facility for women and children seeking asylum from Central America.").

[14] ADAM M. MCKEOWN, MELANCHOLY ORDER: ASIAN MIGRATION AND THE GLOBALIZATION OF BORDERS 2 (2008).

The United States devised a solution that suggests that in global tax policy "so far as the rights of blacks were concerned, race prejudice was, practically, the supreme law of the land."[15] In 1960, anti-Black discrimination was both legal and ubiquitous at home. With Africa's decolonization dawning, it formed an all-white international organization called the Organisation for Economic Co-operation and Development (OECD) and tasked it with tax policy.[16]

As described in Chapter 3, the United States embraced a vision heavily influenced by Edwin Seligman, a Columbia University professor linked to the Dunning School, notorious intellectual apologists for Jim Crow.[17] The treaties Seligman helped craft have been decried for "reallocating tax revenues" by delivering "regressive redistribution—to the benefit of the developed countries at the expense of the developing ones."[18] Jim Crow again made separate unequal, this time on a global scale.

My father learned from monks because King Charles III's grandfather refused to educate him. The need for Global Jim Crow emerged only as independence fueled new demands for public services, including education. It became necessary when colonialism could no longer directly safeguard the interests of such men.

The OECD charter would not be signed until my father was bundled up in the frigid north. As decolonization progressed, the number of newly independent states in the Global South grew, lending them an ever-louder voice in the United Nations. With business interests fearful of the power of those newly enfranchised states, the Organisation for European Economic Co-operation members joined Canada and the United States to create their exclusive group.[19]

[15] Plessy, 163 U.S. at 563. Harlan was speaking of the system that would evolve into Jim Crow not Global Jim Crow. Of course, in practice the two are very different. But the urgency of the impulse to constrain Black agency unites the two.

[16] The United States defines "white" as "having origins in any of the original peoples of Europe, the Middle East, or North Africa. It includes people who indicate their race as 'White' or report responses such as German, Irish, English, Italian, Lebanese, and Egyptian." *Race*, U.S. CENSUS BUREAU (Mar. 30, 2023), https://www.census.gov/topics/population/race.html. Japan joined the OECD in 1964. It would remain the only non-white member until Mexico joined in 1994 and Korea became a member in 1996. More recently, Chile, Columbia, and Costa Rica joined. It has no African members.

[17] *See* Ash & Marian, *supra* note 6, at 168 figs. 1 & 2, 171 fig. 3 (revealing a dramatic change in the trajectory of treaties after the creation of the OECD in 1960).

[18] Tsilly Dagan, *The Tax Treaties Myth*, 32 N.Y.U. J. INT'L L. & POL. 939, 941 (2000).

[19] A key moment in the OECD's rise came in 1954, when the International Chamber of Commerce "formally petitioned these Eurocentric organisations to take up the study of double taxation." *See* NIKKI J. TEO, THE UNITED NATIONS IN GLOBAL TAX COORDINATION 82 (2023).

Within the United States, "African Americans were regarded as a pestilence or as a contagion that necessitated containment or quarantine for fear of its ability to destroy value surrounding it."[20] With African and Caribbean colonies declaring their independence, the OECD served as a critical global bulwark against the source of that virus. As the following chapters will show, that impulse to silence Black voices delivered an impoverished and impoverishing global tax policy that continues to favor global capital over people. In 2023, the OECD declared that its most recent proposal enjoyed the support of "over 90% of global GDP."[21]

The OECD has come to dominate international taxation. Today, it serves as a World Tax Organization in all but name. Deployed at just the right moment to limit the tax sovereignty of Black states, it formed the heart of Global Jim Crow. Embracing its mission "to achieve the highest sustainable economic growth and employment and a rising standard of living in Member countries, while maintaining financial stability, and thus to contribute to the development of the world economy"[22] it would shield the world's wealthy and its multinationals from taxation.[23]

[20] Keeanga-Yamahtta Taylor, Race for Profit: How Banks and the Real Estate Industry Undermined Black Homeownership 18 (2019). ("In the earliest days of the FHA, theories of eugenics and racial inferiority informed its policymaking with regard to Black people. African Americans were regarded as a pestilence or as a contagion that necessitated containment or quarantine for fear of its ability to destroy value surrounding it. Coming to terms with the racism embedded in past federal practices was not about redress, restitution, or repair; instead, it was necessary to contextualize the conditions found in African American communities. Identifying racially inscribed policies, such as redlining, from an earlier era was also critical to implementing new policies that aspired to open up and improve Black housing opportunities. Instead, by ignoring race, new practices that were intended to facilitate inclusion reinforced existing patterns of inequality and discrimination.") Taylor tells the story of continued inequality in US housing as one of racial capitalism in which discrimination fueled the profits of private actors.

[21] Press Release, OECD, 138 Countries and Jurisdictions Agree to Historic Milestone to Implement Global Tax Deal (Jul. 12, 2023), https://www.oecd.org/tax/138-countries-and-jurisdictions-agree-historic-milestone-to-implement-global-tax-deal.htm. Wei Cui offers a skeptical view of the notion of widespread consensus on the OECD's pillar two global minimum tax proposal. Wei Cui, *Strategic Incentives for Adopting the Global Minimum Tax*, 16 J. Legal Analysis 211, 211–212 (2024) ("Many readers of global news headlines may have formed the impression that nations are marching in unison in taxing MNEs. . . . In the USA, however, the global minimum tax remains deeply controversial. . . . Many G20 countries (e.g., China, India, Brazil, and Indonesia) that initially lent support to the OECD proposal have not pursued relevant legislation.").

[22] Convention on the Organisation for Economic Co-operation and Development art. 1, Dec. 14, 1960, 888 U.N.T.S. 12736.

[23] Bret Wells & Cym Lowell, *Tax Base Erosion and Homeless Income: Collection at Source is the Linchpin*, 65 Tax L. Rev. 535, 537 (2012) (detailing how the OECD's treaties "enshrined residency country entitlement to tax residual income as the foundational principle" that "provided the implements to erode the tax base of countries adopting the foundational premise" and "in turn, provided a fertile field for the growth of income that is not effectively taxed in any country").

The Costs of Statehood

During the colonial era, metropoles proved reluctant to authorize spending on education or healthcare. "Colonies that struggled to make their budgets balance were particularly wary of public investments that would commit them to future spending. This included building schools and hospitals, which would need to be maintained and staffed in future years."[24] Devoting revenues collected in the metropoles to pay for such crucial services remained unthinkable.

In the transition to independence, new nations aimed to remedy those failures. Now sovereign, they needed no permission from elsewhere to build schools and hospitals. But even in states that "dramatically increased their spending on services like education and healthcare, neglected during the colonial period . . . these increases were ultimately unsustainable"[25] because of Global Jim Crow.

Education for the masses in newly independent states represented a long-held dream for countless young people. For others, it represented a path to a gratifying career. For wealthy states, though, that public education loomed as a vast entitlement. In the near term, funding paychecks for the teachers, guidance counselors, doctors, nurses, and other public servants necessary to address the long-unmet needs of former colonies would hardly promote the highest living standards within the OECD.[26]

Had the OECD not seized control of global tax policymaking from the United Nations, its members feared indirectly paying those salaries in the form of higher tax burdens on its multinationals. The generosity that helped

[24] Leigh A. Gardner, Taxing Colonial Africa: The Political Economy of British Imperialism 10 (2012) ("Fiscal issues therefore played a central role in the design and implementation of not only those colonial policies related to taxing and spending, but also policies which determined what infrastructure to build and where, which industries should receive government favour, and who should be educated and receive healthcare. The potential impact on present and future budgets was a primary consideration in all policy decisions made by the colonial state, and therefore a dominant influence in shaping African experiences of colonial rule.").

[25] *Id.* at 227. Gardner suggests that the failure of African tax systems not only prevented them from providing the hoped-for social services but contributed to the rise of dictatorships. *Id.* at 245. ("With the transfer of power came widespread optimism that independence would allow for the provision of services, particularly education, at a more generous level than colonial authorities had allowed. However, these hopes were dashed as the tax systems established by colonial governments were unable to cope with the demands of democracy, and the political systems of many independent African countries descended into single-party autocracy and military rule.").

[26] Nana Ama Sarfo, *How the OECD Became the World's Tax Leader*, 98 Tax Notes Int'l 624, 625 (2020) ("When the OECD sat down to discuss double taxation in the wake of World War II. . . . [t]he organization was more concerned with facilitating economic relationships between its member states and boosting those states economically.").

rebuild Europe twice—and that quietly supported a transition to sovereignty for the Philippines in 1946 and for India and Indonesia in the following year—could have helped deliver the freedom colonized people in Africa and the Caribbean had long been denied. Instead, the world has the OECD's vast network of double tax treaties and Global Jim Crow.

The global tax system that the OECD methodically unmade beginning with its creation in 1960—on the same day the UN General Assembly adopted the Declaration on the Granting of Independence to Colonial Countries and Peoples—had already eliminated double taxation. The unlikely story of what is still known as the "foreign" tax credit begins in the closing days of World War I. The United States took an equally principled and practical stand, with Congress offering investors a bargain. If US investors paid income taxes in other countries on cross-border profits the United States would ordinarily tax, the United States would deem those non-US taxes to have been paid to the US Treasury.

That cross-border tax subsidy proved controversial, even when it benefited Europe. Seligman noted that it "represented what was an extraordinarily generous measure for its time: the United States was assuming sole responsibility for the costs of reducing the double taxation of its residents and citizens."[27] On the brink of defeating Germany and demanding billions of dollars in war reparations, the United States made an astonishing "present of . . . revenue"[28] to Germany.

In the wake of World War I, an inward-looking United States had no interest in directly rebuilding Europe. Nor was it willing to stand by while the continent languished. The tax credit reflected a compromise, relying on private investment as a subsidized substitute for direct aid. The United States hoped its "foreign entanglements could remain minimal as long as

[27] Michael J. Graetz & Michael M. O'Hear, *The "Original Intent" of U.S. International Taxation*, 46 Duke L.J. 1021, 1045 (1997).

[28] Edwin R.A. Seligman, Double Taxation and International Fiscal Cooperation 135 (1928). In describing the choice of treaties over the credit, Seligman made no secret of his anxieties over what the credit might mean for a wealthy country. *Id.* at 138 (noting that the "credit, as typified by the practice of the United States, seemed to the committee undesirable for the reasons already mentioned, viz., that unless very carefully restricted it would place the exchequer of each country at the mercy of all the unknown increases of taxation by foreign governments. The committee decided, therefore, in favor of the second principle, namely, the assignment of the income tax to the country of domicile.") Years before, Seligman contributed an essay to a collection on colonial finance for the American Economics Association. Edwin R.A. Seligman, *The French Colonial System*, *in* Essays in Colonial Finance by Members of the American Economic Association 20 (1900). He would have been uniquely positioned to appreciate the potential impact of the credit on the revenues of postcolonial African states.

businessmen were expansionist and public-spirited."[29] The tax credit served that end admirably, paying US investors to serve as private contractors in the effort to rebuild Europe.

Had the OECD's wealthy members been content to be as generous to former African colonies as the United States had been to a defeated Germany, the entire history of global tax policy would have been different. After World War II, the United States doubled down on generosity. It retained the tax credit it had created for Germany and the rest of Europe, now benefiting newly sovereign states in Asia. It also changed course by supplying the direct subsidies it had resisted after World War I.[30] The specter of Africa's decolonization would prompt a different reaction, triggering the creation of Global Jim Crow.[31]

The Cruelty of Global Jim Crow

The cruelty at the heart of Global Jim Crow may seem shocking, but it really should not. The creation of the OECD helped launch an effort to remake the tax landscape—accomplishing indirectly what could no longer be achieved through physical domination—that has all too many parallels. That Kentucky statute—declaring that all corporate property tax revenues should go toward white schools no matter who owned the corporate shares, ensuring that the promise of emancipation would continue to go unfulfilled—offers just one.

A similar story of generosity undone by anti-Black racism appears in *When Affirmative Action Was White: An Untold History of Racial Inequality in*

[29] Emily Rosenberg, Spreading the American Dream: American Economic and Cultural Expansion, 1890–1945, at 139 (1982).

[30] The Marshall Plan delivered billions to Europe's recovery. The lesser-known Point Four did the same for Asia. David Ekbladh, The Great American Mission: Modernization and the Construction of an American World Order 3 (2011) ("[W]hen President Harry Truman announced his global 'Point Four' assistance program . . . the United States abruptly defined much of the world freeing itself of colonial rule as 'underdeveloped.' In this schema, emergence from this historical status could only be accomplished through American aid."). Without the advent of the OECD and Global Jim Crow, Africa would not have benefitted from a postcolonial Marshall Plan. But tax subsidies would have indirectly paid the salaries of its teachers and nurses just as they once did in Germany and France.

[31] It is noteworthy that the shift also exacerbated the impact of globalization, helping fuel Rodrik's hyperglobalization. Dani Rodrik, *Globalization's Wrong Turn: And How It Hurt America*, 98 Foreign Aff. 26, 26 (2019) (noting the influence of the OECD along with the International Monetary Fund and the World Bank in the 1990s "when policymakers set the world on its current hyperglobalist path, requiring domestic economies to be put in the service of the world economy instead of the other way around"). One could argue that without the vast tax treaty network the OECD had built beginning in the 1960s, hyperglobalization would not have been possible.

Twentieth-Century America by Ira Katznelson. That book highlights how excluding Black Americans made the New Deal possible by appeasing Southern Democrats. Katznelson documents the shift in the fortunes of those policies when the demise of Jim Crow made all-white programs impossible. When Black Americans gained access to benefits that had helped countless white families build middle-class lives, those once-popular subsidies suffered.

Heather McGhee offers another example in *The Sum of Us: What Racism Costs Everyone and How We Can Prosper Together*. Faced with the threat of integrating public pools in the mid-twentieth century, McGhee observes that many US cities and towns chose to close them instead. Some, like Montgomery, Alabama, filled those drained pools. Better, it seemed, that nobody have nice things than everyone.

When I began work on this book, I did not suspect that the coded racism of palm trees examined in Chapter 5, which has helped define the last quarter century of global tax policy, had its roots in what may be the ugliest chapter in US history. I intended to expand on my work as a young scholar, exploring the frustrating limitations of global tax policy discourse.

The puzzling embrace of increasingly complex rules at the expense of open-ended standards described in Chapter 1 fascinated me. The faith of experts in facially neutral—but, one might say, inherently unequal—principles like tax harmonization described in Chapter 6 demanded an explanation. I was determined to show how intellectual hubris had allowed good intentions to curdle in the face of growing corporate power.

When I began writing in earnest, it became clear that undue optimism on the part of long-ago experts represented only a fraction of the story. To make sense of a deeply flawed system, today's global tax policy debate needs not more expertise but a different perspective. Its complex rules consistently failed marginalized states not simply because of a lack of capacity or corporate capture but because the fears of another era had corrupted the rulemaking process. I could not truly tell that story without being open about my connection to it. As a result, you will learn about my family as you read about tax credits and the League of Nations.

Many of the failures of today's international tax regime could be traced to a single intervention by a handful of wealthy states that has long gone entirely unnoticed. The convergence of the emancipation of Africa's colonies and the rise of the OECD and its toxic treaties inspired the term Global Jim Crow, echoing a phrase used by Adom Getachew in *Worldmaking After*

Empire: The Rise and Fall of Self-Determination.[32] It served, I thought, as a helpful shorthand for the way racism—not so different from the bias at the heart of the stories McGhee and Katznelson tell—had quietly tainted a critical aspect of international economic law.

The metaphor proved to be eerily apt. Seligman, one of the founding fathers of international tax law and a chief architect of the modern tax treaty, had been appointed to Columbia University's faculty by John W. Burgess. Burgess, Seligman's mentor,[33] hired him as he was assembling what would become an accomplished group of anti-Black scholars.[34] The Dunning School, named after another member of Seligman's Columbia cohort, proved to be talented researchers and educators. And they ruthlessly deployed those skills to marshal flawed histories of the post-US Civil War era, widely inculcating the belief that Black people must not be trusted to wield political power.[35]

To his credit, "William Watson Davis's Columbia doctoral dissertation, published as *The Civil War and Reconstruction in Florida*"—correctly, if somewhat unfashionably in 1913—"insisted that slavery"— rather than states' rights—"was the foundational cause of the Civil War."[36] However, the "scholarly depth and nuance that Davis brought to his study began to crumble when he discussed the role that African Americans played in the Civil War."[37] "In evaluating Davis's book, W. E. B. Du Bois grouped *The Civil War and Reconstruction in Florida* among those works he judged 'Standard—Anti-Negro'" owing to its "dim assessment of African American humanity and agency."[38]

[32] Adom Getachew, Worldmaking After Empire: The Rise and Fall of Self-Determination 21 (2019) (defining a "globalized Jim Crow" as "a set of ideologies and practices of racial domination").

[33] Seligman not only was "attracted to law because of Burgess, his college mentor," but "admired Burgess so much that he sent his son, Eustace, to Amherst College mainly because that was where Burgess was a student." Ajay Mehrotra, *Edwin R.A. Seligman and the Beginnings of the U.S. Income Tax*, 109 Tax Notes 933, 937 (2005).

[34] John David Smith, *Introduction* to The Dunning School: Historians, Race, and the Meaning of Reconstruction 1, 19 (John David Smith & J. Vincent Lowery eds., 2013) ("At Columbia Burgess, and later Dunning, assembled an outstanding social science faculty, including Frank Goodnow in administrative law, Munroe Smith in jurisprudence, Richmond Mayo-Smith in statistics, E. R. A. Seligman in public finance and economic history, Franklin H. Giddings in sociology, John Bates Clark in economics, and Herbert L. Osgood and William M. Sloane in history.").

[35] *See* The Dunning School: Historians, Race, and the Meaning of Reconstruction (John David Smith & J. Vincent Lowery eds., 2013).

[36] Paul Ortiz, *The Not-So-Strange Career of William Watson Davis's* The Civil War and Reconstruction in Florida, *in* The Dunning School: Historians, Race, and the Meaning of Reconstruction 255, 261 (John David Smith & J. Vincent Lowery eds., 2013).

[37] *Id.* at 264.

[38] *Id.* at 267 (Ortiz notes that Davis "variously referred to African Americans as 'semi-barbarous people,' 'slightly above barbarism,' 'hardly above barbarism,'" with "no conception of freedom—except that it exempted them from hard work.").

The Civil War and Reconstruction in Florida became a key Dunning School text. Its enduring success—despite describing Black Americans as "'open-mouthed, thick lipped, insolent, intemperate, offensive, ugly, and incendiary'"[39]—can be credited in part to Seligman. One reviewer acknowledged Seligman by name as he "underscored the book's intellectual pedigree, observing that the text 'has been prepared "under the eye" of Prof. William A. Dunning and with the help of Prof. E. R. A. Seligman.'"[40]

The Global Cost of Silencing Black States

Global Jim Crow contains elements of the selfishness on display in *When Affirmative Action Was White* and the irrational enmity of *The Sum of Us*. Broad frustration with a global tax system that fails to supply the revenues needed for the public services that the whole world expects reveals that it does not only constrain the taxing power of Black—or poor—countries. Displacing the United Nations has done much to ensure that public health expenditures in former metropoles remain far higher than in former colonies. But while its burdens fall heaviest outside the OECD, as the following chapters show, Global Jim Crow has diminished lives everywhere by making it easy for multinationals and wealthy individuals to avoid paying taxes anywhere.[41]

The wealthy world has begun to wonder how it found itself unable to collect the taxes it needs to support the demands of a modern state.[42] Although its experts and media have loudly blamed others—casually deploying racist rhetoric and imagery in doing so—it has become increasingly evident even to critics within the Global North that "the party actually responsible for the roundly decried state of affairs . . . *is us*."[43] Global Jim Crow explains why and the following chapters detail how. To begin to undo the damage Global Jim

[39] *Id.* (quoting Davis).

[40] *Id.* at 256.

[41] *See* Rebecca M. Kysar, *Unraveling the Tax Treaty*, 104 MINN. L. REV. 1755, 1756–57 (2020) ("Instead of alleviating double taxation, a dubious goal in and of itself for many reasons, the treaties are the means to achieve double non-taxation . . . call[ing] into question the widespread assumption that the United States gains revenues through the treaty system.").

[42] France's digital services tax served as a *cri de coeur* in international tax policy. It broadcast that the world's haves had finally joined the world's have-nots in their determination to ensure that the largest corporations not be able to casually shrug off tax burdens.

[43] Wells & Lowell, *supra* note 23, at 602 ("Yet there has been a deafening silence from Washington on the identity of the party actually responsible for the roundly decried state of affairs is identified: *It is us*.").

Crow has caused, the world will need to grapple with the racism that shaped it and that still sustains it. However unlikely a notion to those who believed they knew Seligman and thought they understood the origins of our global tax system, the ugly reality of Global Jim Crow can no longer be ignored.

Chapter 1 offers readers new to global tax policy an overview of the two key challenges it has confronted. Corporations have long enjoyed considerable freedom to engage in complex transactions to minimize their global tax burdens (often with the aid of Swiss subsidiaries). Individuals have tended to take a more direct approach, simply hiding income from tax authorities (with Swiss bankers ready to help by hiding diamonds in toothpaste tubes if necessary).[44] The response to both problems has been to reflexively replace flexible standards with detailed rules. The resulting precision has unintentionally revealed a profoundly unequal world in which powerful states blithely violate the requirements they impose on others. Tax mavens might consider skipping ahead to Chapter 2.

Shifting focus from the esoteric world of transfer pricing to the postage stamp makes it possible to begin to make sense of Global Jim Crow. Chapter 2 uses the humble stamp to paint a picture of the tax landscape as it existed between World War I and Africa's decolonization, before the rise of Global Jim Crow. It explains how an obscure provision—a tax credit—would twice help rebuild a war-torn Europe. The remarkable generosity of those decades—a far cry from the America-first policies of today—has been all but forgotten.

It also sketches the origins of contemporary global tax policy, including the double tax treaty. Seligman and his contemporaries, under the auspices of the League of Nations, imagined a paternalistic post-imperial future for global taxation. They created a new architecture to maintain hierarchy without empire that would remain dormant for decades only to define the last six decades of cross-border taxation.

Chapter 3 tells the story of that delayed victory by describing the rise of Global Jim Crow. Tax law served as one response by wealthy states to racialized fears of a rising Global South. In the 1950s—fearful that the Dunning School's imagined debacle of Reconstruction would play out on a global scale, at great cost to wealthy states—the United States orchestrated the creation of an all-white alternative to the United Nations. Just as the organization stood poised to welcome dozens of majority-Black members—each

[44] Lynnley Browning, *Ex-UBS Banker Pleads Guilty in Tax Evasion,* N.Y. Times (June 20, 2008), https://www.nytimes.com/2008/06/20/business/20tax.html.

determined to deliver the essential services their colonial masters had long denied them—displacing the United Nations served to limit taxing and spending by former African colonies.[45]

Chapter 4 describes the heyday of Global Jim Crow and the power it granted to the United States. Delivering innovations such as John F. Kennedy's Subpart F—echoed in contemporary policies such as global minimum taxes—such policies favor wealthy states by reallocating tax revenues from the most vulnerable states to the most prosperous. Today, in the words of Afton Titus, they serve as a "Death Knell for African Country Taxation."[46] Other US innovations, like the Clinton administration's check-the-box election, would prove equally impactful.

Chapter 5 highlights the continuing dangers of Global Jim Crow, presenting a global tax policy landscape marred by biased algorithms and racist images. It recounts how the OECD, having its leadership challenged, labeled a group of overwhelmingly Black and brown jurisdictions "tax havens" and threatened them with sanctions. Resistance by the US Congressional Black Caucus marked the start of a new era of contestation even as the OECD fought to strengthen its hold over global tax policymaking, in part by exploiting racial bias.

Chapter 6 examines the pyrrhic impact of Global Jim Crow on its architects.[47] Opportunities to address the problems highlighted in Chapter 1 drifted within easy reach but—as described in Chapter 5—the OECD focused instead on the imagined threat of Liberia. Viewing the world dimly through a nineteenth-century lens, the OECD could not see its Switzerland problem. It would take the greed of a rogue banker and another intervention by a member of the US Congressional Black Caucus to catapult global tax policy out of the past.

Chapter 7 considers paths forward for those states most heavily impacted by Global Jim Crow. A 2023 vote in the United Nations represented a direct

[45] The resulting tug of war would see the United Nations Conference on Trade and Development propose the New International Economic Order, a pointed response to Global Jim Crow.

[46] Afton Titus, *Global Minimum Corporate Tax: A Death Knell for African Country Tax Policies?*, 50 INTERTAX 414, 414 (2022) (describing the impact of the global minimum tax on Rwanda's corporate tax incentive structure).

[47] CLIFFORD GEERTZ, THE INTERPRETATION OF CULTURES: SELECTED ESSAYS 220 (1973). In this essay, Geertz wrestles with the meaning and purpose of ideology, attempting to set aside its pejorative connotations. Viewing Global Jim Crow as the product of the process of sense-making he describes—an ideology—helps explain why the OECD resisted opportunities to solve the problems described in Chapter 1. As detailed in Chapter 6, faith in tax harmonization had become just that, forming a belief system in which Liberia represented a meaningful threat to the United States and Europe.

challenge to the OECD's dominance. But what would it take to truly end the era of Global Jim Crow? Imagining what such a future would demand reveals the daunting challenge faced by champions of global tax justice.

Africa in Global Tax Policy

This book builds on scholarship questioning the unjust assumptions at the heart of our global tax system.[48] It highlights that generosity rather than greed defined that system for decades.[49] It explains that while it appears that tax experts have long ignored Africa,[50] precisely the opposite is true.[51]

It does all of that by directly confronting the racial bias that remains the original sin of international taxation. The fall from grace that accompanied an influx of sovereign African states has deprived vulnerable individuals across the globe of opportunities previously offered to others. Facing the uncomfortable truth that fear inspired and continues to shape complex global rules—increasingly making them an obstacle to securing human rights and achieving sustainable development—has become an essential precondition for global tax justice.

[48] *See, e.g.*, ALLISON CHRISTIANS & LAURENS VAN APELDOORN, TAX COOPERATION IN AN UNJUST WORLD (2022) (arguing that wealthy countries have structured the global tax system to serve their greed); Kim Brooks, *Inter-Nation Equity: The Development of an Important but Underappreciated International Tax Value, in* TAX REFORM IN THE 21ST CENTURY 471, 471 (Richard Krever & John G. Head eds., 2009) (noting that "few states have considered how their national tax systems might have important implications for international income flows between high-income and low-income states and how their tax treaties might be used as a mechanism for achieving a fairer distribution of income internationally").

[49] Graetz & O'Hear, *supra* note 27, at 1028 ("Modern policy advocates, of course, may reject the primacy of taxation by countries of source, but they cannot properly claim that such a rejection is simply a continuation of the original U.S. tax policy toward international income.").

[50] *See* Karen B. Brown, *Missing Africa: Should U.S. International Tax Rules Accommodate Investment in Developing Countries*, 23 U. PA. J. INT'L ECON. L. 45, 48 (2002) ("Without radical reconsideration of some of the premises supporting the current U.S. tax regime, Africa's role as a treaty partner will remain negligible and it will continue to be a site of last resort for investment by U.S. businesses. This Article proposes that the United States reverse a historic bias and adopt a network of treaties with sub-Saharan Africa that provide an exemption from U.S. tax for specified income from African sources. The proposal does not call for wholesale implementation of an exemption system, but rather calls for a limited plan for African-source income only, which is designed to provide a platform for increased investment in sub-Saharan Africa by U.S. firms."); Allison D. Christians, *Tax Treaties for Investment and Aid to Sub-Saharan Africa: A Case Study*, 71 BROOK. L. REV. 639, 639 (2005).

[51] *See, e.g.*, Edwin R.A. Seligman, *The French Colonial System, supra* note 28, at 34 (noting, without irony, that the French colonial system in Latin America, Asia, and Africa "has taken away from the colonies the privilege of levying their own tariffs and has imposed upon many of the dependencies a system of taxation more suitable to the interests of the mother country than to those of the colonies themselves").

1
The Perils of Precision

Evasion and Abuse

To convey the urgency of global tax policy to the uninitiated, the puzzles its brightest minds have struggled to solve for a century offer the best starting point. Unsurprisingly, they involve taxing multinationals and wealthy individuals. Increasingly, the response to both challenges has been a torrent of technical complexity. That result has revealed as much about the weaknesses of the institutions leading the charge against corporate tax abuse and individual tax evasion as their strengths.

A contradiction has shaped those reforms. No World Tax Organization exists.[1] Yet the OECD oversees a network of bilateral treaties that serves as the backbone of what many see as an "international tax regime."[2] Such conflicts might not matter if the world had a reliable means of distinguishing good policies from bad.

Unfortunately, over the many decades of its existence, the OECD has failed to craft what H.L.A. Hart called a rule of recognition for global tax policy.[3] As Chapter 6 explains, the OECD has instead preserved nineteenth-century notions like tax harmonization to light the way forward.[4] That approach has

[1] *See* Reuven S. Avi-Yonah, *Globalization, Tax Competition, and the Fiscal Crisis of the Welfare State*, 113 HARV. L. REV. 1573, 1631 (2000) ("It is not an authoritative 'world tax organization' that designs international tax rules, but each country acting separately with its own interests in mind.").

[2] *See* Reuven S. Avi-Yonah, *The Structure of International Taxation: A Proposal for Simplification*, 74 TEX. L. REV. 1301, 1303 (1996) (arguing that the network of treaties anchors a "coherent international tax regime . . . that enjoys nearly universal support").

[3] H.L.A. Hart observed that the laws that govern our behavior draw strength from notions that operate unseen in the background. The spark of "rules of recognition" can transform a lifeless "regime of primary rules" into a dynamic "legal system." H.L.A. HART, THE CONCEPT OF LAW 94 (1994). For international law, Hart concluded that this offers grounds for both optimism and pessimism. On the one hand, "the absence of an international legislature, courts with compulsory jurisdiction, and centrally organized sanctions" does not necessarily mean that international law cannot exist. *Id.* at 214. On the other hand, he acknowledges that crafting a principle—"a basic rule of recognition"—sufficient to judge "the legal 'quality' of international law" will be difficult. *Id.* at 237.

[4] Experts often invoke the benefits principle as a cornerstone of the international tax regime. *See* Reuven S. Avi-Yonah, *International Taxation of Electronic Commerce*, 52 TAX L. REV. 507, 509 (1997) ("The Benefits Principle assigns the right to tax active (business) income primarily to the source jurisdiction, while the right to tax passive (investment) income is assigned primarily to the residence jurisdiction."); Nancy H. Kaufman, *Fairness and the Taxation of International Income*, 29 LAW &

Racial Capitalism and International Tax Law. Steven A. Dean, Oxford University Press. © Steven A. Dean 2025.
DOI: 10.1093/9780197526002.003.0002

failed to produce the vital system Hart suggested could thrive in the cross-border context even without the traditional trappings of lawmaking.

As this chapter explains, in the absence of "secondary rules"[5] that can bring coherence to what might otherwise collapse into mindless detail, global tax policy fell into precisely that trap, drifting toward rules and away from standards. Offering the illusion of progress, that pattern has had an unintended impact. Its precision has cast the global tax system's shortcomings into stark relief, revealing not only that it has winners as well as losers but that those winners just happen to be its architects.

Dominant Standards, Ascendant Rules

Transnational enterprises remain square pegs to the round holes national corporate taxes present.[6] Formulary apportionment[7]—the chief rival of the more established arm's length method[8] of allocating corporate profits among jurisdictions—promises progress. Seeking to counter the threat of individual tax evasion, extraterritorial tax information has become increasingly important, and states have developed elaborate rules to acquire it.

Although not characterized in such terms, both efforts work to replace a standard with a rule.[9] Trading standards for rules promises clear

POL'Y INT'L BUS. 145, 183–88 (1998) (exploring the relationship between benefit theory and international tax rules such as the source rules). More recently, the benefits principle has been reframed as "taxing where value is created." *See* Allison Christians & Laurens van Apeldoorn, *Taxing Income Where Value Is Created*, 22 FLA. TAX REV. 1 (2018). As Christians and van Apeldoorn observe, even that reframing leaves considerable ambiguity regarding the meaning of value, bringing the value of its conclusions into question.

[5] *See* Hart, *supra* note 3, at 91–99 (describing the three functions of secondary rules as making it possible to identify laws, adjudicating disputes, and facilitating changes in those laws over time).

[6] *See* Elizabeth Chorvat, *Forcing Multinationals to Play Fair: Proposals for a Rigorous Transfer Pricing Theory*, 54 ALA. L. REV. 1251, 1252 (2003) ("Perhaps the greatest problem facing the international tax system is the taxation of transfer pricing within related groups of corporations. By guaranteeing that the allocation of profits among related parties reflects the economic reality . . . tax havens, tax competition, and corporate expatriations, would be greatly reduced or eliminated entirely.").

[7] *See* Reuven S. Avi-Yonah & Kimberly A. Clausing, *Reforming Corporate Taxation in a Global Economy: A Proposal to Adopt Formulary Apportionment*, HAMILTON PROJECT, June 2007, at 14–16, https://www.brookings.edu/wp-content/uploads/2016/06/200706clausing_aviyonah.pdf.

[8] The arm's length standard illustrates the allure of rules. *See* Reuven S. Avi-Yonah et al., *Allocating Business Profits for Tax Purposes: A Proposal to Adopt a Formulary Profit Split*, 9 FLA. TAX REV. 497, 506 (2009) (noting that since "neither taxpayers nor enforcement authorities typically have clear standards for judging compliance" with the arm's length standard, "issues involving very large amounts—billions of dollars—of federal revenue are resolved" through a variety of relatively informal administrative procedures).

[9] International tax scholars currently distinguish between features of the international tax regime as either "hard" law or "soft" law. *See, e.g.*, Allison Christians, *Networks, Norms, and National*

benefits.[10] The allure of rules stands out starkly in the contrast between a fifty-five mile-an-hour speed limit and a standard requiring "reasonable and prudent" driving speeds.[11]

This chapter describes the headwinds tax authorities face in enforcing corporate and individual income taxes. It considers the impact of corporate income shifting and individual tax evasion and the trend toward addressing each with rules. It then highlights the hidden costs of that transition.

Despite the superficial appeal of such a shift, rules and standards differ less in substantive terms than one might expect.[12] In this context, the allure of rules lies in the appearance of progress they provide. Beneath a veneer of sophistication, this chapter reveals a profound gap between their promise and the reality they deliver. The resulting disparities raise grave doubts about what Hart calls the "legal quality" of the rules that increasingly make up the international tax regime.

That regime consists of a host of distinct elements. Thousands of bilateral double tax treaties and countless provisions of national law governing the treatment of cross-border transactions can hardly form a seamless whole.[13] Nevertheless, upon careful examination, important patterns emerge.

Tax Policy, 9 WASH. U. GLOB. STUD. L. REV. 1, 34 (2010) ("While scholars and policy-makers debate the relative merits of soft and hard coordinative methods, practitioners and administrators must navigate the uncertainties on a daily basis."); Diane Ring, *Who Is Making International Tax Policy?: International Organizations as Power Players in a High Stakes World*, 33 FORDHAM INT'L L.J. 649, 652 (2010) ("Thus, despite the formal, hard law power of the state over international tax policy, international organizations influence the actual design of international tax policy and tax rules in a variety of ways, up to and including the creation or exercise of 'soft law' power.").

[10] *See* Cass R. Sunstein, *Problems with Rules*, 83 CAL. L. REV. 953, 972 (1995). Sunstein enumerates the virtues of rules, identifying, among others, their "simplifying effects," and their capacity to replace "ambiguous and conflicting guidelines" so that "government officials [and] affected citizens may reliably know their obligations in advance." *Id.* at 972, 976. By specifying outcomes in advance in relatively straightforward terms, both information exchange and formulary apportionment offer the appeal of greater simplicity and clarity and the promise of reduced enforcement costs. *See* Avi-Yonah et al., *supra* note 8, at 498 ("The U.S. [transfer pricing] system is also notoriously complex; observers are nearly unanimous in lamenting the heavy compliance burdens and the impracticality of coherent enforcement.").

[11] *See* Robert E. King & Cass R. Sunstein, *Doing Without Speed Limits*, 79 B.U. L. REV. 155, 155–56 (1999).

[12] As discussed below, the primary difference between rules and standards lies in the timing of decisions on what behavior is proscribed.

[13] Thousands of bilateral treaties exist. The US statutory provisions that govern cross-border transactions are numerous and varied. They govern everything from the treatment of US investors in foreign investment funds to the treatment of cross-border social security payments. *See* I.R.C. §§ 1291–1297 (describing treatment of investments in Passive Foreign Investment Companies); I.R.C. § 871(a)(3) (specifying the treatment of US social security benefits received by a non-resident alien).

Recent efforts to replace long-dominant standards with rules evoke a venerable scholarly debate.[14] Recognizing that recent proposals tread this well-worn path augurs poorly.[15] The primary distinction between a rule and a standard is whether it "is given content ex ante or ex post."[16] Although they may not differ substantively from the standards they replace, the transparency of rules can reveal telling differences between what is and what ought to be.

Corporate Transfer Pricing

Tax authorities may feel like sea captains trying to navigate a round earth with only flat-earth maps to guide them. In both the corporate and individual contexts, the environment in which the modern income tax was conceived has long passed.[17] Yet key aspects of the international tax regime have changed little in decades.[18]

Today's transnational businesses scarcely resemble their predecessors from decades past. Spanning the globe, they defy the notion that they belong to any particular jurisdiction. With fundamentally rootless intellectual

[14] The rules versus standards debate has a long history and an impressive pedigree. *See* Sunstein, *supra* note 10, at 959; Louis Kaplow, *Rules Versus Standards: An Economic Analysis*, 42 Duke L.J. 557, 560 (1992); Colin S. Diver, *The Optimal Precision of Administrative Rules*, 93 Yale L.J. 65, 71–76 (1983); Isaac Ehrlich & Richard A. Posner, *An Economic Analysis of Legal Rulemaking*, 3 J. Legal Stud. 257, 258 (1974).

[15] The trend is sometimes framed as an evolution from "soft" to "hard" law. That framing suggests an inevitable progression from soft standards to hard rules. *See* Reuven S. Avi-Yonah, *International Tax as International Law*, 57 Tax L. Rev. 483, 496–501 (2004) (observing that features of the international tax regime are so widely observed that they may have evolved into customary international—or hard—law); Allison Christians, *Hard Law, Soft Law, and International Taxation*, 25 Wis. Int'l L.J. 325, 332 (2007) (examining the use of the concepts of hard and soft law in international taxation and questioning whether hard law should be viewed as superior to soft law).

[16] Kaplow, *supra* note 14, at 559.

[17] *See* Michael J. Graetz & Michael M. O'Hear, *The "Original Intent" of U.S. International Taxation*, 46 Duke L.J. 1021, 1041 (1997) (describing the emergence of key elements of the international tax regime in the early twentieth century).

[18] Transfer pricing rules, for example, were first introduced in 1917. *See* Reuven S. Avi-Yonah, *The Rise and Fall of Arm's Length: A Study in the Evolution of U.S. International Taxation*, 15 Va. Tax Rev. 89, 89 (1995). The arm's length standard arrived with regulations introduced in 1935. *See id.* The modern transfer pricing regime took shape in the 1960s. *See* James P. Fuller, *Section 482 Revisited*, 31 Tax L. Rev. 475, 476 (1976) (describing circumstances that led to the promulgation of the "far reaching" 1968 regulations, stating that "the most significant period in section 482's history started during 1961 when the Treasury Department urged congress to make numerous changes affecting U.S. taxpayers with foreign affiliates").

property making up an increasing proportion of their value, associating their profit with a specific location becomes more difficult.[19]

It is in that context that tax authorities and corporations attempt to manage the process known as transfer pricing.[20] Transfer pricing involves allocating taxable profits among the many jurisdictions in which transnational businesses create, manufacture, and sell. Although the context makes it seem exotic, transfer pricing abuse closely resembles a small business owner putting her daughter on the payroll to take advantage of the child's lower marginal tax rates.[21]

The term derives from the process related entities undertake when they set a price on goods or services that they transfer to one another.[22] Take a business that makes and sells contact lenses. If it manufactures and sells all its products in the same jurisdiction, there will be no international transfer pricing problem. However, if it manufactures the lenses in Ireland and sells them in the United States, tax authorities must determine how much of the profit on each lens is US profit and how much is Irish profit.[23]

Transnational businesses have developed many techniques for maneuvering profit into jurisdictions with relatively low tax rates. For example, a business might take the dramatic step of moving all of its staff and productive assets from a jurisdiction with a 50 percent tax rate to one with a 10 percent rate. Doing so might allow future profits to be taxed in the low-rate

[19] *See* Avi-Yonah, *supra* note 1, at 1590 (warning that the increasing importance of intellectual property will make it easier for transnational enterprises to shift their operations to reduce global tax burdens).

[20] *See id.* at 1591 (describing transfer pricing).

[21] Such intra-familial income-shifting strategies were once so popular that Congress requires the unearned income of minor children to be taxed at the (higher) marginal tax rate the child's parents would have paid if they had received the unearned income. *See* I.R.C. § 1(g).

[22] *See* Avi-Yonah, *supra* note 18, at 90 ("Suppose that a product (e.g., computers) is manufactured by a corporation in country A, and then sold to a wholly owned subsidiary of the manufacturer in country B, which proceeds to resell it to unrelated customers. In this common situation, the taxable profit of the subsidiary is determined by three factors: (1) the price at which it resells the computers to the unrelated customers, (2) its expenses other than cost of goods sold, and (3) the price which it pays its parent corporation for the computers. The first two of these factors are governed by market forces outside the control of the parent or the subsidiary. However, because the parent controls the subsidiary, the third factor (the price for which the manufacturer sells the computers to the reseller, or the 'transfer price') is wholly within the control of the related parties. Accordingly, the potential for abuse arises because the related parties will seek to increase aftertax profits by manipulating the transfer price. If the effective tax rate in the manufacturer's country is higher, the price will be set as low as possible so as to channel all taxable profit to the reseller. Conversely, if the effective tax rate in the reseller's jurisdiction is higher, the transfer price will be as high as possible, so as to eliminate any taxable profit of the reseller and concentrate the entire profit in the hands of the manufacturer.").

[23] They cannot rely on market forces to provide an allocation since the buyer and seller are related. *See id.* ("The affiliated parties do not care what the transfer price is, since it merely re-allocates profits within the affiliated group.").

jurisdiction.[24] The objective of transfer pricing planning is to achieve the tax results such a relocation would produce without the necessity of relocating—"hiring" a child without actually putting her to work.

A perfect example of a successful transfer pricing strategy involves Bausch & Lomb's contact lens manufacturing business.[25] Bausch & Lomb, a US corporation, established an Irish subsidiary and in 1981 granted that subsidiary a license to manufacture the lenses in exchange for a modest royalty.[26] Bausch & Lomb then purchased most of the lenses produced by its Irish subsidiary.[27]

The result of that series of transactions was that much of the profit produced by Bausch & Lomb's industry-leading technology remained in Ireland. Faced with a challenge by US tax authorities, Bausch & Lomb prevailed by demonstrating that the transfer price charged by its Irish affiliate was comparable to prices charged by other producers.[28] Bausch & Lomb's victory—shifting income from a high-tax jurisdiction to a low-tax jurisdiction merely by transferring intangible assets to a related party—reveals the depth of national tax authorities' challenge in today's global, technology-driven economy.[29]

Individual Tax Evasion

For national tax authorities, the threat posed by individuals is not that they will report a disproportionate amount of their income in Ireland but that they will not report their income anywhere.[30] It can be remarkably easy for

[24] If the high-rate jurisdiction were the United States, the asset transfer itself might be subject to a tax toll charge of sorts on its exit.

[25] *See* Bausch & Lomb Inc. v. Comm'r, 933 F.2d 1084 (2d Cir. 1991).

[26] *See id.* at 1087.

[27] *See id.*

[28] *See id.* at 1090–91. The Tax Court did, however, increase the royalty rate paid by the Irish subsidiary to Bausch & Lomb. *See id.* at 1092.

[29] The nature of the problem could also be presented differently, so that the struggles of the arm's length method of transfer pricing flow primarily from theoretical deficiencies rather than practical challenges. Treating intrafirm transactions as the equivalent of arm's length transactions between independent firms is not consistent with the way modern multinationals operate. Ultimately, the practical and theoretical limitations reinforce one another. The increased importance of intellectual property produces greater cross-border integration, exacerbating the administrative challenges presented by the arm's length method as intellectual property tends to be unique, making comparisons difficult.

[30] "Much of the income from overseas portfolio investments escapes income taxation by either source or residence countries." Avi-Yonah, *supra* note 1, at 1584 (attributing that compliance failure to the lack of information reporting and withholding in the cross-border context).

individuals to neutralize the structural safeguards that have successfully encouraged domestic tax compliance.[31] When, for example, an individual considers whether to pay tax on interest income she receives from a bank, she is far more likely to do so if she can be sure that the bank has already alerted authorities to its existence.[32] Such third-party reporting is routine within individual jurisdictions. However, the situation can be quite different when a transaction crosses one or more borders.

Not long ago, even transactions involving close allies could quickly become anonymous. Assume a French bank pays interest to a US resident. Even if that payment is reported to French tax authorities, who in turn notify US authorities, that may not matter if the information can not automatically be associated with the taxpayer.[33] Such information might prove helpful during an active investigation of that taxpayer. Still, given the rarity with which taxpayers are audited, she might choose not to report the French interest on her US tax return.[34]

The Dominance of Standards

A typical arm's length transfer pricing method does not specify a particular technique transnational businesses must use to associate their profit with individual jurisdictions. Rather than providing a uniform formula for all businesses (the equivalent of a numerical speed limit) the arm's length method provides a flexible standard.[35] Employing the international tax version of a "reasonable speeds" approach simply calls for integrated elements of a single enterprise to behave as though they were unrelated.[36] In other words,

[31] *See* Edward K. Cheng, *Structural Laws and the Puzzle of Regulating Behavior*, 100 Nw. U. L. Rev. 655, 677 (2006) ("The use of structure to encourage tax compliance has been an unqualified success.").

[32] *See* Leandra Lederman, *Statutory Speed Bumps: The Roles Third Parties Play in Tax Compliance*, 60 Stan. L. Rev. 695, 697–700 (2007) (exploring the importance of third-party information reporting and withholding for domestic tax compliance).

[33] *See* Avi-Yonah, *supra* note 1, at 1584 (lamenting the absence of "uniform, worldwide system of tax identification numbers").

[34] Domestic cash-based businesses and others not subject to information reporting or withholding often make the same calculation, contributing to disproportionately low rates of compliance among those taxpayers. *See* Lederman, *supra* note 32, at 698 (explaining that compliance rates fall nearly in half when neither information reporting nor withholding apply).

[35] Formulary apportionment sits at the opposite end of the spectrum, with a one-size-fits-all rule for all transnational businesses. *See* Avi-Yonah & Clausing, *supra* note 7, at 2 (describing application of formulary apportionment).

[36] The premise of the arm's length method has become increasingly problematic as firms become increasingly global and integrated.

it mandates that transactions between commonly controlled entities be reported as though they were occurring at arm's length between independent parties.[37]

This approach leaves businesses with a great deal of responsibility—and freedom—to determine what constitutes an arm's length price.[38] Using a standard inevitably means that much of its content is only specified when applied to a particular set of circumstances.[39] For example, US regulations specify an array of strategies taxpayers may use to demonstrate the compatibility of their transfer pricing methods with the arm's length standard and encourage taxpayers to choose the "best" method.[40] Businesses can even use a method other than one the regulations describe if they can demonstrate that it is superior to the enumerated methods.[41]

Traditionally, the acquisition of extraterritorial tax information about individuals took place pursuant to a different type of standard. Like arm's length, it provided only a broad sketch of the obligations it imposes.[42] For example, the US model double tax treaty provides that the "Contracting States shall exchange such information as may be relevant for carrying out the provisions of this Convention or of the domestic laws of the Contracting States concerning taxes."[43] What that means in any particular circumstance is left to the judgment of the tax authorities tasked with the responsibility of providing and procuring that information.

[37] The arm's length standard contemplates a wide range of approaches in setting transfer prices. *See* Avi-Yonah, *supra* note 18, at 91 ("'Arm's length' refers to methods of determining transfer prices by using comparables . . . [but] can also be used to refer to any method of determining transfer prices that reaches results (i.e., a profit allocation) that are the same as those that would have been reached between unrelated parties.").

[38] The regulations specify a range of methods to be used in different circumstances. *See* Treas. Reg. § 1.482-3(a).

[39] In other words, the content is specified on an ex post basis when a particular allocation method is chosen.

[40] *See* Robert G. Clark, *Transfer Pricing, Section 482, and International Tax Conflict: Getting Harmonized Income Allocation Measures from Multinational Cacophony*, 42 Am. U. L. Rev. 1155, 1191–92 (1993) ("The IRS acknowledged that problems exist with imposing a rigid hierarchy for applying valuation methods and therefore promulgated the 'best method rule.'").

[41] *See* Treas. Reg. § 1.482-3(e) ("Methods not specified in paragraphs (a)(1), (2), (3), (4), and (5) of this section may be used to evaluate whether the amount charged in a controlled transaction is arm's length.").

[42] Here the obligations fall on tax authorities themselves. This is different than the process by which a tax authority receives information domestically. Domestic information reporting typically involves reporting by private entities. There are, however, some circumstances in which federal authorities report information to states and local governments and vice versa.

[43] U.S. Model Income Tax Convention art. 26, ¶ 1 (U.S. Deparment of Treasury 2016), https://home.treasury.gov/system/files/131/Treaty-US-Model-2016_1.pdf.

At one extreme, the tax authorities charged with implementing that standard might negotiate for the right to receive comprehensive, automatic information flows. In theory, that information could play the same structural enforcement role as the information tax authorities receive from private parties pursuant to domestic laws. In reality, the ad hoc flows of information it produced did not.

The long-standing US approach to cross-border information exchange underscores its shortcomings as a structural enforcement mechanism. Domestically, tax authorities count on steady flows of reliable information. However, the official US interpretation of its own model information exchange language specifies that they may not even request such information from treaty partners.[44]

The Rise of Rules

While such standards continue to play a central role, rules have gained a new prominence. The most visible initiatives of the past two decades have aimed to replace standards with rules.[45] Formulary apportionment—the core of the OECD's pillar one proposal—contrasts with the arm's length method by providing the ex ante content the prevailing standard does not.[46] Likewise, the effort to create more effective tools for extraterritorial tax information acquisition has emphasized the up-front specification of rights and obligations.

Formulary apportionment accomplishes the same allocative task as the arm's length method.[47] It identifies a set of readily observable criteria

[44] *See* U.S. Model Technical Explanation Accompanying the U.S. Model Income Tax Convention of November 15, 2006 art. 26, ¶ 1 (U.S. Department of Treasury 2006), https://home.treasury.gov/system/files/131/Treaty-US-Model-TE-2006.pdf ("The information to be exchanged is that which may be relevant for carrying out the provisions of the Convention or the domestic laws of the United States or of the other Contracting State concerning taxes of every kind applied at the national level. . . . However, the language 'may be' would not support a request in which a Contracting State simply asked for information regarding all bank accounts maintained by residents of that Contracting State in the other Contracting State, or even all accounts maintained by its residents with respect to a particular bank.").

[45] *See* Avi-Yonah & Clausing, *supra* note 7, at 2 (proposing the substitution of formulary apportionment for the present arm's length based regime); OECD, Harmful Tax Competition: An Emerging Global Issue 46–47 (1998) https://www.oecd-ilibrary.org/harmful-tax-competition_5lmqcr2klm5g.pdf?itemId=%2Fcontent%2Fpublication%2F9789264162945-en&mimeType=pdf (launching the anti-tax haven effort that culminated in a wave of information exchange agreements).

[46] *See* Avi-Yonah et al., *supra* note 8, at 500 ("There is universal agreement that [the arm's length] standard leaves substantial room for uncertainty as to the 'correct' transfer pricing. . . .").

[47] Avi-Yonah concludes that the two approaches appear quite different but "despite the common practice of contrasting the ALS and the formulary methods of dealing with the transfer pricing

correlated with each jurisdiction's share of global economic activity.[48] Once the "formula" is established, allocating the tax base becomes mechanical.[49] Unlike the arm's length standard, it does not require transnational enterprises and tax authorities to determine how to employ it in any particular case.[50]

Formulary apportionment's pragmatic approach to the problem can be readily appreciated by making another analogy. Although an income tax should target a taxpayer's ability to pay, in practice it sacrifices accuracy for precision (a broken analog watch will provide a precise but nearly always inaccurate time). The US income tax, for example, employs a formula of sorts that focuses on payments received over the course of a year rather than making any real attempt at a comprehensive measure of an overall change in well-being. The result taxes items like salary while ignoring much of the economic income earned each year by the wealthiest Americans.[51] The resulting tax may be imperfect but is relatively easy to administer.

Formulary apportionment likewise makes life easy for tax administrators. It dispenses with the preliminary step of constructing a counterfactual scenario in which each business exists only within a single jurisdiction in order to then allocate profit.[52] It chooses a measure of a global firm's presence

problem, they are actually not dichotomous. Instead, they form the two extreme ends of a continuum." *See* Avi-Yonah, *supra* note 18, at 93.

[48] *See* Avi-Yonah et al., *supra* note 8, at 508 (under formulary apportionment "net income is apportioned among taxing jurisdictions based on a formula that takes into account various factors").

[49] *See* Avi-Yonah & Clausing, *supra* note 7, at 2 ("Under our proposal, the U.S. tax base for multinational corporations would be calculated based on a fraction of their worldwide income. This fraction would simply be the share of their worldwide sales that are destined for customers in the United States.").

[50] Under the best method rule, the determination of the arm's length price is established under a "facts and circumstances" test. Treas. Reg. § 1.482-1(c) ("The arm's length result of a controlled transaction must be determined under the method that, under the facts and circumstances, provides the most reliable measure of an arm's length result. Thus, there is no strict priority of methods. . . ."). The task is complicated by the fact that the standard is fundamentally at odds with economic reality. In particular, its assumption that integrated transnational companies can be disaggregated for tax purposes is highly problematic. *See* Avi-Yonah et al., *supra* note 8, at 501 ("The assumption that each affiliated company within the group transacts with the other members of the group in the same way that it would transact if the members were unrelated . . . defies reality.").

[51] Section 61 of the Internal Revenue Code provides a very broad definition of income. That definition is not so broad that it includes every item that would be considered economic income. For example, the income tax considers only that economic income which has been realized. *See, e.g.*, I.R.C. § 1001 (specifying the calculation of gain on the sale of property). That means that except to the extent that Bill Gates has sold shares of Microsoft stock or received a dividend on those shares, his investment in the corporation has produced no taxable income.

[52] By contrast, the arm's length method calls for taxpayers and tax authorities to disaggregate fully integrated transnational businesses, a task that brings to mind putting toothpaste back in a tube. *See* Avi-Yonah et al., *supra* note 8, at 501 ("For firms that are truly integrated across borders, holding related entities within the commonly controlled group to an 'arms-length' standard for the pricing

in a given country to serve as a proxy for the benefits that jurisdiction provides to that firm.[53] Accepting sales, for example, as a robust measure of a jurisdiction's entitlement would not be so different from focusing on an individual's salary, making it quite easy to calculate each state's share of the global tax base.

The debate between formulary apportionment and arm's length proponents is not new.[54] Well before the OECD's pillar one, Reuven Avi-Yonah and Kimberly Clausing offered a detailed exploration of the costs and benefits of a switch from arm's length to formulary apportionment.[55] After considering the implications of such a change—including efficiency, complexity, and distributional concerns—Avi-Yonah and Clausing judged formulary apportionment to be superior to arm's length. They note that such a switch will inevitably create winners and losers, but "despite concerns about systematic revenue losses in some countries" formulary apportionment "would eventually help many governments by eliminating incentives for tax competition."[56]

The shift to rules has already happened in extraterritorial tax information acquisition. Those more precise mechanisms—two of which are described later in this chapter—have helped create a reality closer to that producing remarkably high rates of compliance in the domestic context. Ideally, taxpayers will soon assume that tax authorities know nearly as much about their offshore income and activities as they do about their domestic income. Rather than adopting a defiant attitude toward tax authorities, taxpayers will volunteer information about their cross-border activities.[57]

of intracompany transactions does not make sense, nor does allocating income and expenses on a country-by-country basis.").

[53] The formula often used in the US domestic context—referred to as the "Massachusetts formula"—combines sales, assets, and employees. *See id.* at 509.

[54] *See* Avi-Yonah, *supra* note 2, at 1339 ("There are two approaches to this problem, which has been the subject of heated debate in the past thirty years. One approach is the arm's-length method . . . and the other is the unitary or formulary apportionment method. . . .").

[55] *See* Avi-Yonah & Clausing, *supra* note 7.

[56] *See id.* at 25.

[57] Like Foucault's panopticon, that transparency would persuade taxpayers that non-compliance will inevitably be discovered and punished. Michel Foucault, Discipline and Punish 201–02 (Alan Sheridan trans., Vintage Books 2d ed. 1995) (1975) (explaining that once they accept that authorities have the capacity to monitor their activities "it is not necessary to use force to constrain the convict to good behavior, the madman to calm, the worker to work, the schoolboy to application, the patient to the observation of the regulations").

Hard Rules, Soft Standards

Instead of a contest between rules and standards, the dynamics of the international tax regime tend to be viewed in terms of hard and soft law.[58] That distinction can be quite useful.[59] It draws attention to the different mechanisms through which the two types of international law influence state behavior and provides a vocabulary for distinguishing between different types of legal instruments.[60]

Hard and soft law can be distinguished across three dimensions: "obligation, precision, and delegation."[61] In matters of taxation, the sovereignty-driven questions of obligation and delegation can steal the limelight.[62] Considered alongside such fraught questions, the more technical question of precision tends to be an afterthought.[63] Rules versus standards provides

[58] *See* Christians, *supra* note 15, at 325 ("Discussion in international tax literature is increasingly using terms such as hard law, customary law, and soft law. . . .").

[59] *See* Kenneth W. Abbott & Duncan Snidal, *Hard and Soft Law in International Governance*, 54 INT'L ORG. 421, 421 (2000) (concluding that the dichotomy of hard and soft law allows commentators to "analyze the benefits and costs of different types of legalization and suggest hypotheses regarding the circumstances that lead actors to select specific forms").

[60] Referring to international law as "soft" does not mean that it has no capacity to influence state action. It may merely influence states through non-legal channels. For example, Hathaway identifies the formal and informal mechanisms that influence state action as "transnational legal enforcement" and "transnational collateral consequences." Oona A. Hathaway, *Between Power and Principle: An Integrated Theory of International Law*, 72 U. CHI. L. REV. 469, 497–512 (2005).

[61] Abbott & Snidal, *supra* note 59, at 422.

[62] *See* Diane M. Ring, *What's at Stake in the Sovereignty Debate?: International Tax and the Nation-State*, 49 VA. J. INT'L L. 155, 156 (2008) ("No significant issue in international tax can be discussed without raising the question of sovereignty. Does a particular outcome or position harm or infringe upon a nation's sovereignty? Is sovereignty advanced by the proposed tax plan? Should a sovereign nation participate in multilateral tax cooperation to solve shared problems?"). Interestingly, the preoccupation that states have with tax sovereignty does not always lead in the same direction on the question of obligation and delegation. The European Union struggled with a situation in which they obligated themselves without delegating. The result is a situation in which the European Court of Justice struck down national tax laws (and the states act as though they are bound to respect those decisions) but the European Parliament cannot pass laws to solve the problem without the unanimous agreement of EU member states (because they have not delegated authority). *See* Michael J. Graetz & Alvin C. Warren, Jr., *Income Tax Discrimination and the Political and Economic Integration of Europe*, 115 YALE L.J. 1186, 1253 (2006); Ruth Mason, *Made in America for European Tax: The Internal Consistency Test*, 49 B.C. L. REV. 1277, 1278–82 (2008).

[63] States bridle at suggestions that they shape their tax policies for the benefit of others and display skepticism toward efforts to delegate authority to resolve intergovernmental tax disputes. States tend to be very reluctant to consider commitments binding. *See generally* Richard L. Doernberg, *Overriding Tax Treaties: The U.S. Perspective*, 9 EMORY INT'L L. REV. 71, 82–116 (1995) (providing the history of US tax treaty overrides). States are even less willing to delegate authority to third parties. Kenneth W. Abbott et al., *Concepts of Legalization*, 54 INT'L ORG. 401, 415 (2000) ("The characteristic forms of legal delegation are third-party dispute settlement mechanisms authorized to interpret rules and apply them to particular facts (and therefore in effect to make new rules, at least interstitially) under established doctrines of international law."). With the exception of the recent advent of a limited amount of binding arbitration in the double tax treaty context, states simply do not delegate the interpretation or adjudication of international tax rules. *See* Ring, *supra* note 9,

a rich set of tools that brings that important dimension into focus. Also, unlike the hard versus soft debate, it implies no hierarchy between rules and standards.[64]

Defining the "optimal precision" of legal requirements as falling somewhere between "administrative underprecision" and "excessive regulatory rigidity" suggests both the importance of striving for that goal and the impossibility of achieving it.[65] No matter how well tailored to a particular context, a highly specified rule is likely to be perceived as unduly rigid in at least some cases. By the same token, even the most elegant standard will fail to provide adequate guidance in others.

The critical difference between rules and standards is timing. A numerical speed limit embodies up-front content specification, while a reasonable speed requirement demands a case-by-case determination.[66] In that sense, a rule is a mass-produced legal instrument and a standard the work of a skilled craftsman. By providing "an advance determination of what conduct is permissible" that may apply to hundreds or thousands of events, a rule creates the potential for economies of scale.[67] Of course, like any other mass-production process, creating a rule entails significant up-front costs.

The two most significant are "the cost of obtaining and analyzing information about the rule's probable impact, and the cost of securing agreement among participants in the rulemaking process."[68] To put it bluntly, a standard

at 689–99 (2010) (tracing the history of the inclusion of binding arbitration features in the OECD model double tax treaty). The binding arbitration was carefully designed "to assuage countries' sovereignty concerns. . . ." Hugh J. Ault, *Reflections on the Role of the OECD in Developing International Tax Norms*, 34 Brook. J. Int'l L. 757, 775 (2009); *see* Hugh J. Ault, *Improving the Resolution of International Tax Disputes*, 7 Fla. Tax Rev. 137, 139 (2005) (noting that most international tax disputes are resolved pursuant to Mutual Agreement Procedures and that "the individual case is not considered on its merits but [as] part of a larger tradeoff between the countries").

[64] By contrast, viewing legal regimes through the lens of hard and soft law can create an expectation that soft law will—or should—blossom into hard law. *See* Abbott & Snidal, *supra* note 59, at 422–23 ("Others justify soft law only as an interim step toward harder and therefore more satisfactory legalization."). As a result, through the hard versus soft law prism, the arm's length standard may seem like little more than "a way station to harder legalization" such as formulary apportionment. *Id.* at 423. The soft law label itself can become a liability. *See id.* ("The implication is that soft law—law that 'falls short' on one or more of the three dimensions of legalization—is a failure."). The rules versus standards framework, by contrast, does not suggest a comparable hierarchy as between rules and standards. Each offers advantages and disadvantages and neither is viewed as inferior to the other.

[65] Diver, *supra* note 14, at 65.

[66] *See* Kaplow, *supra* note 14, at 560.

[67] *Id.* at 560, 583.

[68] Diver, *supra* note 14, at 73.

minimizes lawmakers' initial outlay by deferring difficult decisions.[69] Nevertheless, it offers no guarantee of lower overall costs. Given a large number of instances in which a standard applies, the need for private parties and authorities to repeatedly implement the standard could make it more costly over time.[70]

The economies of scale that a rule offers do not come without risk. One of the "conventional arguments against precise statutory guidelines . . . stresses the need for flexibility for responding to changed circumstances. . . ."[71] In other words, not even the most efficient production process can compensate for a change in technology or tastes that renders a product—or a law—obsolete. In such cases, lawmakers' up-front investment may, in retrospect, appear foolish.

Rules and Standards in International Taxation

The intuitive appeal of rules is not difficult to grasp. One need only compare the indeterminacy of the arm's length standard to the clarity of formulary apportionment to appreciate why rules seem essential to the international tax regime's future.[72] Rather than asking transnational businesses and national tax authorities to craft bespoke solutions to increasingly common allocative problems, formulary apportionment promises a dependable off-the-rack alternative.

Bausch & Lomb paints a compelling picture of the limits of the arm's length standard. The long, expensive fight over allocating the profits derived

[69] The parallels between the hard/soft law and the rules/standards distinctions are particularly apparent when we focus on the nature of the costs they entail. *See* Abbott & Snidal, *supra* note 59, at 434 ("A major advantage of softer forms of legalization is their lower contracting costs. Hard legalization reduces the post-agreement costs of managing and enforcing commitments, but adoption of a highly legalized agreement entails significant contracting costs.").

[70] An imprecise standard could, for example, spawn a large number of disputes. *See* Diver, *supra* note 14, at 95 (offering the "staggering" number of cases challenging Immigration and Naturalization Service's exercise of its discretion to adjust the status of aliens to permanent residence pursuant to the Immigration and Nationality Act of 1952 as an example of the impact of a lack of precision).

[71] Cass R. Sunstein, *Constitutionalism After the New Deal*, 101 Harv. L. Rev. 421, 481 (1987).

[72] Of course, the clarity rules provide does not come without costs. If substituting rules for standards were an easy cure for chronic ailments like those that afflict the international tax regime, the rules versus standards debate would hardly have been the subject of decades of sustained scholarly attention. Choosing between rules and standards is never easy. Similar contests between rules and standards persist in all sorts of settings. One particularly heated and long-running debate focuses on the appropriate way of policing the behavior of public companies. *See* James J. Park, *The Competing Paradigms of Securities Regulation*, 57 Duke L.J. 625, 625 (2007) (contrasting "principles-based" and "rules-based" securities law enforcement actions).

from a product as prosaic as a contact lens does not inspire great confidence in the arm's length standard's capacity to address disputes regarding more complex products and services. The opacity of financial firms' operations, for example, has long taxed the capacity of the extant regime.[73] It seems safe to conclude that our increasingly digital future will contain more, not less, of that complexity.

Against that backdrop, formulary apportionment's rule—dispensing with the need to delve too deeply into the nature of an organization's idiosyncratic technologies and structures—holds great appeal. Unfortunately, embracing formulary apportionment can create new problems. Some of the drawbacks of rules are obvious.

As described above, while it might significantly lower post-implementation costs, those savings could be dwarfed by increased rulemaking costs. Even assuming the costs of designing a rule remain modest, the costs of achieving consensus may not be. Forging agreement among states with differing interests and capacities may be extremely difficult.[74]

As Cass Sunstein succinctly put it, "sometimes people can agree on a standard when they cannot agree on its specification. An incompletely specified provision may be the best the political (or judicial) system can do."[75] The indeterminacy of the arm's length standard may indicate its status not merely as a lowest common denominator but also as a high-water mark in political terms.[76]

The evolution of the mechanisms through which information is exchanged among national tax authorities provides another illustration of the extent to which the international tax regime long deferred content specification. It also illustrates a second cost of switching from standards to rules. Not only

[73] *See* Lisa M. Nadal, *Reproposed Global Dealing Regs Similar to 1998 Regs*, 117 Tax Notes 307, 307 (2007) (describing the long saga of creating regulations governing the allocation of profits of financial firms).

[74] *See* Alvin C. Warren, Jr., *Alternatives for International Corporate Tax Reform*, 49 Tax L. Rev. 599, 611 (1994) (arguing that structural differences among countries make it "seem very unlikely that a consensus would develop in the foreseeable future" regarding an appropriate formula by which to apportion income). Some commentators argue that a high level of coordination is not necessary, but concede that some coordination would be required. *See, e.g.*, Reuven S. Avi-Yonah & Ilan Benshalom, *Formulary Apportionment—Myths and Prospects: Promoting Better International Tax Policy by Utilizing the Misunderstood and Under-theorized Formulary Alternative*, 3 World Tax J. 372, 392 (2011).

[75] Sunstein, *supra* note 10, at 965 (emphasis omitted).

[76] *See* William J. Wilkins & Kenneth W. Gideon, *Memorandum to Congress: You Wouldn't Like Worldwide Formula Apportionment*, 65 Tax Notes 1259, 1261 (1994) (contrasting the "difficulty in achieving international agreement on formula apportionment and its details" against "the arm's length approach, which is capable of brief and noncontroversial treaty expression").

are rules costly to construct, but once they exist, they create new barriers to future reform.

It is difficult to contemplate the double-tax-treaty-based information exchange infrastructure without acknowledging the inadequacy of the ad hoc information flows it generated. Still, it embodies the flexibility that is so prized in a standard.[77] Even as national income taxes and the global economic landscape have changed dramatically, treaty information exchange provisions have remained unchanged.[78]

Had they been more precisely specified, those treaty-based mechanisms might have made it difficult for national tax regimes to evolve.[79] The profound changes in states' domestic laws over the past century would have been made more daunting by the existence of a highly specified, rules-based information exchange regime.[80] In the context of domestic tax information acquisition, administrators constantly battle to keep pace with change. It is not difficult to understand that the more highly specified a rule becomes, the more vulnerable it would be to even incremental adjustments.[81] In other words, switching from a standard to a rule might merely replace the ex post costs of providing content for a standard with the not-inconsiderable expense of constant modernization.[82]

[77] The information exchange articles themselves change little over time. The commentaries provide more flexibility.

[78] *Compare* U.S. MODEL INCOME TAX CONVENTION art. 26 (U.S. DEPARTMENT OF TREASURY 2006), https://www.irs.gov/pub/irs-trty/model006.pdf, *with* U.S. MODEL INCOME TAX TREATY art. 26 (U.S. DEPARTMENT OF TREASURY 1976). Before the recent wave of change the switch from the "is necessary" threshold to the newer "may be relevant" standard would have seemed dramatic. Footnote 44, *supra*, provides a portion of the official US commentary on that change, suggesting that the new language may not even represent as significant a change as it appears.

[79] For example, US tax authorities require borrowers to report not only the cash interest they pay to lenders, but also interest that economically accrues without being paid in cash. *See* I.R.S. Form 1099-OID (2024), https://www.irs.gov/pub/irs-pdf/f1099oid.pdf. The highly specified information exchange provisions created during the first half of the twentieth century did not require reporting of that deferred interest, referred to as Original Issue Discount. As a result, even if those early agreements had not been supplanted by the modern information exchange standard, they would not have provided today's authorities with information comparable to the information they receive from domestic sources.

[80] *See* STAFF OF J. COMM. ON TAXATION, 104TH CONG., JCS-5-96, IMPACT ON INTERNATIONAL COMPETITIVENESS OF REPLACING THE FEDERAL INCOME TAX 96–114 (Comm. Print 1996) (addressing international implications of dramatic changes in the US tax system). Of course, some of the investment in information technology infrastructure could be salvaged and repurposed to create a new information exchange regime. By the same token, the cooperative relationships among participating states would survive that switch.

[81] *See* Sunstein, *supra* note 10, at 994 ("Rules may badly misfire under new conditions.").

[82] The same would be true if a formulary apportionment regime were introduced. *See* Julie Roin, *Can the Income Tax be Saved? The Promise and Pitfalls of Adopting Worldwide Formulary Apportionment*, 61 TAX L. REV. 169, 174 (2008) ("Replacing the current international tax rules with a system of formulary taxation would entail tremendous institutional and transition costs in the

Legitimacy

In the international context, the potency of rules and standards derives from the push and pull generated by the underlying principles.[83] States can be expected to comply with legal regimes when that compliance is perceived to be in their own national interest, however that is understood.[84] More difficult to understand is why states comply even against their own apparent interests. Legitimacy offers one explanation.

That dynamic has been described as "compliance pull."[85] Compliance pull refers to the capacity of a regime to "secure compliance when, as in the international system, there are no other compliance-inducing mechanisms."[86] Why, for instance, does a state accept an adverse ruling from an international body? There may be circumstances in which the short-term burden of doing so will be more than offset by the long-term benefits of membership in that body. In other cases, legitimacy may play the more important role in cultivating commitment to a regime. Simply put, regimes that are perceived to be legitimate elicit more compliance than those that are not.

Legitimacy can be disaggregated into input and output legitimacy.[87] Thomas Franck identifies input legitimacy as "that quality of a rule which

United States and elsewhere. Further, achieving and maintaining the degree of legal uniformity necessary for such a system to operate to its full potential would have its own costs.").

[83] Without Hart's secondary rules, a set of obligations will not develop into a "legal system." *See* Hart, *supra* text accompanying note 3. Franck echoes the importance of such secondary rules to the success of international law. *See* Thomas M. Franck, *Legitimacy in the International System*, 82 Am. J. Int'l L. 705, 752 (1988) ("Primary rules of obligation that lack adherence to a system of secondary rules of process are mere ad hoc reciprocal arrangements."). Franck and Sunstein both make the observation that rules divorced from principles are less likely to be successful. Sound principles provide the foundation that makes rules—and standards—strong. *See* Sunstein, *supra* note 10, at 966 ("[R]ules are justified by principles, usually political or moral in character."). Posner and Ehrlich make a similar observation about the relationship between rules and principles. *See* Ehrlich & Posner, *supra* note 14, at 260 ("Properly understood, 'principles' are simply the considerations that are relevant in determining the content of a rule."). As Hart put it, a rule of recognition represents a means by which "other rules of the system" can be "assessed, and in virtue of which the rules constitute a single system." Hart, *supra* note 3, at 233.

[84] *See* Claire R. Kelly, *Realist Theory and Real Constraints*, 44 Va. J. Int'l L. 545, 547 (2004) (observing that states will abide by rules that do them a short-term disservice in order to secure greater long-term benefits). Such incentives are the explanation typically offered for the remarkable success of the double tax treaty network. States offer concessions with regard to their taxation of foreign residents in order to secure equivalent benefits for their own residents. *See infra* note 95.

[85] Franck, *supra* note 83, at 713.

[86] *Id.* at 706.

[87] *See* Fritz Scharpf, Governing in Europe 2 (1999) (distinguishing "input-oriented authenticity" and "output-oriented authenticity" as two distinct sources of legitimacy); Robert O. Keohane & Joseph S. Nye, Jr., *The Club Model of Multilateral Cooperation and Problems of Democratic Legitimacy*, *in* Efficiency Equity and Legitimacy 264, 265 (Roger B. Porter ed., 2001) ("The

derives from a perception on the part of those to whom it is addressed that it has come into being in accordance with right process."[88] Congruence between a regime's objective and its real-world impact generates a second type of legitimacy: output legitimacy. If a law succeeds in meeting its goals—whether limiting noise pollution, reducing crime, or promoting investment—it may command respect independent of its origins.

International legal regimes and institutions can acquire legitimacy in both ways. Acceptance of the process that produced it—the Bretton Woods Conference, for example—determines the input legitimacy of the International Monetary Fund. The perceived success or failure of the Fund's efforts to resolve financial crises will either burnish or detract from its output legitimacy.[89]

The rise of rules has come to threaten the legitimacy of the international tax regime. Their precision ensures that when states do not meet their obligations, that failure becomes plain for all to see. When the results favor the powerful, that too can become evident, inviting scrutiny of the processes that produce those rules.

In extreme cases, the transparency of rules can make hypocrites of even their most stalwart champions. "On March 18, 2010, the US Congress passed . . . the Foreign Account Tax Compliance Act (FATCA). The act obliges foreign financial institutions to automatically report US clients and their capital income to the IRS."[90] Although no substitute for the information it receives from domestic sources, FATCA went a long way toward that goal.

FATCA embodies the best and the worst of rules. It makes perfectly clear what information the United States receives from abroad about its taxpayers. Thanks to FATCA, the United States no longer relies on vague assurances that it might, at some future date, be provided with the modest amount of information it is permitted to request.

Unfortunately, it also clarifies what the United States does not provide to other states. Despite pledging that it would supply other states with comparable information, "the Obama administration eventually refused

legitimacy of institutions is affected both on the 'input' side—in particular, through procedures for accountability—and on the 'output' side, in terms of effectiveness.").

[88] Franck, *supra* note 83, at 706 (emphasis omitted). Although Franck uses the concept of "input legitimacy," he does not use that label.

[89] *See* Keohane & Nye, *supra* note 87, at 286.

[90] *See* Lukas P. Hakelberg, The Hypocritical Hegemon: How the United States Shapes Global Rules Against Tax Evasion and Avoidance 4 (2020).

to reciprocate."[91] In the years that followed FATCA, more and more information has flowed across borders pursuant to such rules. But not from the United States, which has become "the world's preeminent tax haven."[92]

Compared with the information exchange provision included in a typical double tax treaty, FATCA and a second regime that followed it—the OECD's Common Reporting Standard (CRS)—both articulate the rights and obligations of each party with great precision. CRS encompasses a comprehensive, automatic system of extraterritorial tax information acquisition.[93] For the better part of a decade, more than 100 countries, both OECD members and non-members, have swapped information about taxpayers. However, the United States has remained stubbornly on the sidelines.

Qualified Intermediaries

The US position on information exchange forms part of a damning pattern. Before FATCA, the United States embraced "qualified intermediaries" to collect extraterritorial tax information. A qualified intermediary is a private firm deputized by US tax authorities to collect taxes imposed on US income earned by foreign individuals and businesses.[94]

It is a quirk of the international tax regime that relatively few cross-border payments are taxed at the statutory tax rate.[95] As a result, the qualified

[91] *Id.* at 5.

[92] Reuven S. Avi-Yonah, *Does the U.S. Have to Be a Tax Haven*, 117 Tax Notes 1009, 1009 (2024). Avi-Yonah observes that "[t]he main argument for why the United States should not tax foreign investors or collaborate with exchanges of information to enable the investors' countries of residence to tax them is that the United States needs the investment and if the United States imposed that tax or collected that information, the funds would simply flow elsewhere."

Id. at 1012.

[93] OECD, Standard for Automatic Exchange of Financial Account Information in Tax Matters (2d ed. 2017).

[94] A qualified intermediary is defined under the regulations as a "foreign financial institution" or a similar entity "that is a party to a withholding agreement with the IRS." Treas. Reg. § 1.1441-1(e)(5)(ii).

[95] The high statutory rate serves merely as a penalty default encouraging taxpayers to identify themselves in order to qualify for a lower rate. *See* John F. Avery Jones, *Are Tax Treaties Necessary?*, 53 Tax L. Rev. 1, 3 (1999) (concluding that the "high withholding taxes on nonresidents" are intended to make those non-residents, and by extension their states of residence, to "want treaties" to reduce those rates). In the United States that nominal rate on dividends, interest, and similar periodic payments is 30 percent. I.R.C. §§ 1441–42. Historically, one benefit of the scheme is that in order to secure the lower non-statutory rate, a non-resident must generally provide documentation establishing his or her entitlement to that rate. Tax authorities can provide that information—specifying the taxpayer's identity and residence—to tax authorities in the recipient's residence jurisdiction. Having received information about the income of one of its residents in this roundabout manner, that jurisdiction may then impose a tax on the investment income of its resident. The rise of

intermediary routinely assesses the eligibility of overseas taxpayers receiving interest or dividends from within the United States for rates below the high statutory withholding tax rate.[96] Only after it examines the documentation proving that a French recipient is eligible for the reduced rates provided by a double tax treaty between the United States and France, for instance, will it ensure that the appropriate amount of tax is remitted to US authorities.

Privatizing a process previously carried out directly by US tax authorities has distinct advantages for the United States. As is often true, privatization offers the possibility of significant operational savings. The savings may be more substantial here than in a typical privatization scenario. That is because qualified intermediaries not only perform a complex, labor-intensive task on behalf of US tax authorities, they do so without compensation.[97]

Although uncompensated, those services nonetheless proved remunerative.[98] Clients of qualified intermediaries benefit from access to US financial markets without sacrificing their anonymity.[99] That irresistible combination generates business for qualified intermediaries while producing privacy and higher returns for foreign investors and more foreign investment and tax revenues along with lower administrative costs for the United States.

The result appears to be a win–win–win for the United States, qualified intermediaries, and their clients. The primary losers are those states that

qualified intermediaries disrupts the flow of information from non-resident taxpayers to their home jurisdiction.

[96] The obligations of the qualified intermediary are specified by each intermediary's withholding agreement. *See* Treas. Reg. § 1.1441-1(e)(5)(iii)(B) ("The agreement shall specify the type of certifications and documentation upon which the qualified intermediary may rely to ascertain the classification . . . and status . . . of beneficial owners and payees who receive payments collected by the qualified intermediary and, if necessary, entitlement to the benefits of a reduced rate under an income tax treaty.").

[97] Rather than receiving information with respect to individual taxpayers, qualified intermediary withholding agreements may provide for the qualified intermediary to provide aggregate, rather than individualized information regarding non-resident taxpayers. *See id.* In effect, US tax authorities receive a convenient summary, sparing them the burden of processing the information themselves.

[98] As Michael McIntyre put it, being a qualified intermediary benefits financial intermediaries by making it possible for them to "handle anonymously the investments in the United States by foreign tax cheats." Michael J. McIntyre, *How to End the Charade of Information Exchange*, 56 Tax Notes Int'l 255, 259 (2009) ("Hundreds of billions of dollars flow into the United States under this system.").

[99] Qualified intermediaries need not "disclose the identity of beneficial owners and payees" when those payees are non-residents. Treas. Reg. § 1.1441-1(e)(5)(iii)(B). As a result, US tax authorities do not receive that information and cannot exchange that information with their foreign counterparts. Even before FATCA, the existence of the qualified intermediary at a time when the United States urged states to enter into Tax Information Exchange Agreements (TIEAs) represented "brazen hypocrisy." *See* McIntyre, *supra* note 98, at 255.

have agreed to exchange information with the United States. Because the qualified intermediary receives and reviews the documentation that entitles our hypothetical French taxpayer to a low treaty withholding rate, the United States does not possess and cannot provide that documentation to France.

The Swiss banking scandal explored in Chapter 6 highlights the risk that increased precision will reveal flaws standards might have kept hidden.[100] As a qualified intermediary, a major Swiss bank agreed to satisfy the program's exacting requirements. As has become clear, the bank then breached those clearly defined obligations spectacularly. That scandal, FATCA's absence of reciprocity, and the US stance on CRS have all drawn attention to the structural imbalances that sustain Global Jim Crow—and that Global Jim Crow sustains—extracting meaningful costs in legitimacy terms.

Neither Rules Nor Standards

The OECD's pillar one captures all of the hopes and fears of formulary apportionment advocates. The OECD's involvement dates back to 2008. The G20—a group of countries with large economies—enlisted the OECD to explain why multinationals enjoyed such freedom to avoid taxation. The OECD responded with what is now unofficially known as BEPS 1.0, offering thousands of pages of analysis but few answers. In the years that followed, the OECD proved either unable or unwilling to craft an answer to the intertwined questions of which multinationals should bear the burden of higher taxes and which states deserve to collect them. A decade later, in an about-face, it offered two proposals it called pillars. Pillar two describes the misleadingly named global minimum tax that will be examined in the coming chapters. Pillar one proposed a ban on—and a formulary alternative to—a new tax.

[100] David Kocieniewski, *Whistle-Blower Awarded $104 Million by I.R.S.*, N.Y. Times (Sept. 11, 2012), https://www.nytimes.com/2012/09/12/business/whistle-blower-awarded-104-million-by-irs.html.

An observer could be forgiven for dismissing pillar one as a cynical attempt to sabotage a potent new tax. With so-called digital services taxes gaining momentum,[101] the OECD abandoned its exploration of the "idea of an allocation of profits based on user contributions to value."[102] Instead, it embraced "an outright formula apportionment of profits to market [countries], but limited to very large corporations."[103]

As the foregoing discussion suggests, the details of pillar one have prompted sharp disagreement. As Clausing and Avi-Yonah predicted, the proposal produced clear winners and losers. The losers—disproportionately nonmembers of the OECD—have, quite understandably, objected.

Because the proposal was a rule, its impact could be clearly measured. Estimates reveal which countries would benefit from the OECD's proposal. One study indicates that nearly all of the billions in tax revenues generated by one of its key provisions would go to members of the OECD.[104]

Conclusion

As the following chapters reveal, at a crucial moment, generosity yielded to fear in global tax policy. Even had that not happened, expertise might still be more prized than empathy. In an episode recounted in Chapter 3, when the OECD's predecessor first focused on tax, the United Nations—then the global tax policy leader—offered it technical assistance.

Had the United Nations known that what was then the Organisation for European Economic Co-operation—explicitly tasked with promoting European interests—would eventually set the tax agenda for the world, it might have chosen to plant different seeds. The rise of rules during the OECD era has alleviated some problems while amplifying others. It has left little doubt that the United States refuses to play by the rules it imposes on others. It also makes it plain that the OECD favors its own.

[101] Young Ran Kim & Darien Shanske, *State Digital Services Taxes: A Good and Permissible Idea (Despite What You Might Have Heard)*, 98 Notre Dame L. Rev. 741, 757 (2022) ("Unable to rely on the traditional tax system, certain market countries have started imposing a new tax on the large digital platforms unilaterally, the DST. Maryland's DST is modeled in part on these foreign DSTs.")

[102] Cong. Rsch. Serv., R47988, The OECD/G20 Pillar 1 and Digital Services Taxes: A Comparison (2024).

[103] *Id.* The report's reference to "market companies" rather than "market countries" appears to be a typo.

[104] Mona Barake & Elvin Le Pouhaër, *Tax Revenue from Pillar One Amount A: Country-by-Country Estimates* Int'l Tax Pub. Finance 2024).

Thanks to FATCA and CRS, far more extraterritorial tax information finds its way to those charged with enforcement than in decades past. The United States' steadfast refusal to join CRS or to live up to its pledge of reciprocity profoundly undermines the legitimacy of the international tax regime. More than a decade after the creation of FATCA, US law still does not allow authorities to collect basic ownership information about US corporations.[105]

Before the rise of rules, standards helped keep such conflicts hidden. The procedural and substantive unfairness of global tax policies remained obscure. Rules lay both disagreements and bias bare. As Chapter 7 describes, Kenya and Nigeria forcefully rejected the OECD's pillars. The United States rejects CRS simply because it can.

The rise of rules has been a mixed blessing for the international tax regime. Predictably, a focus on precision has led to conflicts over the content of those rules. The growing clarity of obligations has revealed patterns of willful non-compliance.

Both developments highlight the consequences of Global Jim Crow displacing a political body with technical experts. They also hint at why those untroubled by a continent's disenfranchisement might nevertheless question the OECD's continued dominance. As Chapter 6 shows, its weaknesses are its strengths.

The OECD's increasingly sophisticated rules remain lifeless, not the dynamic legal system Hart envisioned. Thanks to an intervention by the Africa Group described in the final chapter, that could change. The advent "of a UN Framework Convention on International Tax Cooperation . . . should initiate a process that increases the legitimacy, stability, resilience, and fairness of international tax rules."[106] Whether the United Nations' return to global tax policy can deliver the future the OECD's leadership has not remains

[105] In 2021, the United States passed a law providing law enforcement with information about the ownership of corporations and other entities critical to uncovering tax evasion and money laundering. It had still not gone into effect thanks to litigation from a range of interests including small businesses when the Trump administration pulled back on enforcement of the provision. *See, e.g.*, Small Businesses Ask Court to Reject Corporate Transparency Act in Amicus Brief, NFIB (Jan. 30, 2025), https://www.nfib.com/news-article/small-businesses-ask-court-to-reject-corporate-transparency-act-in-amicus-brief/; Press Release, Treasury Department, Treasury Department Announces Suspension of Enforcement of Corporate Transparency Act Against U.S. Citizens and Domestic Reporting Companies (Mar. 2, 2025), https://home.treasury.gov/news/press-releases/sb0038.

[106] Senator The Honorable L. Ryan Pinder K.C., Attorney General and Minister of Legal Affairs for the Commonwealth of The Bahamas, Statement at the ECOSOC Special Meeting on International Cooperation in Tax Matters (Mar. 18, 2024).

uncertain. But it has become evident that merely replacing standards with rules will not.

Understanding its past is the key to global tax policy's path forward. Global Jim Crow dashed billions of dreams by sidelining the United Nations decades ago. Breathing new life into those hopes will not be as simple as creating a new UN tax convention. But, as Chapter 2 suggests, answers to the biggest questions are out there and can sometimes be found in the smallest of objects.

2

A Surprising Generosity

Stamps

One of my best childhood memories is visiting the building that once housed my father's primary school in Nassau. The small building had long before been converted into a post office. We stopped by after school nearly every day to pick up our mail.

The highlight came whenever a magazine arrived. Each month, The National Wildlife Federation's *Ranger Rick* and *National Geographic World* transported me beyond the bounds of my little island. Although I did not know it, those deliveries had once threatened a small marvel of the modern world. Chapter 1 used the contact lens to show how multinationals routinely flout tax rules. This chapter turns to the stamp to deliver a message about tax justice.

The postage stamp represents just one of many miracles across "countless areas of technology, communication and cross-border trade"[1] that we now take for granted. Such innovations revolutionized "weights and measures, international mail . . . railroad gauges, train timetables, coinage" smoothing the way for a rapidly changing world.[2] That change was not always easy.

At times, even stamps and time zones proved controversial. In 1891, France was unwilling to accept a British standard, so Paris time filled the role of Greenwich Mean Time served everywhere else. For several decades, France stubbornly remained nine minutes and twenty seconds ahead.[3]

[1] *See* JÜRGEN OSTERHAMMEL, THE TRANSFORMATION OF THE WORLD: A GLOBAL HISTORY OF THE NINETEENTH CENTURY 510 (Patrick Camiller trans.) (2015).
[2] *Id.*
[3] *Id.* at 71.

Racial Capitalism and International Tax Law. Steven A. Dean, Oxford University Press. © Steven A. Dean 2025.
DOI: 10.1093/9780197526002.003.0003

International Tax Policy

As Chapter 1 suggests, one could spend lifetimes studying international tax law without appreciating every aspect. But a straightforward fact explains much of it. Rich countries have more capital than poor ones.

Some tax rules reward countries that export capital. And some deliver more revenue to those that import it. The choice between the two can have enormous distributional consequences.

Idealists who take a cosmopolitan view of the world favor the latter. Crucially, they see the world as a collection of equally important individuals who happen to live in different countries. Since poor countries need both capital and tax revenue, cosmopolitan policies benefit capital importers.

Statists see the world as a field of combatants. Each country crafts policies that deliver results for itself and its residents. In such a world, the strongest countries naturally fight for their prerogatives as capital exporters.

The last century's two most important US international tax policy interventions fall neatly into statist and cosmopolitan camps. This chapter focuses on a distinctly cosmopolitan US tax credit that encourages US multinationals to pay tax *overseas*. Embodying an idealism one might not expect, that credit disproportionately benefits countries with fewer resources. Chapter 3 explores the rise of a second, treaty-based mechanism that favors wealthy states in part by shielding global businesses from taxes abroad.

A Global Tax System

Chapter 1 makes it easy to understand why a global tax system could never be all things to all countries. That did not discourage long-ago experts from attempting to build one. Under the auspices of the League of Nations, experts tackled the challenges of international taxation. Their efforts were prompted in part by fears that relatively new income taxes swollen by wartime revenue demands would become an obstacle to cross-border investment. They also sought another way to bind states together in the wake of conflict.

The League's experts recognized that navigating a world where each country maintained a separate system would be challenging. International mail used to be no different. Sending a letter across the Atlantic once posed a daunting challenge. The journey of a single piece of mail from Philadelphia to the Netherlands over the course of December 1845 captures the essence of the problem. Without the benefit of the not-yet-introduced postage stamp, paying for the letter's delivery presented a logistical nightmare.

The sender first paid 5 cents to send the letter from Philadelphia to New York.[4] From New York, it made its way to Le Havre in France, through Belgium, and then to the Netherlands. Upon arrival in Haarlem, it would be "marked for 85 Dutch Cents postage due" of which "50 Dutch Cents belonged to the French and 35 Dutch Cents to the Netherlands for internal postage."[5]

Each leg of the journey demanded separate payment. But how could our sender in Philadelphia pay a ship sitting in New York harbor, much less the French, Belgian, and Dutch carriers? The system worked, but it took faith. The complex arrangement relied on a letter's recipient being willing to pay the Dutch and the French portions. One letter, two payments, split three ways.

That complexity seems both familiar and inevitable for an international tax lawyer steeped in transfer pricing and other cross-border tax conflicts. Substitute far-away tax authorities for foreign postal services, and the fears of those League of Nations experts begin to come into focus. An investment by a Philadelphia resident in Haarlem presents the same fundamental challenge as that letter. Each jurisdiction the transaction touches could demand payment for its passage.

Determining who to pay and how much represents a formidable challenge. Paying a faraway tax collector might be no easier. In technical terms, Philadelphia, where the investor resides, would be the residence jurisdiction. The Netherlands would be the source of income and, therefore, the source jurisdiction in tax parlance.

Mediating between the claims of residence and source forms the heart of international tax policy. And because of the basic truth that rich countries have the capital that poor countries need, how those claims get reconciled can have an enormous impact. Who collects taxes on cross-border transactions—or who sold the stamps on my *Ranger Rick*—can matter a great deal.

[4] *Transatlantic cover to Haarlem, Netherlands*, Smithsonian Nat'l Postal Museum, https://postalmuseum.si.edu/object/npm_1992.2053.1.

[5] *Id.*

The Four Economists

We no longer worry about multiple payments across different jurisdictions when we send a letter.[6] However, as would have been true in 1845, any location where an investment generates profits may still impose a source tax. Complying with two sets of tax laws imposes a meaningful administrative burden on cross-border transactions. Even today, making sense of and complying with tax rules abroad remains difficult. A hundred years ago, the prospect would have been daunting.

The other risk lies not in more paperwork but in a bigger tax bill. Both the source and the residence country might tax the same profits. Just as one plus one equals two, income bears a double tax if the residence and the source jurisdictions tax the same transaction. The question of double taxation—when "one taxpayer is being taxed twice while the majority of men similarly situated are being taxed only once"[7]—attracted the attention of tax experts from the start.

In one of the best-known episodes in international taxation, four economists devised a solution. The men tasked with the job represented a handful of countries. "Professor Edwin R.A. Seligman of the United States, Sir Josiah Stamp of Great Britain, Professor G.W.J. Bruins of the Netherlands, and Professor Luigi Einaudi of Italy" collaborated to produce a report for the League of Nations in 1923.[8] A small circle of men laid the groundwork for the model treaties the League would publish later that decade.

Those economists' work wrestled with whether source or residence taxation should be prioritized. They chose residence.[9] By the decade's end, the League would develop those principles into treaties designed to be adopted between pairs of states.

[6] The postage stamp created a much simpler system. A Philadelphia sender would only need to purchase a single stamp right at home, delivering an elegant solution to a complex problem.

[7] Thomas S. Adams, *International and Interstate Aspects of Double Taxation*, 22 Nat'l Tax Ass'n Proc. 193, 197 (1929).

[8] Michael J. Graetz & Michael M. O'Hear, *The "Original Intent" of U.S. International Taxation*, 46 Duke L.J. 1021, 1074 (1997). Recent scholarship has offered evidence that the Dutch contributor made limited contributions to the project and that the Italian economist simply "consented for his name to be put to the Report." *See* Sunita Jogarajan, *Stamp, Seligman and the Drafting of the 1923 Experts' Report on Double Taxation*, 2013 World Tax J. 368, 391 (2013).

[9] Graetz & O'Hear, *supra* note 8, at 1077 ("The 1923 Report recommended a scheme that rested on a distinction between taxes on global income and all other taxes. The former were to be levied based solely on residence, while the latter were to be divided between residence and source based on the principle of economic allegiance, a principle that turned out to be quite generous to residence.")

Although highly technical, these treaties basically serve as tiebreakers between source and residence taxation. For example, those early models embraced the notion of "permanent establishment."[10] Treaties that include a permanent establishment threshold help shield business profits from source taxation. Unless the business maintains a sufficient footprint abroad—physical or otherwise—such a treaty would award taxing rights to the residence jurisdiction.[11] That is, of course, a win for wealthy states.

Surprising Generosity

As Chapter 3 details, bilateral tax treaties, much like those proposed by the League, would eventually become key features of international tax law. But before they became ubiquitous, the League's treaties languished in obscurity. Some treaties existed as early as the nineteenth century, notably within "the German Empire, particularly the Kingdom of Prussia."[12] But even decades after the League introduced its model, the number of treaties remained small.

Today, thousands of such treaties populate the globe. Despite the apparent advantages of paying at home—a key benefit of the postage stamp and residence taxation—treaties did not take hold until well after the League vanished. The turbulent events that would engulf the League offer one possible explanation for the long interval between their design and their embrace. Another is that double taxation had proven to be a paper tiger, more fearsome in theory than in practice.

Double tax treaties were, from the beginning, a solution in search of a problem. The United States had already embraced another method of limiting double taxation. Even before the war's end—or the League's creation—a generous American tax credit served as a bulwark against the threat of double taxation. Reflecting a circuitously cosmopolitan view that "much double taxation is caused not by unfair treatment of the foreigner, but by unfair and

[10] *Id.* at 1088–89.

[11] Only when a business opens an office—establishing a permanent place of business—in a source jurisdiction can its profits be taxed. Despite earning significant profits in a source country, a foreign business would only be taxed once it has that fixed presence. Merely earning profits without having a permanent establishment leaves a business exempt from source taxation. Such a business would pay tax on its profits, but only in its country of residence.

[12] Sunita Jogarajan, *Prelude to the International Tax Treaty Network: 1815–1914 Early Tax Treaties and the Conditions for Action*, 31 Oxford J. Legal Stud. 679, 681 (2011) Jogarajan suggests that "the advanced nature of the study of political economy in Germany at the time as compared to other countries" helps explain why treaties took root there during that period. *Id.* at 701.

thoughtless treatment of the citizen by his own state or country"[13] that tax credit prioritizes source country taxation.

The credit, devised by US experts to shield US taxpayers from US taxation to facilitate their taxation abroad, represented something remarkable. The United States unilaterally handed over whatever residence tax revenues it could have collected to source jurisdictions. It asked nothing in return.

Of course, what at first glance appears selfless may not be. Reciprocity can transform both apparent generosity and greed. For example, if a state keeps all the revenues it earns by selling postage stamps, the result may appear selfish. But if a pair of states both do it, that apparent greed may produce equal outcomes for both. The more similar the states involved, the more likely reciprocity will work such a change.

That was not the circumstance the United States found itself in when it enacted its tax credit in the waning days of World War I. The sacrifice was real and breathtakingly vast when it deferred to source jurisdictions. Investment flowed overwhelmingly in one direction. Rebuilding Europe after the war demanded an enormous amount of capital and—subsidized by the cosmopolitan credit—US investors supplied it.

Tax Credits

That tax credit works no differently than any number of other tax incentives. Purchasers of some electric cars, for example, qualify for a tax credit. The Internal Revenue Code simply says, "[t]here shall be allowed as a credit against the tax imposed by this chapter" some of the purchase price of a "new clean vehicle placed in service by the taxpayer during the taxable year."[14] Up to a given amount, each dollar of tax you owe can be offset by amounts spent on the right kind of vehicle. The tax credit serves as a kind of universal rebate, subsidizing the purchase of an electric car.

The tax credit the United States offered more than a century ago in the wake of World War I provides the same result for "the amount of any income . . . taxes paid or accrued during the taxable year to any foreign country"[15]

[13] Adams, *supra* note 7, at 196.
[14] I.R.C. § 30D.
[15] I.R.C. § 901(b)(1). In the absence of a foreign tax credit, a business might be allowed to deduct foreign taxes just as it would any other business expense, from employee salaries to the costs of leasing office space. But that would not be nearly as appealing.

effectively subsidizing rival governments. Assume a US investor paid a dollar of German income tax. If they also owed a dollar of US income tax, the German payment could entirely eliminate their US tax. They would pay only one dollar of tax. They would pay it all to Germany.[16]

At the risk of understatement, the credit can quickly become much more complicated than this example suggests. A modern business may operate in a dozen countries that impose taxes at a dozen different rates, with each tax potentially qualifying for the credit. Headlines like "Electric Vehicle Tax Credit Rules Create 'Chaos for Consumers'"[17] suggest the complexity that can come with any tax credit's generosity.

Understanding the intricacies of this US tax credit for non-US taxes changes little about its bottom-line result. When a US taxpayer's investment triggers tax elsewhere—in Germany or the Netherlands for example—the risk of double taxation stays low. The United States would offset any payment of overseas income tax against the taxpayer's US tax obligations.[18] When the US tax collector comes calling, the investor can—however implausible it may sound—satisfy its demands by offering evidence that it paid someone else.

The Rise of Cosmopolitanism in US International Tax Policy

By the end of World War I, there may have been German investments in the United States. But for every one of those, there would have been many

[16] A deduction would reduce their US income tax burden, but by pennies on the dollar. If their marginal tax rate were 20 percent, they would save 20 cents of tax but would still owe 80 cents in US tax. Better than no tax break at all—which would doom our investor to the dreadful fate of paying a combined two dollars of tax—but paying one dollar in tax will always beat paying $1.80.

[17] Lawrence Ulrich, *Electric Vehicle Tax Credit Rules Create "Chaos for Consumers,"* N.Y. Times (Apr. 20, 2023), https://www.nytimes.com/2023/04/20/business/electric-vehicle-tax-credits-consumers.html.

[18] Every tax credit presents its own unique challenges. If, for example, the Netherlands imposed an exceedingly high rate of tax, it would generate a correspondingly large foreign tax credit. That credit could offset US tax on income earned in the United States. One of the first big changes to the foreign tax credit came in 1921, intended to avoid that result. Congress has since revisited the foreign tax credit many times, leaving no shortage of complexity in its wake. Michael J. Graetz, *The David R. Tillinghast Lecture: Taxing International Income: Inadequate Principles, Outdated Concepts, and Unsatisfactory Policies*, 54 Tax L. Rev. 261, 263 (2001) ("[T]he method for determining the limitation on foreign tax credits has taken a variety of forms over the years, having been computed based on a taxpayer's overall foreign source income when first enacted in 1921, limited to the lesser of an overall or per-country amount in the 1930's, 1940's, and early 1950's, and computed country by country in the latter half of the 1950's. Beginning in 1960, taxpayers were given the option of an overall or per country limitation until 1976 when the per country limitation was repealed and the law returned to its 1921 shape.").

more US investors helping rebuild the former adversary. Because of the war, Germany and the rest of Europe desperately needed capital to rebuild. The United States delivered. "In 1914, the United States was a net debtor on international account by $3.7 billion. By 1929, it was a net creditor by more than $10 billion."[19]

The United States enacted its tax credit precisely when it would be sure to lose the most by doing so. That surprised no one more than the man who designed it. The credit's creator, T.S. Adams, hoped it would prevent cross-border investors from "being taxed twice . . . by the same tax."[20] But he seemed startled that it actually became law.

Britain offered a similar tax credit, but only within its empire.[21] Adams insisted that he had "no notion . . . that it would ever receive serious consideration"[22] in the cross-border context. He viewed double taxation as a question of principle—"grounded in concerns for fairness"[23]—and seemed delighted to see the credit thrive despite its enormous cost to the US Treasury.

The credit appalled Seligman. Prioritizing the needs of outsiders over the interests of the United States, it prompted Seligman to observe that "[i]n a country which already has many foreign investments or where much business is already carried on abroad, this would put its exchequer at the complete mercy of the foreign country. . . . It is an over-generous and one-sided arrangement."[24] Seligman conceded that the credit might be "endurable or even desirable for a country which is anxious to favor the business enterprises carried on abroad by its own nationals; and which is ready to make sacrifices for that end" but condemned the credit for "making a present of the revenue to other countries."[25]

[19] Sunita Jogarajan, Double Taxation and the League of Nations 13 (2018).

[20] Adams, *supra* note 7, at 197.

[21] Britain provided an offset against UK taxes for taxes paid within its empire. Income earned outside the British Empire was exempted from tax until remitted to the UK. *See* Mitchell B. Carroll, Prevention of International Double Taxation and Fiscal Evasion: Two Decades of Progress Under the League of Nations 8 (1939).

[22] Adams, *supra* note 7, at 198.

[23] Graetz, *supra* note 18, at 296.

[24] Edwin R. A. Seligman, Double Taxation and International Fiscal Cooperation: Being a Series of Lectures Delivered at the Académie de Droit International de La Haye 135 (1928).

[25] *Id.*

The Tax Subsidy

The dispute between Adams and Seligman highlights the conflict at the heart of global tax policy. Two "competing philosophical theories of cosmopolitanism and statism" echo their divergent views of the credit.[26] The credit would be easy for "proponents of cosmopolitan justice" to embrace. They argue that "justice should prevail between individuals irrespective of their national affiliation."[27] A cosmopolitan would shrug off Seligman's objection since the credit would favor poor countries.

By contrast, statists insist that "justice is a duty that is a derivative of political institutions and focus on the state as the primary forum for justice."[28] They would respond to the credit as forcefully as Seligman did. Since states owe their primary loyalty to their own citizens and such a gift of revenue conflicts with that duty, the credit represents a failure from a statist perspective, even if it helps outsiders more than it hurts insiders.

A statist might accept such a tax credit on humanitarian grounds, acknowledging that helping others in extreme circumstances matters more than helping their own. Empathy for a devastated Europe—for instance—might have moved a statist to accept the credit. The resulting loss of revenue would be justified by the imperative to ensure that outsiders' basic needs were met.[29]

When the United States volunteered to shield cross-border transactions from double taxation unilaterally, it knowingly made a present of its revenue to other countries. At the end of World War I, its enviable place in the world left no doubt that it would overwhelmingly be the residence country rather than the source country. But it did not hesitate. Whether it did so in recognition of the demands of justice or despite them, it proved that solving the

[26] Tsilly Dagan, International Tax Policy: Between Competition and Cooperation 9 (2018).

[27] *Id.*

[28] *Id.*

[29] Kysar offers a realist explanation for rejecting an extreme beggar-thy-neighbor approach. Rebecca M. Kysar, *The Global Tax Deal and The New International Economic Governance*, 74 Tax L. Rev. 171, 219 (2024) ("One lingering question might be why nations should care about the well-being of other less fortunate ones. A realist view would posit that nations act only on self-interest and bargaining power, with international relations defined as a struggle between nations for their own defense and security. But even from this narrow vantage point, a wealthy nation's building of alliances with emerging and developing economies not only reflects those economies' increased bargaining power in today's world but can also further the wealthy nation's national security interests by, for instance, making those economies less beholden to unwanted influences and including them in the pursuit of more resilient supply chains").

problem of double taxation was no problem at all, easily addressed by the action of a single sovereign.

The credit was also good business. For US ventures to prosper, they needed European consumers to purchase their goods. The credit served as a discreet way of supporting Europe's rebuilding effort. The United States could have been less subtle, but the tax credit delivered cash to former allies and enemies without attracting unwanted scrutiny.[30]

The credit dovetailed with a US preference to "exercise economic leadership yet maintain a limited government and minimize diplomatic conflict."[31] A credit favoring private investment in Europe also benefited from the public's blind spot for tax subsidies.[32] As an alternative to "instituting government foreign loans, lowering tariffs, or canceling debts—all of which they considered politically impossible—the Republicans encouraged private loans abroad as the primary way of recycling cash for purchase of more American exports."[33] The tax credit quietly provided a boost to such efforts.

Substituting Order for Anarchy

As the 1923 report acknowledges, the League of Nations saw a world made up not merely of different countries but of different types of countries.[34]

[30] Emily Rosenberg, Spreading the American Dream: American Economic and Cultural Expansion, 1890–1945, at 143 (1982) ("The United States, which emerged from World War I with a great surplus of capital and owned a majority of the world's gold, could hardly expect to sell exports without first transferring some of its wealth to foreign buyers. There were several ways to recycle America's wealth to foreign customers. Many people in the international business community favored large government programs for foreign lending, but both the Wilson and Harding Administrations rejected that on ideological and political grounds. Another partial solution was to cancel the Allies' war debts to the United States so that the Allies would reduce the heavy reparations they levied on Germany.").

[31] *Id.* at 146. ("By encouraging lending through private banking channels, Hoover hoped America could exercise economic leadership yet maintain a limited government and minimize diplomatic conflict."). Measured simply in terms of the amount of private lending that took place during the 1920s, the effort seems to have been successful. Jogarajan, *supra* note 19, at 13 ("Between 1920 and 1929, American private lenders furnished $7.6 billion in foreign loans.").

[32] Stanley S. Surrey, Pathways to Tax Reform: The Concept of Tax Expenditures 136 (1973) ("[M]any tax incentives look, and are, highly irrational when phrased as direct expenditure programs structured the same way. Indeed, it is doubtful that most of our existing tax incentives would ever have been introduced, let alone accepted, if so structured, and many would be laughed out of Congress").

[33] Rosenberg, *supra* note 30, at 145.

[34] G.W.J. Bruins et al., Econ. & Fin. Comm'n, League of Nations, Report on Double Taxation Submitted to the Financial Committee 51 (1923) ("Looking forward to the future, the influence of example by others and the spirit encouraged by the operations of the League of Nations indicate the possibility of a development away from localised ideas and from the earlier stages of economic thought typified by strict adherence to the principle of origin. Moreover,

Creating a structure capable of weaving the world's heterogeneity into stability represented the League's core mission. However focused its tax experts may have been on questions of source and residence, that broader mission helps explain why the credit's existence did not preempt the League's work on international taxation.

As the four economists began their push, the League urged them to find a way of "substituting international order for the international anarchy which reigns" in international taxation.[35] The League clearly outlined how that order should be achieved, urging "the promotion of international conventions." Well before the four economists' 1923 report but after the creation of the US credit, the League called for "a model convention upon which actual conventions between countries could be based."[36]

The League's mandate to create stability explains that preference for structure, urging states to "conduct their foreign policies through certain machinery, in certain conferences, and on the basis of certain obligations providing for international co-operation and peaceful settlement of disputes."[37] Perhaps inevitably, given that preference for diplomacy, the 1923 report would prove to be "something of a repudiation of the American credit."[38] Even if unilateral approaches like the credit adequately addressed the threat of double taxation, they did not curb the anarchy the League feared.

as semi-developed countries become more industrialised, with the resulting attenuation of the distinctions between debtor and creditor countries, the principle of personal faculty at the place of residence will become more widely understood and appreciated and the disparity between the two principles will become less obvious, so that we may look forward to an ultimate development of national ideas on uniform lines toward [residence taxation], if not as a more logical and theoretically defensible economic view of the principles of income taxation, at least as the most practicable solution of the difficulties of double taxation.").

[35] Sunita Jogarajan, *Stamp, Seligman and the Drafting of the 1923 Experts' Report on Double Taxation*, 5 World Tax J. 368, 372–73 (2013) (quoting Letter from F.H. Nixon to Stamp (Jan. 4, 1922), *in* Edwin Robert Anderson Seligman, Box 44, Folder Box 118, League of Nations—Committee on Double Taxation, Correspondence & Notes, 1921-23 (Rare Book & Manuscript Library)).

[36] *Id.* at 373.

[37] C. Howard-Ellis, The Origin, Structure & Working of the League of Nations 58 (1929).

[38] Graetz & O'Hear, *supra* note 8, at 1076 n.220 (suggesting that "as a progressive tax on worldwide income, the American income tax, under the reasoning of Seligman and the other League economists, should not have deferred in any sense to foreign source-based levies").

The Costs of Stability

The waning of empire's constraining influence demanded new tools for producing stability.[39] The League's Mandate System illustrates its efforts to construct alternatives to direct imperial control. Tradition would have allowed the war's victors to claim the colonies once held by its losers. But after World War I, the world's appetite for that sort of colonialism had declined. Under the Mandate System, former colonies—"peoples who could not *yet* stand on their own"[40]—would be nominally independent but subject to external control.

The Mandates were classified according to their perceived proximity to fitness for true independence. A Mandates, B Mandates, and C Mandates would be each governed by clearly defined rules specifying their degree of autonomy. A Mandates (including former parts of the Ottoman Empire) would possess the most, and C Mandates (including "South West Africa, New Guinea and small Pacific islands like Nauru") would have the least.[41] Such mechanisms would—the League hoped—"uphold imperial authority and strengthen the prestige and legitimacy of alien, non-consensual rule."[42]

While delivering a subsidy to US businesses helping rebuild Europe and solving what even experts like Seligman seemed to dismiss as a primarily theoretical[43] problem, the tax credit accomplished none of the League's broader priorities. The model double tax treaties that the League would produce later in the decade did. Like the Mandate System, those treaties would bind nominally independent states, imposing external constraints on their autonomy without compromising their formal sovereignty.

Thanks to those treaties, international taxation could have been rescued from anarchy. Instead, few treaties took root for decades. It would not be

[39] Adom Getachew, Worldmaking After Empire: The Rise and Fall of Self-Determination 10 (2019) (arguing that "Woodrow Wilson and Jan Smuts excised the revolutionary implications of the Bolshevik right to self-determination and repurposed the principle to preserve racial hierarchy in the new international organization").

[40] Ntina Tzouvala, Capitalism as Civilisation: A History of International Law 97 (2020).

[41] *Id.* at 101.

[42] Susan Pedersen, The Guardians: The League of Nations and the Crisis of Empire 13 (2015). The racial subtext of the League's hierarchy was not terribly subtle. *See* Getachew, *supra* note 39, at 42 (observing that the League's supporters "argued that racially backward people were not suited for democracy but could partake in minimal forms of consent and were owed some modicum of respect").

[43] *See* Jogarajan, *supra* note 35, at 379 (noting that in their correspondence "Seligman . . . queried whether Stamp was in fact of the opinion that any effort to avert double taxation was unnecessary as there was virtually no such double taxation").

until after the League's collapse that its "certain machinery" and "certain obligations" would flourish.[44]

Statism, Cosmopolitanism, and the Postage Stamp

The Mandate System offers a stark demonstration of what may seem surprising to those tempted to equate international cooperation with cosmopolitanism: international cooperation can be a form of "predatory inclusion."[45] The League's work could—and in the case of the Mandate System did—serve as a more palatable form of imperialism.[46] Under the League's new architecture, independence did not mean equality.[47]

The Mandate System offers an example of international legal frameworks producing unequal results. Many forms of international cooperation produce clear winners and losers.[48] Sometimes, as with France's quixotic struggle

[44] In other words, those treaties helped ensure that "empire could end" while "private property rights were protected worldwide and the free flow of capital and goods disciplined the behavior of postcolonial states." Quinn Slobodian, Globalists: The End of Empire and the Birth of Neoliberalism 220 (2018).

[45] Keeanga-Yamahtta Taylor, Race for Profit: How Banks and the Real Estate Industry Undermined Black Homeownership 5 (2019) ("Predatory inclusion describes how African American homebuyers were granted access to conventional real estate practices and mortgage financing, but on more expensive and comparatively unequal terms. These terms were justified because of the disproportionate conditions of poverty and dilapidation in a scarred urban geography that had been produced by years of public and private institutional neglect.").

[46] The colonization of Africa offers an even starker example of international law facilitating exploitation. *See* Getachew, *supra* note 39, at 18 ("[T]he colonization of Africa in the late nineteenth century was facilitated through international treaties and conferences.").

[47] Getachew shows that through innovations like the Mandate System, a "globalized Jim Crow . . . a set of ideologies and practices of racial domination, emerging out of the experience of New World slavery, were internationalized." *Id.* at 22. She explains that:

> Smuts's mandates system embodied this differentiated application of self-determination. According to Smuts, the [League of Nations] would be guided by the general principles of "no annexation and the self-determination of nations." And yet the "self-determination of nations" would have to be fitted for the capacities of different peoples. While nations like Poland could be immediately granted statehood, many of the nations under Ottoman rule were capable of autonomy but would need "the guiding hand of some external authority." At the bottom of Smuts's hierarchy were the German colonies in the Pacific and Africa. Smuts viewed these colonial subjects similarly to black South Africans and argued, "It would be impracticable to apply any idea of political self-determination in the European sense" to the inhabitants of these territories.
>
> *Id.* at 49 (footnotes omitted).

[48] This problem is not, of course, unique to the Mandate System. *See id.* at 23 ("[E]ven if the international order secured full membership and sovereign equality to all states, relations of economic dependence and inequalities of political power between states would continue to create the conditions in which postcolonial states would be subject to the arbitrary wills of powerful states and other international actors.").

against Greenwich Mean Time, cooperation threatens little more than pride. But often, the stakes are higher, which brings us back to the postage stamp.

The postage stamp revolutionized global communications, streamlining sending mail internationally. Eventually, the world changed, and so did the hidden machinery that made cross-border correspondence effortless. The postage stamp had long succeeded because of its simplicity. It survived by adapting.

For nearly a century, the country selling a stamp kept whatever it collected. All the other members of the Universal Postal Union did the same. That consensus ensured that every letter and package reached its intended destination with only one payment at the point of origin.

Then came the existential threat posed by my *Ranger Rick*. Initially, it "was assumed that a letter gives rise to a reply and that the total number of letters dispatched from a country therefore approximates to the total number of letters sent in the opposite direction."[49] That may have been true initially, but much changed as the postage stamp neared its 100th birthday.

Over time, asymmetries emerged in the flow of mail and of commercial deliveries in particular. Simply put, more media was sent from wealthy states than to them. For the stamp's "first 95 years, mail was transferred without compensation"[50] but the growing imbalance in the flow of commercial mail made that arrangement untenable. No American kids subscribed to Bahamian nature magazines, so the Bahamas would have been forced to deliver mine for free.

Those states that sold fewer stamps and delivered more than their share of mail insisted on a new approach. At the United Nations, Colombia proposed providing "justice for the young countries receiving large quantities of mail, especially from the industrialized countries."[51] Adopted by secret ballot in 1969, the new compensation system went into effect in 1971. The payment of terminal dues "ensures that the designated operator of the destination country is compensated for the costs associated with the handling,

[49] Paulus Schoorl et al., Universal Postal Union, Terminal Dues: New Frontiers for a Changing World 107 (2021), https://www.upu.int/UPU/media/upu/files/postalSolutions/remuneration/Research%20and%20publication/Terminal-dues-New-frontiers-for-a-changing-world_2.pdf.

[50] *Id.* at 5.

[51] *Id.* at 116.

transporting and delivering of the postal items it receives from the sending designated operator."[52]

In other words, the terminal dues system delivered global postal justice, saving the postage stamp. By categorizing countries according to their ability to "self-finance postal development," those terminal dues provide more resources to states that need them. By a formula that considers per capita incomes and the "average costs per letter reflect[ing] the difficulties" of delivering mail, that system keeps mail flowing seamlessly around the globe.[53]

Conclusion

The terminal dues system came at the end of a decade in which global tax policy took a different path. After playing second fiddle to the cosmopolitan credit, the League's decades-old double tax treaties suddenly flourished. Terminal dues sought to help poor countries; the League's treaties to control them. Thanks to the United Nations, terminal dues embraced a business-friendly cosmopolitan vision. The double tax treaty never came up for a vote.

As detailed in Chapter 3, US multinationals such as Citibank and General Motors had long sought treaty protection from foreign taxes. But now they succeeded. US experts had promoted the League's treaties for decades with little success. Somehow, just as the United Nations stood poised to create the global tax equivalent of terminal dues, the world finally listened to them. Chapter 3 contextualizes the dramatic turnabout in the fortunes of the tax treaty, describing the origins of Global Jim Crow.

As African colonies began gaining sovereignty, Europe and North America feared the "increased taxation" that those "independent governments and non-white rule"[54] might produce. Forsaking the increasingly diverse United Nations, they reached back in time to embrace the League's treaties. Designed

[52] *Terminal Dues*, UNIVERSAL POSTAL UNION, https://www.upu.int/en/Postal-Solutions/Programmes-Services/Remuneration/Terminal-dues.
[53] *Id.*
[54] Vanessa Ogle, *'Funk Money': The End of Empires, the Expansion of Tax Havens, and Decolonization as an Economic and Financial Event*, 249 PAST & PRESENT 213, 214 (2020). Ogle describes the "deep-seated racist convictions" that made decolonization so frightening to Europeans that they "simply could not imagine economic life continuing in regular form after independence." *Id.*

as a form of legitimized, alien, non-consensual rule to suppress source taxation, those treaties helped produce a "globalized Jim Crow."[55] Treaties and the new, all-white organization that championed them ensured that "empire could . . . accommodate itself to the loss of direct control by deploying the international structures of unequal integration."[56]

[55] GETACHEW, *supra* note 39, at 21. Getachew applies the notion of a global Jim Crow to refer to "a set of ideologies and practices of racial domination." *Id.* The Mandate System and double tax treaties both represent such structures.

[56] *Id.* at 22.

3

The Rise of Global Jim Crow

Dream

My parents married the same year Congress marked Jim Crow's end. That came just two years after Martin Luther King Jr. delivered his "I Have a Dream" speech in 1963. Often remembered for an optimistic vision of a post-racial future, King's remarks began with a sobering reminder that under Jim Crow, "America ha[d] given the Negro people a bad check, a check which has come back marked insufficient funds."[1] Thanks to Jim Crow, King observed, a century after emancipation, "the Negro lives on a lonely island of poverty in the midst of a vast ocean of material prosperity."

As King related in his speech, he had four little children, just like my parents. And they, like King, may have dreamed that we would one day live in a nation where we would not be judged by the color of our skin but by the content of our character. But that imagined tomorrow was not my parents' reality. Even though Jim Crow had ended, racism would haunt their union from the start.

Because my father was Black, my mother's parents disowned her. After having their first two daughters while living not far from where Minneapolis police officers would one day murder George Floyd, they left for the Bahamas. They never moved back to the United States.

The Fairy Tale of Global Tax Policy

As complex as the rules of global tax policy may be, its history is simple. The League of Nations identified the threat of double taxation and created double

[1] Martin Luther King Jr., I Have a Dream speech at the Lincoln Memorial in Washington, D.C. (Aug. 28, 1963).

Racial Capitalism and International Tax Law. Steven A. Dean, Oxford University Press. © Steven A. Dean 2025.
DOI: 10.1093/9780197526002.003.0004

tax treaties to tame it. With that elegant framework in place, nothing changed for a century.[2]

The lie at the heart of that fairy tale can be measured in decades. It can also be weighed in the many billions of dollars quietly shifted from the Global South to the Global North. The modern double tax treaty has been fibbing about its age to the tune of about forty years. It has also been less than forthcoming about its parentage. This chapter shows why that matters for anyone concerned about human rights or sustainable development.

Seligman's statist treaty eclipsed Adams's cosmopolitan credit in the 1960s (not the 1920s). The rise of the treaty formed part of a broader transformation, anticipatorily rejecting demands for postcolonial economic justice. Had he survived to the 1970s, King would have recognized the complaint at the heart of the UN's New International Economic Order, discussed in the closing chapters. The treaty's preemptive challenge hinged on the ouster of the United Nations and the rise of the OECD as the home of global tax policy. The OECD published its first model tax treaty in 1963—the year King spoke—marking the end of the era of source taxation with a bad check for newly independent African states.

The Importance of Resources

The two eras of global tax policy described in this chapter and in Chapter 2 offer a jarring contrast. The distance between the extravagant generosity of the tax credit and the brutality of sanctions considered in Chapter 5 reveals an extraordinary transformation. This chapter describes the upheaval that triggered that fall from grace.

The pull of statism can offer only a partial answer. The push of fear played a key role as well. The constraints on tax sovereignty that define Global Jim Crow reflect multinationals' success in resisting rising tax burdens. The xenophobia and racism that have become an accepted feature of mainstream global tax policy discourse suggest a more complex picture.

[2] Rebecca M. Kysar, *The Global Tax Deal and The New International Economic Governance*, 74 Tax L. Rev. 171, 183–84 (2024). Kysar offers a standard telling of that false story ("the jurisdictional bargain struck in the 1920s League of Nations held for nearly a century, with its general division of taxing rights embodied in the OECD Model Tax Convention, which nearly all countries follow regardless of their OECD membership"). That telling highlights the decades-long gap in the story of tax treaties that has long hidden in plain sight.

The OECD displaced the United Nations at a particular moment in history. The end of colonial rule offered a brighter future for Africans. Fueled by the same dreams that made King's speech so memorable, independence offered new nations the freedom to author their own destinies. Racial fears that Seligman helped legitimate and institutionalize would dash those hopes.

For newly independent African states, the promise of fiscal sovereignty proved empty. Thanks to Global Jim Crow, independence would leave African states without the resources necessary for stability and sustainable development. "For administrators of the new states, public resources were key to resolving what they believed were the most serious problems inherited from the colonial period, particularly economic inequality, poverty, and unemployment."[3] Unfortunately, the cosmopolitanism that defined the first decades of global tax policy dissipated, allowing African dreams to give way to autocracy.[4]

During Jim Crow, tax law played a key role in making separate unequal in the United States. As decolonization remade the world, the United States helped Jim Crow's inequality transcend its borders. This chapter tells the story of the disenfranchisement of Africa's new states from the global tax policymaking process.

The racism the Dunning School helped leverage into decades of segregation and legal discrimination within the United States created a path for the OECD to displace an increasingly diverse United Nations. That would devastate newly formed African governments, starving them of urgently needed tax revenues. The fallout continues to be felt across the globe, affecting rich and poor countries.

As the following chapters show, the successful effort to create an undemocratic governance structure for global tax policy did more than deny African states the means to shape their own future. Not for the first time, racism left

[3] Leigh A. Gardner, Taxing Colonial Africa: The Political Economy of British Imperialism 226 (2012).

[4] Gardner argues that "the rapid move towards single-party rule amongst African governments was closely related to the weakness of the fiscal foundations which their democracies had inherited from their colonial predecessors." *Id.* at 227. Tax sparing, famously rejected by Stanley Surrey—or something equally generous—could have been that missing piece. *See* David R. Tillinghast, *The Contributions of Stanley S. Surrey to the International Aspects of Taxation*, 38 Nat'l Tax J. 267, 268 (1985) (explaining that Surrey rejected tax sparing because he saw it as "mindless perversion"). Of course, even with the benefit of the cosmopolitan foreign tax credit, Europe would prove susceptible to autocracy.

deep self-inflicted wounds. Better for no one to have access to revenue than for everyone to have it.[5]

In the waning days of Jim Crow, as King spoke to more than a quarter of a million people in Washington, a stable and successful global tax architecture was being quietly upended. The power of racial bias and corporate greed combined with disastrous results. A collection of majority-white countries would create an organization devoted to the well-being of its members, setting it on a path toward becoming a World Tax Organization in all but name.

The US Civil War and Reconstruction

Understanding Seligman's complex contribution to Global Jim Crow requires an examination of the role of the Dunning School in fueling Jim Crow, the violent system of subordination that delivered King's bad check. It all started with Reconstruction. That era began in earnest with the end of the US Civil War.

The nation had been devastated by what remains the Western Hemisphere's bloodiest contest.[6] President Lincoln had signed the Emancipation Proclamation years before the Thirteenth Amendment finally abolished slavery. However, neither answered the question of how to integrate four million newly free individuals into the country's civic life.

Nor did the end of fighting mean an end to conflict. On April 9, 1865, the Confederate General Robert E. Lee surrendered to General Ulysses S. Grant. President Lincoln would be assassinated less than a week later.

On the day he was shot, Lincoln's Secretary of War "presented his Cabinet with a tentative plan to appoint military governors for Virginia and North Carolina."[7] Lincoln had previously done the same for other Confederate

[5] In this case, the damage recalls Heather McGhee's lost swimming pools. McGhee explains that even when policymakers do not make "racial stereotypes an explicit part of their communications strategy" bias can be harnessed to favor powerful interests at the expense of ordinary Americans. Heather McGhee, The Sum of Us: What Racism Costs Everyone and How We Can Prosper Together xiv (2022). McGhee describes overhearing a legislator invoking racial stereotypes to justify opposing bankruptcy reform as one example of how racism has made it difficult for "generations of American leadership to solve big problems and reliably improve the quality of life for most people." *Id.* at xi.

[6] The number of US military deaths in the Civil War approach those in both World Wars combined and exceed the number lost during the Vietnam War by an order of magnitude.

[7] Eric Foner, Reconstruction: America's Unfinished Revolution 1863–1877, at 75 (2014).

states under Union control. Such federal interventions made Lincoln a target.

Lincoln's successor, President Johnson, took a more modest approach. His vision of Reconstruction largely left Southern states free to create their own post-Confederacy legal framework. During that first phase of Reconstruction, that took the shape of Black Codes. Representing an "indisputable attempt on the part of the Southern States to make Negroes slaves in everything but name,"[8] those Black Codes varied in their details. Still, none offered anything resembling citizenship or equality.

Black Codes offered "the right to hold property" and "to sue and be sued."[9] They also ensured that "family relations for the first time were legally recognized."[10] But those rights remained profoundly compromised. In North Carolina, Black Americans could testify only where "rights of persons or property of persons of color shall be put in issue" with their testimony ignored in all other cases.[11] Interracial marriage remained unlawful. It would continue to be illegal in some states even after my parents married (but it had never been outlawed in Minnesota).

Black Codes did not attempt to be subtle. "Mississippi simply reenacted her slave code" with rules once applying to enslaved persons now targeted at freedmen.[12] One Louisiana town imposed a law providing that any freedman discovered in public after 10 pm without written permission from an employer could be forced to work for five days without compensation.[13]

Johnson's Presidential Reconstruction gave way to Congressional—or Radical—Reconstruction. The 1866 election provided Congressional Republicans with large majorities in both the House and the Senate. Those comfortable margins offered protection from the threat of a Johnson veto. Legislators used that power to send Federal troops to former Confederate states to oversee a series of constitutional conventions. Those constitutions succeeded in every state except Alabama and Mississippi.[14]

Radical Reconstruction's success in protecting the rights of Black Americans triggered a "wave of counterrevolutionary terror" by paramilitary

[8] W. E. Burghardt Du Bois, Black Reconstruction: An Essay Toward a History of the Past Which Black Folk Played in the Attempt to Reconstruct Democracy in America 167 (1935).
[9] *Id.*
[10] *Id.*
[11] *Id.* at 176–77.
[12] *Id.* at 177.
[13] *Id.*
[14] Foner, *supra* note 7, at 332.

organizations such as the Ku Klux Klan.[15] Violence "swept over large parts of the South between 1868 and 1871" on a scale without "counterpart either in the American experience or in that of the other Western Hemisphere societies that abolished slavery in the 19th century."[16] Federal military and legal intervention at the direction of then-President Ulysses S. Grant proved necessary to bring the Klan to heel.[17]

The Myth of Reconstruction

The story of Reconstruction offers three crucial lessons for global tax policy. First, inclusion does not always come easily. Black Codes made a mockery of freedom. Even well-intentioned attempts to deliver voting rights to formerly enslaved people met with limited success. The Fifteenth Amendment—the third Constitutional revision during Reconstruction—guaranteed Black men the right to vote. But when federal troops withdrew, its promises proved meaningless.[18]

With the end of Reconstruction came the start of Jim Crow. Reconstruction Amendments notwithstanding, states employed "ingenious methods of limiting black voting power" such as poll taxes to "undermine the legal and political gains blacks had achieved."[19] Black men had the right to vote, but they could not exercise it.

The second lesson is the ease with which gains can be lost. Reconstruction eventually yielded to a conflagration of fraud and terror, but before it did, Black men voted for and served as judges and legislators. John Mercer Langston became the first Black Congressman from Virginia in 1888. The next would not be elected until 1992.

[15] *Id.* at 425 ("the Klan was a military force serving the interests of the Democratic party, the planter class, and all those who desired the restoration of white supremacy . . . it sought to affect power relations, both public and private . . . and restore racial subordination in every aspect of Southern life").

[16] *Id.*

[17] The resulting litigation involved more than 700 indictments of Klansmen in Mississippi alone. In South Carolina, soldiers "root[ed] out" the Klan. Ultimately, the Federal government's "willingness to bring its legal and coercive authority to bear" had the desired effect. *Id.* at 457–59. By 1872, the Federal government "had broken the Klan's back and produced a dramatic decline in violence throughout the South." *Id.* at 459.

[18] The withdrawal of most Federal troops from the South by 1877 left the Ku Klux Klan once again free to terrorize. Conditions "varied considerably from state to state. . . . But in the Deep South, where electoral fraud was widespread and the threat of violence hung most heavily over the black community" political rights progressively eroded. *Id.* at 590.

[19] *Id.* at 422–23.

The third lies in the story of Reconstruction itself and how it would come to be told. With few notable exceptions—such as the book *Black Reconstruction* by W.E.B. Dubois—the real history of Reconstruction, of meaningful progress undone by violent white resistance, would not be told until almost a century after the end of the Civil War. Instead, Reconstruction would be offered as a different kind of cautionary tale.

Historians explained Reconstruction's "failure" as the product of Black incompetence and corruption.

> This rewriting of Reconstruction's history was accorded scholarly legitimacy—to its everlasting shame—by the nation's fraternity of professional historians.... The views of the Dunning School shaped historical writing for generations and achieved wide popularity through D. W. Griffith's film *Birth of a Nation* (which glorified the Ku Klux Klan and had its premiere at the White House during Woodrow Wilson's Presidency).... Few interpretations of history have had such far-reaching consequences as this image of Reconstruction.[20]

The Dunning School insisted that "negro incapacity" had made "childlike blacks . . . unprepared for freedom and incapable of properly exercising the political rights" Reconstruction "thrust upon them"[21] thanks to interfering Northerners. The 1956 edition of a history textbook by Stanford University professor Thomas Bailey, which might have been part of my mother's high school curriculum, taught the same lies. Now in its 17th edition and still in widespread use today, the book taught that formerly enslaved people "were so 'hapless' and incompetent, so unable to exist in freedom, that after the Civil War scores of them simply lay down and died."[22]

Only with a burgeoning civil rights movement fueled partly by Cold War politics would the attitudes and assumptions at the heart of the Dunning School become untenable. "How could American democracy be a beacon during the Cold War, and a model for those struggling against Soviet oppression, if the United States itself practiced brutal discrimination against

[20] *Id.* at 609–10.

[21] *Id.* at xviii. (quoting Coulter) ("The fact that blacks took part in government wrote E. Merton Coulter in the last full-scale history of Reconstruction written entirely within the Dunning tradition [in 1947], was a 'diabolical' development, 'to be remembered, shuddered at, and execrated.'").

[22] Donald Yacovone, Teaching White Supremacy: America's Democratic Ordeal and the Forging of Our National Identity 267 (2022).

minorities within its own borders?"[23] The end of Jim Crow's legal discrimination may not have meant an end to discrimination and exploitation[24] but the change it brought helped to break the Dunning School's spell.

Scholars finally acknowledged the accuracy of Dubois's account—rejecting the falsehood that Reconstruction served as an indictment of Black governance—in the 1960s and 1970s. Eric Foner's definitive history of the era, *Reconstruction: America's Unfinished Revolution, 1863–1877*, published in 1988, completed the dismantling of the intellectual pedigree of such ideas. But in the 1950s, as decolonization began to sweep across Africa, the Dunning School narrative's hold on the nation's collective imagination remained firm, deeply entrenched from high schools to elite universities.

The Dunning School's impact would extend well beyond the United States. Just as it did at home, "the alleged failure of Reconstruction became part of the ideology of the white man's burden, cited all over the world to demonstrate the incapacity of nonwhite peoples for self-government."[25] Visions of "Reconstruction as a time of corruption and misgovernment caused by the enfranchisement of the former slaves"[26] had lasting economic consequences everywhere, but particularly for Africa.

Within the United States, "'the alleged horrors of Reconstruction' did much to freeze the mind of the white South in unalterable opposition to outside pressures for social change and to any thought of . . . eliminating segregation or restoring suffrage to disenfranchised blacks."[27] The scientific racism at the heart of the Dunning School "also justified Northern indifference to the nullification of the Fourteenth and Fifteenth Amendments."[28] When

[23] Mary L. Dudziak, Cold War Civil Rights: Race and the Image of American Democracy 1 (2011). Dudziak offers ample evidence confirming Derrick Bell's conclusion that an interest convergence between Black and white Americans opened the door to Civil Rights breakthroughs, including landmark Supreme Court victories.

I contend that the decision in *Brown* to break with the Court's long-held position on these issues cannot be understood without some consideration of the decision's value to whites, not simply those concerned about the immorality of racial inequality, but also those whites in policymaking positions able to see the economic and political advances at home and abroad that would follow abandonment of segregation. First, the decision helped to provide immediate credibility to America's struggle with Communist countries to win the hearts and minds of emerging third world peoples.

Derrick A. Bell Jr., *Brown v. Board of Education and the Interest-Convergence Dilemma*, 93 Harv. L. Rev. 518, 524 (1980).

[24] Taylor demonstrates how "predatory inclusion" prevented the end of Jim Crow from providing Blacks meaningful opportunities to participate on equal footing in the real estate market. Keeanga-Yamahtta Taylor, Race for Profit: How Banks and the Real Estate Industry Undermined Black Homeownership 17–19 (2019).

[25] Foner, *supra* note 7, at xxxix.

[26] *Id.*

[27] *Id.* at 610.

[28] *Id.*

decolonization finally arrived in Ghana in 1957, Nigeria in 1960, and Kenya in 1963, Jim Crow and the Dunning School remained America's reality.

In Seligman's time, even Black leaders such as Booker T. Washington presented Africa "as a cultural, linguistic, and moral void."[29] They imagined slavery as "an anguished but perhaps necessary passage to a new age for the black race" beyond "their African legacies of 'ignorance,' 'poverty,' and 'immorality.'"[30] As African colonies gained independence, Europeans and Americans held "deep-seated racist convictions about the absence of business acumen among native populations" and private capital fled the continent.[31] With Reconstruction fixed in the popular memory as a moment when Black Americans demonstrated their inability to govern, they "simply could not imagine economic life continuing in regular form after independence."[32]

The "Redemption" of Newly Independent African States

After Reconstruction's premature end, neo-Confederate "Redeemers" took control. With Black Americans silenced, "the tax system became increasingly regressive, as those with the least property bore the heaviest proportional burden."[33] Spending on "[p]ublic education—described as a luxury by one Redeemer governor—was especially hard hit, as some states all but dismantled the public infrastructure established during Reconstruction."[34] "Mississippi and Alabama abolished statewide school taxes" while Florida "was left without any institution of higher learning, public or private" and "Alabama's Redeemers closed public hospitals."[35]

Global Jim Crow would deliver similar results as the United States seized an opportunity to "redeem" newly free African states. The United States had already shaped much of the postwar economic order to its liking and continued to wield enormous influence during the 1950s. The enduring myth of Reconstruction made it easy to dislodge the United Nations from its central

[29] David W. Blight, Race and Reunion: The Civil War in American Memory 319–20 (2003).
[30] *Id.* at 320.
[31] Vanessa Ogle, *'Funk Money': The End of Empires, The Expansion of Tax Havens, and Decolonization as an Economic and Financial Event*, 249 Past & Present 213, 214 (2020).
[32] *Id.*
[33] Foner, *supra* note 7, at 589.
[34] *Id.*
[35] *Id.*

role in global tax policy to stave off the threat of increased taxation by new African states.[36]

The "sensationalist bestseller of the 1920s, *The Tragic Era*, described Louisiana's Reconstruction legislature as a 'zoo.'"[37] After the United States insisted on inviting a diverse group of countries to a conference on what would become the World Bank and International Monetary Fund, the British economist John Maynard Keynes "expressly objected to the inclusion of such participants."[38] In a cable to the British Treasury, he derided the invitees—including Liberia and Ethiopia—as "the most monstrous monkey-house assembled for years."[39]

For men like Keynes, Reconstruction mattered even if everything they knew about it was wrong. Thanks to the complicity of scholars like Seligman, Reconstruction taught them to fear Black governance. "Around the world, the 'key history lesson'... of Reconstruction was taken to be the impossibility of multiracial democracy."[40]

In 1960, the United States, Canada, and Europe joined forces to create the OECD. With little fanfare, global tax governance shifted toward it and away from the United Nations. The transformation was blessed[41] by experts like Stanley Surrey, John F. Kennedy's chief tax advisor. Surrey, a Harvard Professor and one of the most widely admired figures in twentieth-century tax policy, made no secret of his contempt for the Haitian economist appointed to a key UN policy role. In his autobiography, Surrey took pains to highlight that the help he provided to the United Nations in the 1970s represented his own personal white man's burden.[42]

[36] Ogle, *supra* note 31, at 214.

[37] Foner, *supra* note 7, at xxxii.

[38] Sundhya Pahuja, Decolonising International Law: Development, Economic Growth and the Politics of Universality 15 (2011).

[39] *Id.*

[40] Foner, *supra* note 7, at xxxix-xl.

[41] Stanley S. Surrey, A Half-Century with the Internal Revenue Code: The Memoirs of Stanley S. Surrey 284 (Lawrence A. Zelenak & Ajay K. Mehrotra eds., 2022) ("In the Treasury I had agreed that the United States would be a party to the development of that [OECD] treaty.").

[42] Surrey's autobiography highlights his contempt for developing country experts. *Id.* Surrey's work on behalf of developing countries reveals what might generously be described as sympathy for their plight. He helped create a less harmful alternative to the OECD model but managed to do so in a way that created a "personal enemy" out of a key developing country expert. *Id.* at 290 Pierre Benoit, a Haitian economist appointed as the head of the Fiscal and Financial Branch of the UN Department of Economic and Social Affairs "was furious" when Surrey published work he and his students had done at Harvard as a "the only draft covering the entire scope of the U.N. group's work". Surrey drily noted that "From the start of his appointment Benoit had appeared to resent my assistance to the [UN effort], apparently because he saw it reflecting adversely on the competence of the Secretariat and his own competence—he was correct on both points." *Id.* at 289–90.

The Threat of Tax Sovereignty

The recovery of the history of Reconstruction does not mitigate the consequences of its loss. When the OECD took control of international tax policy with the blessing of men like Surrey, the Dunning School still taught the world that Black governance represented a grave threat. The United States offered a reassuringly all-white OECD as an alternative to the United Nations as the forum for global tax policymaking.

As described below, in the 1930s, US experts had already demonstrated a ruthless determination, using threats to persuade France to sign a double tax treaty. In the 1940s, they worked to shield US multinationals from taxation in Latin America by performing an elaborate masquerade designed to clothe corporate demands as altruism. By the 1950s, a fear of African decolonization made such gamesmanship superfluous.

If newly independent African states had been able to carry through with their promises of improved public health and education, they might have financed those expenditures with increased source taxation on OECD businesses. Whether Surrey and his peers shared Keynes' sentiments or merely exploited widespread skepticism of Black governance hardly matters. Creating another ingenious method of limiting Black voting power—silencing African voices by stripping the United Nations of its role in global tax governance—delivered results US experts had pursued for decades.

The League of Nations tackled international tax questions starting in the 1920s. After World War II, the United Nations succeeded it. The OECD disrupted that inclusive pattern. In 1963, when King warned of a bad check, the OECD delivered its own with its first model double tax treaty. With that treaty, the OECD asserted its claim as the League of Nations' true successor. The OECD's ascendance muted a vibrant debate within the United Nations over the future of taxation and, in particular, the importance of source taxation.

Global Jim Crow would disproportionately harm African states just achieving independence, helping make Africa another lonely island of poverty in a vast ocean of material prosperity. The OECD's rise also secured a victory for US multinationals in a decades-long effort to shield their profits from taxation. As Chapter 2 explains, the United States had already tamed double taxation with its tax credit. By design, such mechanisms encouraged other states to tax, leaving multinationals at the mercy of jurisdictions beyond their influence. Treaties sheltered them from those tax burdens with concepts like permanent establishment.

The Birth of the OECD

In May 1956, two dozen men from across Europe helped set Global Jim Crow in motion at the first session of what would become the OECD's fiscal committee at the Chateau de la Muette in Paris.[43] Joined by two Americans and a Canadian along with an observer from the United Nations who generously "said that the Fiscal Division of the United Nations would be very pleased to assist in the work of the Committee," they laid out their task.[44] Their first order of business would be "[t]he concept of permanent establishment."[45]

Decades before, a tax credit had invited source jurisdictions to tax US multinationals.[46] Inevitably, those multinationals worked to reduce the burden of source taxation. In its early days, those efforts were complicated by the fact that the credit provided a generous subsidy to vulnerable allies. Nevertheless, US experts persevered, working to limit its impact.

Other countries had been only too happy to capitalize on the US credit. Less content were US multinationals. And they made their displeasure known. In the 1930s, General Motors and what was then the First National City Bank of New York had a fierce fight with France over its efforts to tax them.

With France's need for cash to rebuild and to pay its debts growing less acute, multinationals became increasingly restive. Congress's generosity had shocked even its creator when it enacted the credit. Now, that selflessness clashed with a parochial impulse to protect US multinationals.

General Motors and Citibank urged the United States to embrace a treaty to curb French source taxation. Influential figures proved sympathetic. Amid the fray, leading US experts could be observed traveling to Europe to

[43] ORGANISATION FOR EUROPEAN ECONOMIC CO-OPERATION, Minutes of Sessions of Fiscal Committee – 1956: Minutes of the 1st Session 1, 3 (1956) https://archives.eui.eu/en/files/documents/15007.pdf.

[44] *Id.* at 6. The scope of the Committee's work seemed somewhat unclear even for participants. *Id.* at 8 ("The Representative of Canada said that he understood that the Committee proposed to confine work to Europe. If that was not to be the case, he would like to be given ample time to refer the matter to his Authorities.").

[45] "The concept of permanent establishment" was literally item "1" at the first meeting of the OEEC's Fiscal Committee. *Id.* at 5.

[46] The credit's generosity was somewhat curtailed over the years. An early technical change ensured that the foreign tax credit would not go so far as to prevent the United States from taxing US taxpayers on profits earned in the United States. But even after that change, the credit remained generous. It allowed foreign governments to dictate how heavily US multinationals would be taxed on income earned overseas while reducing tax revenue for the United States.

"pressur[e] the French into ratifying a treaty that the latter viewed as much too favorable to American interests."[47]

Such experts knew treaties offered the perfect tool to blunt the impact of source taxation. Some of them had, after all, helped design them.[48] Those same experts pushed for treaties with Latin America during World War II. They revealed "almost complete concern for US foreign enterprise, with no consideration of the . . . revenue concerns of the Latin American countries."[49]

For those US experts, protecting US multinationals from source taxation was a serious business. Accordingly, they used all the tools at their disposal to promote treaties. They used strong-arm tactics even with their closest allies. By threatening French firms with retaliatory taxes, the United States eventually secured the treaty it sought. Madeline Woker puts it bluntly: "[t]he French caved in only under the direct threat of reprisal taxes, introduced for the occasion in an obscure corner of the IRS code."[50]

During World War II, Latin America became the object of US efforts to deploy tax treaties. The United States, unwilling or unable to apply the same leverage in wartime, enjoyed less success. Like France, Latin American countries understood that double tax treaties served "as an American ramp to keep them from taxing American enterprises as heavily as they wished."[51] Unlike France, Latin America successfully fended off US efforts to create tax treaties.

In the years before the OECD's rise, US experts proved willing to play hardball with allies to help US multinationals. A report published by one of the American experts personally involved in each episode described above appears to have intentionally misrepresented the existence of a consensus on the arm's length method described in Chapter 1 to bolster it against the

[47] Madeline Woker, *Global Taxation Is a Mess. Here's How to Start Fixing It*, THE NATION (Dec. 20, 2019), https://www.thenation.com/article/archive/france-tax-wine-tariff/ (Woker notes the involvement of Mitchell Carroll in a dispute over tax bills handed to First National City Bank of New York—later Citibank, General Motors, and "other brand names").

[48] US representatives—including Mitchell Carroll—worked to "relieve[] its businesses of much foreign taxation with the permanent establishment rule, while preserving the spirit of source-based taxation" with the League of Nations model treaties in the 1920s. Michael J. Graetz & Michael M. O'Hear, *The "Original Intent" of U.S. International Taxation*, 46 DUKE L. J. 1021, 1087–89 (1997).

[49] Teo retells the story of the 1943 "Mexico" draft treaty, revealing that what has long been seen as an inclusive effort that lent legitimacy to the tax treaty concept was in fact primarily a US-led effort—orchestrated in large part by Carroll—greeted with skepticism by Latin American countries. Carroll executed the effort with "almost complete concern for US foreign enterprise, with no consideration of the essentially one-way investment flows and revenue concerns of the Latin American countries." NIKKI J. TEO, THE UNITED NATIONS IN GLOBAL TAX COORDINATION 29–45 (2023).

[50] Woker, *supra* note 47.

[51] TEO, *supra* note 49, at 29 (quoting a League representative's assessment).

encroachment of formulary apportionment.[52] Such experts went to great lengths to legitimize the notion of tax treaties. A model treaty known as "the Mexico draft" appears to have been part of an elaborate ruse orchestrated by the United States to persuade Latin America to enter into treaties.[53] Although presented as the work of the League of Nations, the Mexico draft was little more than US stagecraft.[54]

The Fear of African Taxation

The ascendance of the OECD and its 1963 model treaty represented a decisive loss for source taxation. The struggle between source and residence taxation has been fierce since the first days of the modern income tax. As early as 1923, "battle lines were drawn, with the capital-exporting British rejecting any semblance of source-based taxation, and the capital-importing debtor nations of continental Europe, principally France and Italy, defending source-based taxation."[55] Over the next three decades, as their fortunes rose and fell, states would find source taxation more or less appealing. Wealthier states would prefer residence taxation while their less prosperous counterparts favored source.

Nothing about the 1963 model, little more than another retread of the League's long-dormant work, suggested it would enjoy a different fate than its predecessors. But 1963 would indeed be different; after a decades-long doldrum, treaties flourished.[56] "In 1939, there were 20 treaties between OECD members, 85 at the time of the 1963 Draft, 179 at the time of the 1977

[52] Woker notes that the key conclusion of a report that would "turn the tide" in favor of the United States on a highly technical but very important point was factually incorrect ("Contrary to what Carroll would later claim, there was no clear consensus in the survey on the separate accounting method."). Woker, *supra* note 47.

[53] Teo, *supra* note 49, at 53 (highlighting the "many problematic aspects concerning the motivations and legitimacy of the League's efforts during this period, especially concerning its engagement with Latin America"). Teo notes that the League Council had ceased to exist by 1939 well before the publication of the Mexico draft. *Id.* at 52. Teo also documents that the Rockefeller Foundation played a key unacknowledged role in funding these efforts. *Id.* at 55.

[54] *Id.* at 52–53 ("Although the publication of the Mexico Model alongside the London Model in the *Tenth Session Report* legitimised the former, and both are today regarded as 'the Fiscal Committee's legacy to the international fiscal community', in reality, two-thirds of the Committee were not formally appointed members, and the *Tenth Session Report* and *Mexico/London Models Commentary* were never approved by the Council or Assembly.").

[55] *See* Graetz & O'Hear, *supra* note 48, at 1072.

[56] Omri and Ash offer a visually striking illustration of that trend. *See* Elliott Ash & Omri Marian, *The Making of International Tax Law: Empirical Evidence from Tax Treaties Text*, 24 Fla. Tax Rev. 151, 168 fig. 2 (2020).

Model Treaty and 475 (out of a possible 552) in 1995."[57] Today, thousands of these treaties crisscross the globe.

That resurgence reflected a new consensus rather than a new approach. The tax treaty worked no differently than in the 1930s, when France unsuccessfully resisted it, and in the 1940s, when Latin America managed to do so. As in the 1920s, treaties served as "a repudiation" of the US embrace of source taxation.[58] By the early 1960s, that repudiation had simply ceased being controversial.

After World War II, the United Nations replaced the League of Nations. In some ways, it offered a sharp departure. In other respects, it delivered more of the same. The General Assembly's one-country, one-vote equality juxtaposed against the Security Council's inequality reveals that the United Nations delivered continuity and change. Former Mandates like Nauru—placed under UN trusteeship—may have found little difference between them.[59]

In other respects, the changes would be dramatic. Decolonization would ensure that by the end of the 1950s, "new states enjoyed a significant majority in the General Assembly."[60] A wave of independence that had swept across Asia in the 1940s arrived in Africa, transforming the UN's makeup.

In 1957, Kwame Nkrumah renamed the Gold Coast "Ghana" after an ancient empire. In a speech declaring the nation's independence, Nkrumah announced that "the Black man is capable of managing his own affairs."[61] Becoming only the fourth Black state, "for those in the audience in Accra that night and observers across the world, the world historical significance of the first sub-Saharan colony to gain independence was palpable."[62]

For some, that moment held great promise. But others would have heard Nkrumah's words differently. That would have been particularly true in the United States. Its experience over the prior century made the prospect

[57] John F. Avery Jones, *The David R. Tillinghast Lecture: Are Tax Treaties Necessary?*, 53 Tax L. Rev. 1, 3 (1999).

[58] Graetz and O'Hear insist that "modern claims that the U.S. international tax regime gives primacy to residence-based taxation should be understood as a repudiation—not a continuation—of its original intent." *See* Graetz & O'Hear, *supra* note 48, at 1041.

[59] Antony Anghie, Imperialism, Sovereignty and the Making of International Law 1 (2005) ("Nauru was administered by Australia . . . first as a mandate territory under the League and then, as a trusteeship territory under the United Nations.").

[60] *Id.* at 216.

[61] Adom Getachew, Worldmaking After Empire: The Rise and Fall of Self-Determination 1 (2019).

[62] *Id.*

of sovereign African states like Ghana acutely troubling. For a nation still bound by the strictures of Jim Crow, the simple prospect of a racially integrated global governance structure would have been unnerving.

Racism remained a hard fact of American life. An all-white alternative to the United Nations promised a range of benefits. Dudziak shares the story of African representatives encountering the reality of 1960s Jim Crow:

> A source of particular concern was Maryland's Highway 40, the route taken by many diplomats on the drive from the United Nations in New York City to the nation's capital. Time after time, when African diplomats stopped for a bite to eat, they were refused service at Maryland restaurants. . . . Upon hearing of these incidents, President Kennedy's initial reaction was that African ambassadors shouldn't be driving on Highway 40. They should fly. "It's a hell of a road," he said. "I used to drive it years ago, but why would anybody want to drive it today when you can fly? Tell these ambassadors I wouldn't think of driving from New York to Washington. Tell them to fly!"[63]

Even for those who did not themselves disapprove of race mixing, an all-white alternative to the United Nations would eliminate opportunities for embarrassing incidents and conflict.[64]

Racial fears also dovetailed with worries about the economic consequences of independence. In the "1950s and 1960s . . . [d]istrustful of newly independent governments and non-white rule, fearing resentment, increased taxation or possibly even nationalization, Euro-American businesses active in the colonial world divested from empire."[65] The prospect of the decolonization of Africa prompted many Europeans and Americans to withdraw capital from the continent.[66]

[63] DUDZIAK, *supra* note 23, at 168.

[64] Dudziak notes the ways that domestic race discrimination complicated US relationships with diplomats from Africa and its efforts with the United Nations. *Id.* at 153 ("One concern—a motivating issue since the late 1940s—was how race discrimination in the United States would affect Cold War alignments. Would race discrimination make it less likely that African and Asian nations would ally themselves with the United States and against the Soviet Union? There were practical consequences for United Nations politics as well. Would race discrimination make it more difficult for the United States to gain support for its positions in the UN from African and Asian nations? Would that affect the usefulness of the UN as a forum for the nation to further its interests in the global community?").

[65] Ogle, *supra* note 31, at 214.

[66] "With the end of white rule in the Congo in 1960 and fresh memories of the anti-colonial Mau Mau rising in Kenya, beginning around 1960, settlers sought to move money out of the East African territories." *Id.* at 228.

Global Jim Crow responded to those fears. In the decades to come, international law would embrace various strategies to guard against the risks posed by decolonization. For example, nationalization threats would be addressed through bilateral investment treaties.[67]

Double tax treaties had long had their champions. With few exceptions, their efforts produced little in terms of results. The arrival of African states like Ghana would transform the fate of tax treaties. With fears over the economic impact of decolonization growing and an increasingly diverse United Nations proving a welcoming venue for source taxation, the time had come for a new strategy.

Enhanced Source Taxation

Nikki Teo observes that in the early 1950s, the United Nations served as the site of concerted efforts to expand source taxation. In particular, "the principle of exclusive source-country taxation of income from foreign investments in underdeveloped countries, with corresponding residence-country exemption of taxation of foreign-source income by capital-exporting countries" became the subject of numerous resolutions.[68] Cuba repeatedly sponsored those efforts.[69]

Despite embracing source taxation decades before, the United States used its influence to prevent its expansion in the United Nations. In 1953, the UN Fiscal Commission considered the possibility of exclusive source country taxation. That the Commission had a "membership composed of seven First World countries, five developing countries (the largest in any session so far), two Soviet countries and China" concerned the United States.[70]

With the changing complexion of the United Nations, the US State Department worried that expanded source country taxation might eventually become a reality. It warned the US delegation of the possibility of the introduction of a pro-source resolution "by a Latin American delegation,

[67] Pahuja, *supra* note 38, at 160 ("Capital exporting states . . . were making attempts in other fora . . . to concretise obligations at international law to protect foreign investment, to pay 'prompt, adequate and effective' compensation for any nationalisations, and to respect agreements entered into before independence.").

[68] Teo, *supra* note 49, at 241.

[69] *Id.* at 325–26, 330.

[70] *Id.* at 318.

which would draw the support of Pakistan, India, South Africa, other Latin American countries and possibly the Soviet bloc, making for a majority vote."[71] Cuba obliged, but what the UK delegation derided as "the old Cuban taxation gambit"[72] failed despite US fears.

The Cold War would create new imperatives for the United States as it squared off against its rival. As described above, Soviet complaints of hypocrisy dampened opposition to the civil rights movement.[73] Despite Cuba's persistent efforts, the Soviet Union would not push the United States on global tax policy.

The Soviets had no appetite for an approach—exemption—that they suspected would ultimately benefit "US capitalist business."[74] And India had its own reasons to side with the Soviets. In effect, Soviet ambivalence ended the threat of the old Cuban tax gambit.

Conclusion

The Dunning School insisted on a version of Reconstruction's history that omitted crucial information in service of its biased narrative. Mainstream versions of tax history likewise omit all the twists and turns of the years between 1928 and 1963. They make no mention of the old Cuban tax gambit. They draw a straight line between the publication of the League's model treaties and the OECD's.[75]

[71] *Id.* at 320.
[72] *Id.* at 334.
[73] DUDZIAK, *supra* note 23, at 3.
[74] TEO, *supra* note 49, at 337.
[75] *See* Michael J. Graetz, *Taxing International Income: Inadequate Principles, Outdated Concepts, and Unsatisfactory Policies*, 26 BROOK. J. INT'L L. 1357, 1358–59 (2001). ("In 1928, the League of Nations issued drafts of model bilateral income tax treaties for the reciprocal relief of double taxation of international income. . . . It is remarkable that not only the fundamental structure of the system for taxing international income today, but also many of the core concepts used to implement that structure—concepts such as permanent establishment, corporate residence, and arm's length pricing—date from a time when airplanes were first becoming a regular means of travel, and when the 'wireless' was a relatively new instrument of communication, and when Dorothy Parker, Robert Benchley, and Haywood Broun were holding court in the lobby of the Algonquin Hotel. . . ."). Graetz makes a similar claim more recently in a book that tells a story reminiscent of this book, but focused on the US domestic taxes and locating the start of the anti-tax movement after the start of Global Jim Crow, overlooking the global anti-tax movement the OECD and its treaties represented. MICHAEL GRAETZ, THE POWER TO DESTROY: HOW THE ANTITAX MOVEMENT HIJACKED AMERICA 1 (2024) ("During the half century from the late 1920s until the late 1970s. . . people across the land complained about taxes but did nothing about it.").

Had today's "rules for taxing international income" actually been "put in place following the First World War" to be "tweaked from time to time"[76] it would be accurate to say that

> Nothing comparable to the thoroughgoing multilateral restructurings of international monetary and trade relationships that followed the Second World War (which themselves have been substantially revised and refined since) has affected the system of international income taxation.[77]

But that is not what happened.[78] The structure of international taxation underwent a profound change in the 1950s and 1960s, both in terms of process and substance, as the United States helped shift control from the United Nations to a brand-new OECD. The remaining chapters explore the consequences of that shift, not least its impact on the taxation of multinationals.[79]

Nkrumah's independence address and King's speech highlight the link between Jim Crow and its global counterpart. King's words almost seem a warning to Nkrumah, albeit one delivered too late. America's past, a reality my parents fled before I was born, would become part of Ghana's future. Jim Crow—the source of the bad check that King described—a system of laws designed to deliver empty promises of freedom and opportunity to Black Americans by denying them the resources generously provided to others would soon visit Ghana in the form of the OECD and its treaties. The Jim Crow system that defined life in the United States for more than half a century would be echoed on a global scale.

[76] *Id.* at 1359.

[77] *Id.*

[78] Thomas Rixen, *From Double Tax Avoidance to Tax Competition: Explaining the Institutional Trajectory of International Tax Governance*, REV. INT'L. POL. ECON. 197, 207 (2011) (Rixen explains that as late as the 1950s "the regime was still of limited practical significance").

[79] *Id.* at 197–98 ("From the 1960s onwards, under-taxation—comprising the related phenomena of tax competition, tax evasion and tax avoidance—became a pressing issue.").

4

US Power and Global Jim Crow

Structure

If you ask my mother about my father's work, she may tell you about a plaque in downtown Nassau. The sign acknowledges his design work on the Central Bank of the Bahamas. A man who loved his job—he never found a construction site less than riveting—dad understood that the most effective approach need not be complicated. Sometimes, a simple structural choice can prove quite powerful.

That might mean nothing more than paying attention to the placement of a building's windows. After returning to the Bahamas, he designed sophisticated cooling systems like the one serving its Central Bank. Still, he never stopped evangelizing for the power of cross ventilation. He believed there was no better way to ensure a room would stay cool than to build it so that a steady ocean breeze would pass through it.

Dad would have—grudgingly—admired the decision to quietly wrest control of global tax policy from Keynes's "monkey house" by creating the OECD out of the Organisation for European Economic Co-operation. Displacing the United Nations tamed the threat posed by the growing influence and great need of newly sovereign African states. Thanks to that masterstroke, the United States never needed to worry about the old Cuban taxation gambit again.

The transformation also accomplished something more. That structural intervention has left a lasting imprint on global tax policy, creating a hierarchy of power that has overwhelmingly benefitted the wealthiest states. In addition to providing protection from newly sovereign states, the creation of the OECD allowed the United States to wield affirmative power quietly. It may be an overstatement to say, "the United States takes the lead, the OECD and its members reach a compromise, and the rest of the world follows the OECD."[1] But it contains more than a grain of truth.

[1] Jinyan Li, *Global Profit Split: An Evolutionary Approach to International Income Allocation*, 50 Can. Tax J. 823, 867 (2002) (discussing transfer pricing).

Racial Capitalism and International Tax Law. Steven A. Dean, Oxford University Press. © Steven A. Dean 2025.
DOI: 10.1093/9780197526002.003.0005

Over the decades, the impact on global tax rulemaking has been extraordinary.[2] The popularity of double tax treaties serves as a rough proxy for the OECD's influence. One might also look at the long decline in corporate tax revenues that began in the 1950s.[3] In the years since, corporate tax abuse flourished in tandem with the OECD's treaties.

Chapter 3 highlighted racial fears' pivotal role in the OECD's story. Chapter 5 details how that history of bias has continued to shape its role, finding expression in its blacklist and its coconut trees. This chapter describes how the United States has exploited the power Global Jim Crow lent it. It tells that story through the lens of three US legal innovations: Subpart F, FATCA, and the check-the-box election. Each would reinforce the pattern of US impunity outlined above. Thanks to its dominant role in the OECD, its policies—no matter how much they diverged from established practice—were always tolerated by the OECD and often embraced by its members.

Subpart F and Enhanced Residence Taxation

Having convinced the world that its quiet stewardship of thousands of treaties dispatched a grave threat to the world's welfare—double taxation—the OECD remains widely admired.[4] The truth is far more complicated. As Chapter 2 demonstrates, the League's treaties long proved a solution in search of a problem. When they finally did take root, they harmed wealthy and poor states by shielding multinationals from taxation.[5]

[2] Allison Christians, *BEPS and the New International Tax Order*, 2016 BYU L. Rev. 1603, 1604 (2017) (observing that the OECD's recent initiatives have served to "entrench the OECD's monopoly over tax policy making"); Ruth Mason, *The Transformation of International Tax*, 114 Am. J. Int'l L 353, 354 (2020) (arguing that the OECD's recent efforts have produced "major changes in the participants, agenda, institutions, norms, and legal instruments of international tax").

[3] Press Release, U.S. Department of the Treasury, Testimony of Kimberly A. Clausing, Deputy Assistant Secretary, Tax Analysis, Before the Senate Committee on Finance (Mar. 25, 2021), https://home.treasury.gov/news/press-releases/jy0079 ("corporate taxes as a percentage of GDP have been trending downwards in the United States since the 1950s").

[4] Dad would also have appreciated the irony of the League of Nations' double tax treaty legitimizing the OECD's efforts. On reflection, it becomes easy to recognize the League as a thinly disguised version of the imperialism it claimed to reject. But—thanks to the myth of its tax treaties—within the international tax community the League's reputation remains unimpeachable.

[5] Rebecca M. Kysar, *Unraveling the Tax Treaty*, 104 Min. L. Rev. 1755, 1757 (2020) ("Although recent scholarship laments the revenue losses imposed by the treaty system on developing countries, even developed countries may lose revenue if they are net capital-importing.").

The OECD's pillar two serves in part as a response, expanding its members' tax reach at the expense of the rest of the world.[6] The OECD embraced a concept, referred to as a global minimum tax, first proposed during the Obama administration and adopted under President Trump. Like domestic minimum taxes, this cross-border counterpart sidesteps the standard cat-and-mouse battle between taxpayers and authorities. Instead, it creates a simplified alternative.

Like pillar one, it offers a complex formula that obviates thorny questions in favor of a precise answer. The US version purports to target Global Intangible Low-Taxed Income (GILTI).[7] Inverting the logic of permanent establishment, GILTI identifies overseas profits not linked to factories or other physical investments and deems them intangible income, therefore ripe for an enhanced form of residence taxation.[8] Pillar two dispenses with the pretense of targeting wayward intangible income, pitching its tax simply as a way of ensuring that multinationals pay some tax somewhere.

Coding and Corporate Tax Abuse

Both GILTI and pillar two can trace their roots as far back as 1961. Early in his presidency, John F. Kennedy took an interest in tax policy. He delivered a Special Message to Congress, decrying the abuses that allowed US multinationals to shield their overseas income from US taxation. Behind the scenes, Kennedy's team of tax experts engaged in an extraordinary effort to gauge the scope and nature of the threat. Stanley Surrey personally oversaw an investigation of US corporations engaging in tax abuse.

Kennedy made no secret of the abusive transactions in his crosshairs. Bausch & Lomb would later use much the same structures to avoid tax on its contact lenses. Eventually, Google and Apple would deploy them—one

[6] The immediate impetus for its most recent effort is its Base Erosion and Profit Shifting (BEPS) initiative. In 2013, the OECD identified fifteen distinct issues related to BEPS and published more than a thousand pages of research on those topics in 2015. Despite that extensive analysis, little became of what has come to be known as BEPS 1.0. Its successor, BEPS 2.0, doubled down on its longstanding embrace of enhanced residence taxation.

[7] I.R.C. §951A (imposing a US tax on US shareholders of certain foreign corporations on the "net CFC tested income" of those corporations).

[8] Unlike the Subpart F rules, which identify a limited universe of income subject to tax, §951A includes all of a foreign corporation's income in the definition of net CFC tested income. It arrives at the GILTI amount by subtracting the foreign corporation's "net deemed tangible income return"—which is 10 percent of the corporation's "qualified business asset investment"—from the net CFC tested income.

incarnation of which is the double Irish Dutch sandwich described below—as their profits surged.

Subpart F responded to corporate tax abuse by US multinationals in Switzerland.[9] Kennedy's transactions exploited a pre-OECD US treaty with Switzerland. Subpart F counteracts that abuse by claiming tax revenues that the arm's-length method assigns to other—often less prosperous—jurisdictions.

The double Irish Dutch sandwich typifies the legal coding Katharina Pistor describes in *The Code of Capital: How the Law Creates Wealth and Inequality*.[10] Designed—and named—by high-priced experts and relying heavily on Ireland's extensive network of tax treaties,[11] it allows multinationals to avoid taxes on their profits. While perfectly legal, the structure prompted outrage when the public learned it allowed "American companies to cut their tax bills by hundreds of billions of dollars."[12]

Like the global minimum taxes that would follow, Subpart F asserted an unprecedented and expansive notion of residence taxation. Wealthy residence jurisdictions claimed broad categories of income ordinarily assigned to source jurisdictions. Subpart F and the OECD's treaties combined to offer those states an appealing mix of expansive residence and curtailed source jurisdiction. OECD members in particular prospered as treaties proliferated and residence states embraced Subpart F.[13]

The OECD's two pillars offer similar benefits for wealthy states. Pillar one addresses a new type of source taxation: digital services taxes. Pillar one imposes a moratorium on those taxes. In their place, pillar one offers an alternative at once narrower and more expansive. Although its reach extends beyond digital ventures, its complex mechanism shields all but a handful of multinationals from an anemic source tax. Even for those ventures subject to

[9] Nir Fishbien, *From Switzerland with Love: Surrey's Papers and the Original Intent(s) of Subpart-F*, 38 Va. Tax Rev. 1 (2018).

[10] Katharina Pistor, The Code of Capital: How the Law Creates Wealth and Inequality (2019).

[11] Google's notorious double Irish Dutch sandwich, for example, relies on Ireland's treaty network. *See* Edward D. Kleinbard, *Stateless Income*, 11 Fla. Tax Rev. 699, 712 n.19 (2011) ("Ireland has a good tax treaty network whose treaties often reduce the tax rate on royalties paid between firms in the two treaty countries to zero.").

[12] Edward Helmore, *Google Says It Will No Longer Use 'Double Irish, Dutch Sandwich' Tax Loophole*, Guardian (Jan. 1, 2020), https://www.theguardian.com/technology/2020/jan/01/google-says-it-will-no-longer-use-double-irish-dutch-sandwich-tax-loophole.

[13] Reuven S. Avi-Yonah, *International Tax as International Law*, 57 Tax L. Rev. 483, 488 (2004) (arguing that as "other countries began to copy the CFC regime: Germany in 1972, Canada in 1976, Japan in 1978, France in 1980, and the UK in 1984" controlled foreign corporation regimes became so commonplace that they might be considered customary international law).

it, pillar one's rules sharply limit the profits subject to and the jurisdictions eligible to tax. Pillar two introduces a global minimum tax. Like Subpart F and GILTI, it invokes corporate tax abuse, allowing residence jurisdictions to assert expansive tax claims.

A cycle of first enabling and then selectively combatting tax abuse has produced mixed results for the United States and the OECD. For decades, treaties and Subpart F delivered a stable—if not entirely satisfying—balance. They offered multinationals great flexibility in structuring their tax affairs while providing wealthy states with tools to expand their taxing jurisdiction to offset some of the resulting losses.

The Check-the-Box Rules and the Demise of Subpart F

The bombshell that disrupted that status quo came from an unlikely source. When the check-the-box rules were first announced, Washington was adjusting to the Republican victory in the 1994 elections. Congressional Republicans railed against the costs that regulations impose on businesses. The Clinton administration[14] responded to that deregulatory push[15] with a plan emphasizing regulation's benefits.[16]

In a February 21, 1995, speech, President Clinton announced the administration's rejoinder to Republicans.[17] The Clinton administration

[14] In the 1990s, Republicans such as Newt Gingrich may have been the more forceful advocates of regulatory reform, but the Clinton administration supported their own reform initiatives. The 1993 Clinton–Gore report, "From Red Tape to Results: Creating a Government That Works Better and Costs Less," underscored the extent to which the "consumer paradigm" had transformed the way politicians and the public viewed the relationship between individuals and businesses on the one hand and the government on the other. LIZABETH COHEN, A CONSUMERS' REPUBLIC: THE POLITICS OF MASS CONSUMPTION IN POSTWAR AMERICA 396 (2003).

[15] "This week the congressional calendar was jammed with 'regulatory reform' hearings, news conferences and floor debate—more evidence that the Republicans continue to move at warp speed to produce a grand plan to turn the federal regulatory system inside out, if not disable it." Cindy Skrzycki, *Clinton's Answer to a Juggernaut: Show Who Gets Hurt*, WASH. POST, Feb. 24, 1995, at F1, F1-2.

[16] *Id.* (noting Clinton's emphasis on how private parties would be hurt by the proposed regulatory moratorium). It is noteworthy that even though the consumer paradigm informed the regulatory reform proposals of both congressional Republicans and the Clinton administration, their respective approaches suggest starkly different visions of the role regulations play in the consumer paradigm. While conservative Republicans appeared to view regulations as inherently burdensome and therefore problematic, Clinton administration reforms, such as the introduction of the check-the-box regulations, imply support for the position that simply eliminating regulations is not always in the interests of the private sector. *See, e.g.*, Hal Gann & Roy Strowd, *Reducing the Mounting Tax Compliance Burden*, 66 TAX NOTES 427, 427 (1995) (suggesting that well-designed tax regulations are often a net benefit to the business community).

[17] Remarks on Regulatory Reform, 31 Wkly. Comp. Pres. Doc. 278 (Feb. 21, 1995).

attempted to steal the Republicans' thunder. They embraced a "highly deliberative plan that tells regulators to inventory their rulemakings and come up with some to cut or change by June."[18]

One result of that effort was Notice 95-14, published in early April. With it, the Internal Revenue Service announced the arrival of elective entity classification rules. Those new rules delivered on President Clinton's call for regulatory reform,[19] serving as one answer to the Republican anti-regulation push.[20] With "remarkable speed"[21] the Notice's radical idea would be transformed into regulations. The source of that urgency, a desire on the part of the Clinton administration to demonstrate a commitment to creating regulations that benefitted rather than burdened private actors, delivered the proposed rules before the 1996 election.

The reaction to what became known as the check-the-box rules was distinctly positive. The most common response was "enthusiasm."[22] The shift received "strong support"[23] from the tax bar and was "widely praised as an important, simplifying improvement in the tax law."[24]

The new entity classification regulations declared that some domestic and foreign entities would automatically be classified as corporations for tax purposes. France's societe anonyme and Germany's aktiengesellschaft, along with Delaware corporations, were not granted a choice. The owners of every other entity in those jurisdictions could choose its tax classification.[25]

[18] Skrzycki, *supra* note 15; Remarks on Regulatory Reform, *supra* note 17, at 270 (quoting President Clinton as stating, "By June 1st, I want to know which obsolete regulations we can cut and which ones you can't cut without help from Congress.").

[19] *See* Victor Fleischer, *"If It Looks Like a Duck": Corporate Resemblance and Check-the-Box Elective Tax Classification*, 96 COLUM. L. REV. 518, 518 (1996).

[20] *See* Skrzycki, supra note 15.

[21] *See* George K. Yin, *The Taxation of Private Business Enterprises: Some Policy Questions Stimulated by the "Check-the-Box" Regulations*, 51 SMU L. REV. 125, 125 (1997). Notice 95-14 is dated March 29 and was published in the Internal Revenue Bulletin in April of 1995. Final regulations were issued in December of 1996.

[22] *Id.*

[23] Letter from Carolyn Joy Lee, Chair, New York State Bar Association Tax Section to Leslie B. Samuels, Assistant Secretary (Tax Policy), Department of the Treasury, & Margaret M. Richardson, Commissioner, Internal Revenue Service (Aug. 31, 1995), *reprinted* in NYSBA Strongly Endorses Check-the-Box Entity Classification Proposal, TAX NOTES TODAY, Sept. 5, 1995, at 173–74.

[24] Yin, *supra* note 21, at 125. Yin expressed some skepticism, suggesting that "such praise is very premature" because "important policy questions need to be resolved before we can accurately gauge the wisdom of the new rule." *Id.*

[25] Treas. Reg. 301.7701-3(a). Most of the provisions that were enacted in 1996 and became effective at the start of 1997 have not been subsequently modified. Then, as now, a foreign eligible entity with multiple owners, none of whom are liable for the debts of or claims against the entity, would be an association under the default rules. Treas. Reg. 301.7701-3(b)(2)(i) (treating foreign entities as associations if all members have limited liability). By making an election, the owners of the entity could instead decide to cause the entity to be classified as a partnership for US tax purposes. The election is made on I.R.S. Form 8832—originally one page and now ballooned to three—and is effective

Despite initial wariness about the risks, the Clinton administration made check-the-box available to foreign entities.[26] It quickly became apparent that doing so had gutted Subpart F.[27] New regulations—the ill-fated "extraordinary transaction" amendments—attempted to take away the proverbial punch bowl. Proposed in 1999 only to be withdrawn in 2003[28] in the face of heavy criticism, those amendments tried—and failed—to save Subpart F.

That unsuccessful effort targeted transactions that relied on the taxpayers' new ability to change the classification of a foreign eligible entity shortly before its sale. Because Subpart F was created in a pre-check-the-box world, it treated corporate status as an immutable trait. Taxpayers suddenly had the power to reduce their Subpart F burdens significantly. It would be an overstatement to say that Subpart F became as elective as entity classification, but it would never be the same.

on the date specified on the form (which can be up to seventy-five days prior to the date the election is made or up to one year after the election is made). Treas. Reg. 301.7701-3(c)(1).

[26] The election was made available to foreign, as well as domestic, entities. *See supra* note 25; NYSBA Tax Section, Report on the "Check the Box" Entity Classification System Proposed in Notice 95-14, Part 1, *reprinted* in *NYSBA Strongly Endorses Check-the-Box Entity Classification Proposal*, Tax Notes Today, Sept. 5, 1995, at 173–74 (noting the difficulty US tax lawyers faced under prior law in collaborating with foreign counsel to apply resemblance criteria to foreign entities); *See also* I.R.S. Notice 95-14, 1995-1 C.B. 297, 298–99. Notice 95-14 makes clear that when the election was first announced it was intended primarily as a domestic reform. *Id.* at 298. That the election was to be made available to foreign, in addition to domestic, entities was not a foregone conclusion. *See id.* ("Because the complexities and resources devoted to classification of domestic unincorporated business organizations are mirrored in the foreign context, the Service and Treasury are considering simplifying the classification rules for foreign organizations in a manner consistent with the approach described above for domestic organizations."). Had check-the-box elections been available only to domestic entities, one of its two primary simplification benefits would not have been realized.

[27] Lawrence Lokken, *Whatever Happened to Subpart F? U.S. CFC Legislation After the Check-the-Box Regulations*, 7 Fla. Tax Rev. 186, 187 (2005) ("[A] principal reason for the enactment of subpart F was to curb U.S. companies' ability to shelter income from taxation in tax haven countries. However, evidence collected by Altshuler and Grubert indicates that subpart F has not, in recent years, been effective in preventing U.S. multinational enterprises from using corporations organized in countries commonly considered to be tax havens as vehicles for sheltering large amounts of income from significant taxation by any country. In particular, they conclude that the United States' adoption of the so-called check the box regulations in 1996 has allowed U.S. multinational enterprises to significantly reduce the effective rates of taxation of their non-U.S. incomes. They estimate that 'in 2002 U.S. companies paid $7 billion less in host country taxes compared to 1997 by using intercompany payments deductible in the paying country but exempt from tax in the recipient.' As shown in Part III, the check-the-box regulations facilitate structures accomplishing such no-tax results.").

[28] Prop. Treas. Reg. § 301.7701-3(h)(1), 64 Fed. Reg. 66,591, 66,594 (Nov. 29, 1999), *withdrawn*, I.R.S. Notice 2003-46, 2003-28 I.R.B. 53.

The Swiss Treaty

Corporations do not hide profits; they code them. Employing rules like check-the-box entity classification and strategies such as those described in Chapter 1, multinationals shift profits from one jurisdiction to another. Subpart F and minimum taxes demonstrate that a corporation's income can be measured precisely, even when legally shielded from taxation.

In his 1961 message to Congress, Kennedy detailed the strategy the largest US corporations still employ to minimize their tax obligations.[29] Kennedy explained that multinationals had formed "foreign subsidiaries" to "exploit the multiplicity of foreign tax systems and international agreements in order to reduce sharply or eliminate completely their tax liabilities both at home and abroad." Kennedy related practices familiar from Chapter 1—including "artificial arrangements between parent and subsidiary regarding intercompany pricing, the transfer of patent licensing rights, the shifting of management fees"[30]—but did not mention secrecy or hiding. The same approach would form the heart of Bausch & Lomb's schemes and Google's and Apple's structures.

Kennedy also named the jurisdiction where US multinationals executed this tax avoidance strategy.[31] Behind the scenes, Switzerland had been the intense focus of Kennedy's team of tax experts from the very start of his administration. Surrey's private papers still contain the organizational chart for Chrysler's Geneva operations.

Even as Global Jim Crow took shape, Kennedy knew how and where corporate tax abuse took place. He knew that Switzerland and its "international agreements" lay at the core of the problem. Yet Kennedy neither confronted Switzerland nor abandoned the US–Switzerland treaty.

Any number of factors could explain that decision. A concerted corporate response undoubtedly played a role. Executives from Heinz, Chrysler, IT&T, and Procter & Gamble testified in Congress, warning about the impact of the Kennedy administration's effort on American multinationals. Surrey wrote placating letters to each of them to offer reassurances that "the draft bill on the tax treatment of 'tax haven' profits" had been weakened to reflect "a more limited purpose than the original recommendations respecting deferral on

[29] *See Text of Special Message on Taxes Submitted by President Kennedy to Congress*, N.Y. Times, Apr. 21, 1961, at 18.
[30] *See id.*
[31] *See id.*

income derived generally by American firms through foreign subsidiaries in other industrialized countries."[32]

Fierce resistance from Switzerland played a role as well. The US investigation elicited a threat of prosecution from the Swiss Attorney General.[33] Surrey's team worked to gather information on the number of Swiss subsidiaries formed by US corporations. Initially, due to concerns expressed by the US ambassador that "the Swiss government might have some objection to"[34] the investigation, Surrey hired a Swiss firm to do the work. Ultimately, they shifted gears after concluding that "a private contractor could not proceed with the compilation without running heavy risks."[35]

Whether corporate pressure and Swiss threats would have been enough to frighten Surrey off remains unclear. Ultimately, the fact that Switzerland had begun to play a key role mediating between the United States and Cuba as Cold War tensions escalated may have been at least as important. Switzerland's role as a go-between during the Cuban Missile Crisis, perhaps the most dramatic moment of the Cold War, could easily have persuaded Kennedy of the need to bear the cost of its tax treaty with Switzerland.[36] Seven minutes to midnight—according to the so-called Doomsday Clock—hardly represented an opportune time to confront Switzerland about its tax treaty.

Whatever the reason, Subpart F—still in effect today, albeit neutered by check-the-box—did not single out particular jurisdictions (Switzerland) nor did it target individual companies (Chrysler). It did not, as Kennedy had initially envisioned, "tax each year American corporations on their current share of the undistributed profits realized in that year by subsidiary corporations organized in economically advanced countries." In the end, Subpart F achieved only part of Kennedy's vision by challenging the use of:

[32] *See, e.g.*, letter from Stanley S. Surrey to H.J. Heinz II, Chairman, H.J. Heinz Co. (Nov. 13, 1961) (on file with author) (discussing only the mentioned topics, and not, for example, Switzerland).

[33] The Kennedy Administration conducted a short-lived cloak-and-dagger effort to challenge Switzerland's rise as a tax haven. *See* Steven A. Dean, *Surrey's Silence: Subpart F and the Swiss Subsidiary Tax that Never Was*, 86 LAW & CONTEMP. PROBS. 73 (2023).

[34] Memorandum from Nathan N. Gordon, U.S. Department of the Treasury, to Stanley S. Surrey (undated) (on file with author).

[35] *Id.*

[36] By 1962, Switzerland had become vital to US interests, prompting a key advisor to President Kennedy to say that "[i]f neutral Switzerland did not exist," the United States would have "had to invent it." Robert Rakove, *Neutrality/Nonalignment and the United States, in* THE OXFORD RSCH. ENCYC. OF AM. HISTORY (2016). Switzerland would play a role during the Cuban Missile Crisis that year. It would continue to represent US diplomatic interests in Cuba for more than half a century.

> the "tax haven" device anywhere in the world, even in the underdeveloped countries, through the elimination of tax deferral privileges for those forms of activities, such as trading, licensing, insurance and others, that typically seek out tax haven methods of operation. There is no valid reason to permit their remaining untaxed regardless of the country in which they are located.[37]

Before Subpart F, profits earned by overseas subsidiaries would have only been subject to source taxation (unless and until the subsidiary paid a dividend to its US shareholders).

The Tax Haven Device

Borrowed from the individual tax evasion context, the notion of a corporate tax haven resonates as a way of describing corporate tax abuse. Of course, if a tax haven means a place that keeps tax collectors at bay with privacy, there is no such thing. Again, corporations code their profits rather than hide them to avoid taxation.

Much of the power of the term tax haven derives from confusion about both how (implying hiding rather than planning) and where (suggesting white sand instead of snow) abuse takes place. Conflating the distinct phenomena of corporate tax abuse and individual tax evasion explored in Chapter 1 invites that misunderstanding. It indicates that, just as a corrupt individual might evade taxes by hiding money on a faraway island, corporate tax abuse involves secret cash hoards rather than complex coding.

The double Irish Dutch sandwich has been described as "a tax maneuver used by technology companies that involves routing patent royalties through several European subsidiaries before sending the funds to a tax haven."[38] That characterization—actually a subtle mischaracterization—draws from a New York Times article describing Apple's role in popularizing the technique, explaining that it "reduces taxes by routing profits through Irish subsidiaries and the Netherlands and then to the Caribbean."[39]

[37] *See* N.Y. TIMES, *supra* note 29, at 18.

[38] VANESSA WILLIAMSON, READ MY LIPS: WHY AMERICANS ARE PROUD TO PAY TAXES 264 n.21 (2017).

[39] Charles Duhigg & David Kocieniewski, *Apple's Tax Strategy Aims at Low-Tax States and Nations*, N.Y. TIMES (Apr. 29, 2012), https://www.nytimes.com/2012/04/29/business/apples-tax-strategy-aims-at-low-tax-states-and-nations.html.

The telling difference—replacing "the Caribbean" with "a tax haven"—falsely implies that neither of the European jurisdictions deserves the label. The transaction earned its epithet for a reason. Thanks to "Ireland's treaties with European nations, some of Apple's profits could travel virtually tax-free through the Netherlands—the Dutch Sandwich."[40] Kennedy had warned that multinationals had learned to abuse international agreements to avoid taxes. Yet Surrey and the United States helped paper the world with them.

Like Kennedy, in the first months of his presidency, Biden delivered remarks on corporate tax abuse. Biden boasted that he could generate the revenue to make "a once-in-a-generation investment in America unlike anything we've done since we built the Interstate Highway System and won the Space Race decades ago"[41] without imposing politically painful tax increases on the middle class. He offered a simple alternative, which was misleading and false in equal parts. He proposed making it impossible for "companies ... to hide their income in places like the Cayman Islands and Bermuda, in tax havens."[42]

FATCA's Focus on Personal Income Taxation

Chapter 3 highlights a shift that profoundly altered the balance of power between poor states and rich ones. It did the same between multinationals and states. Not to put too fine a point in it, the creation of the OECD in 1960 set the table for the double Irish Dutch sandwiches that allowed Google, Apple, and other global giants to avoid taxes. By the 2000s, once the full impact of check-the-box was evident, the damage had become too obvious to ignore.

Most observers offered unsparing assessments of the state of international taxation.[43] Each scholar diagnosing the disease threatening the global tax system saw the problem differently. Aging rules whose authorship could be

[40] *Id.*

[41] Joseph R. Biden Jr., President of the US, Remarks by President Biden on the American Jobs Plan (Apr. 7, 2021), https://www.whitehouse.gov/briefing-room/speeches-remarks/2021/04/07/remarks-by-president-biden-on-the-american-jobs-plan-2/ (falsely stating that multinationals "hide their income in places like the Cayman Islands and Bermuda, in tax havens").

[42] *Id.*

[43] Depending on your perspective, the problem might, of course, represent an opportunity. A leading practitioner offered a remarkably upbeat assessment. H. David Rosenbloom, *The David R. Tillinghast Lecture: International Tax Arbitrage and the "International Tax System"*, 53 Tax L. Rev. 137, 164 (2000) (identifying the "network of international tax conventions ... that represents, cumulatively, a triumph of international law in the field of taxation").

traced to the League of Nations seemed the culprit to some.[44] Others pointed to a complex mix of factors, including a lack of state coordination and aggressive tax planning by multinationals.[45]

Each assessment contained elements of truth. None, of course, mentioned Global Jim Crow's transformation of the global tax system. They did not highlight its disparate impact on wealthy and poor states. The decline of source taxation and the expansion of residence taxation offered clues, but experts ignored them.

For wealthy states, the collapse of the corporate tax mattered. But the individual income tax mattered more. In contrast to their poorer counterparts, wealthy states rely more heavily on personal income taxes. To address its needs, the United States devised a solution. In 2010, in one of his last acts as chairman of the lead US tax legislative committee, Congressman Charles Rangel oversaw the creation of FATCA.[46] FATCA answered a call to "enhance the availability of extraterritorial tax information" to bolster US tax authorities' "ability to enforce their taxes. . . by giving them access to ex ante extraterritorial tax information that is tailored to their unique needs."[47]

After engineering the rise and fall of Subpart F, the United States once more remade the global tax landscape by requiring banks everywhere to provide extraterritorial tax information under the threat of draconian financial penalties.[48] It used a stick to incentivize participation, echoing Rangel's

[44] *See* Michael J. Graetz, *Taxing International Income: Inadequate Principles, Outdated Concepts, and Unsatisfactory Policies*, 54 Tax L. Rev. 261, 262 (2001) ("[N]ot only the fundamental structure of the system for taxing international income today, but also many of the core concepts used to implement that structure—concepts such as permanent establishment, corporate residence, and arm's length pricing—date from a time when airplanes were first becoming a regular means of travel.").

[45] Reuven S. Avi-Yonah, *Globalization, Tax Competition, and the Fiscal Crisis of the Welfare State*, 113 Harv. L. Rev. 1573, 1577 (2000) ("In the last decade, competition for inbound investment" and "the relative ease with which an integrated multinational corporation can relocate production facilities in response to tax rates . . . enable multinationals to derive most of their income from abroad, free of host-country taxation.").

[46] Hiring Incentives to Restore Employment (HIRE) Act, Pub. L. No. 111–147, 124 Stat. 71 (Mar. 18, 2010).

[47] Steven A. Dean, *The Incomplete Global Market for Tax Information*, 49 B.C. L. Rev. 605, 611 (2008). Prior to FATCA, the approach favored by the OECD for enforcement relied on a "barter system" to "allow pairs of governments to barter with one another, each supplying information that the other can use to enforce its taxes." *Id.* at 608. It was too much of that system, rather than not enough, that made tax evasion possible.

[48] FATCA's "dragnet" avoided targeting particular countries, but its breadth would do serious damage to vulnerable individuals. Shu-Yi Oei, *The Offshore Tax Enforcement Dragnet*, 67 Emory L.J. 655, 662 (2018) (warning of "disproportionate and unfair burdens on immigrants, American expatriates, and accidental Americans").

controversial campaign decades earlier against Apartheid.[49] Anticipating the use of threats as leverage that would help define the early days of President Trump's second term, FATCA penalized banks unless they provided information on US individuals holding accounts.

FATCA showcased the vast power the United States acquired when the OECD displaced the United Nations. Subpart F had remade the corporate tax landscape decades before. Now, FATCA did the same for individual income taxes. Once the United States took the lead with FATCA, its approach would be widely imitated, just as Subpart F had been.

A Death Knell for African Tax Policy

The stories of Subpart F, of check-the-box, and of FATCA all bear the hallmarks of Global Jim Crow. They reveal a global tax landscape shaped by US aspirations and fears. Its choices, ratified and disseminated by the OECD, have taken the world on a wild ride.

The twists and turns of those decades have made it clear that the OECD, with the backing of the United States, deserves both cheers and jeers for the evolution of global tax policy. FATCA, as Chapter 6 highlights, revealed that OECD inaction had aided tax evasion by individuals just as its treaties shielded multinationals. A decade before, the OECD had insisted it had no power to address the problem. The OECD protested that it could not be held responsible for failing to curb cheating by its own taxpayers. It lamented "the limitations on the effectiveness of unilateral actions."[50]

As the following chapters detail, the OECD instead blamed others. FATCA left no doubt that the OECD could indeed have addressed its concerns unilaterally.[51] Predictably, the OECD quickly aligned with the new US approach. The rest of the world had little choice but to fall in line with US priorities

[49] That earlier effort is described in Chapter 5 in which the penalties came in the form of lost tax credits. Multinationals could no longer offset taxes paid to Apartheid-era South Africa against their US obligations.

[50] OECD, Towards Global Tax Co-operation: Progress in Identifying and Eliminating Harmful Tax Practices 24 (2000), https://www.oecd.org/content/dam/oecd/en/publications/reports/2001/04/towards-global-tax-co-operation_g1ghgcc1/9789264184541-en.pdf.

[51] Avi-Yonah had already demonstrated this as a theoretical matter. He blamed "the effective end of withholding taxation by developed states" for individuals' ability to earn tax-free income. Avi-Yonah, *supra* note 45, at 1576. He explained that the OECD could solve the problem of individual tax evasion unilaterally by reintroducing a withholding tax.

and methods, fixing a problem that mattered more for wealthy states than for poor.

The OECD boasts that over 90 percent of global gross domestic product (GDP) has endorsed its pillars.[52] Given the stark reality of global inequality, that statement is revealing in a way the OECD may not intend.[53] Africa's contribution to global GDP is roughly 3 percent, far lower than its nearly 20 percent share of the world's population. Its role in shaping the development of international tax policy—or, more accurately, its lack thereof—can be traced to Global Jim Crow.

The corporate coding long facilitated by the OECD weighs heavily on the rest of the world. The United States has viewed efforts to push back against that coding skeptically. Speaking to a room filled with high-priced lawyers, President Biden's chief international tax negotiator during the design of the pillars, Itai Grinberg, explained that the pillars had been crafted to prevent "the jungle growing back."[54]

Boasting one of Africa's biggest economies, Nigeria has been among the most strident opponents of the OECD's pillars. Along with other holdouts like Kenya, Nigeria had imposed a digital services tax. Precisely how much revenue those taxes have generated remains unclear. Even conservative figures suggest tens of millions in much-needed tax.[55] Objections to pillar one's

[52] Press Release, OECD, 138 Countries and Jurisdictions Agree to Historic Milestone to Implement Global Tax Deal (July 12, 2023), https://www.oecd.org/tax/138-countries-and-jurisdictions-agree-historic-milestone-to-implement-global-tax-deal.htm.

[53] Even 1 percent of global wealth could represent a majority of the world's population. According to a 2023 study, "[t]he richest 1% hold 45.6% of global wealth, while the poorest half of the world have just 0.75%." OXFAM INTERNATIONAL, SURVIVAL OF THE RICHEST 16 (2023), https://oxfamilibrary.openrepository.com/bitstream/handle/10546/621477/bp-survival-of-the-richest-160123-en.pdf.

[54] Before making that statement, Grinberg asked whether any reporters were in the room and asked that nobody tweet his remark. The anthropologist Johanna Mugler documents that "racialized assumptions" continue to inform the OECD policymaking process. *See* Johanna Mugler, *Sharing beyond the State: International Tax Norm Negotiations at the OECD*, *in* ANTHROPOLOGY AND TAX: ETHNOGRAPHIES OF FISCAL RELATIONS 337 (Johanna Mugler et al. eds., 2024) ("a delegate from a wealthy country, whose domestic tax system facilitates shifting MNE profits away from poorer countries, indicated that she did not feel obliged to give more taxing rights to these states: 'Why should we give more to African countries? I do not see the sense. If the money does not even reach the wider population . . . They must first get organised.' While acknowledging that more money could benefit people in these countries, she delegitimised their demands for more revenue from the global profits of MNEs by pointing to domestic wealth inequalities in various postcolonial states, and also by drawing racialised assumptions about the inefficiency and corruption of 'native' states. In her understanding, each nation-state is solely accountable for economic and social justice within its borders.").

[55] *Social Media: Nigeria Got $1.3 Billion Taxes from Digital Firms*, TRT AFRIKA (Aug. 25, 2023), http://www.trtafrika.com/business/social-media-nigeria-got-dollar13-billion-taxes-from-digital-firms-14675659.

digital services tax prohibition need little explanation. Poor countries want to tax profitable multinationals championed by wealthy states.

Concerns regarding pillar two's minimum tax, by contrast, require some context. Global minimum taxes might seem precisely what the world—and poor countries in particular, given their reliance on corporate tax revenues—needs. Unfortunately, like Subpart F and GILTI, global minimum taxes primarily help residence countries. Pillar two has been modified to permit source countries to participate, but it remains unclear how effective those changes will be in delivering revenue to poor states. As a result, those countries that might seem natural constituencies for a global minimum tax have reason to be skeptical.

The design of pillar two underscores the extent to which Global Jim Crow continues to produce policies that favor wealthy states.[56] For instance, the relatively recent pro-source revisions to pillar two create a complex mechanism to permit source states to attempt to extract a share of global minimum tax revenue. Known by the fittingly inscrutable abbreviation QDMTT, short for qualified domestic minimum top-up tax, they reject a far simpler alternative.

Pillar two could have been restructured as withholding tax collected by residence states on behalf of source states. But Global Jim Crow ensured that such an option would never have been considered. Thanks to Africa's disenfranchisement, even basic design details—like the rate chosen—respond to demands from Ireland rather than from countries like Nigeria or Kenya.[57]

To truly appreciate the impact of decades of Global Jim Crow, consider Rwanda.[58] Rwanda designed its corporate tax system to be consistent with international standards. As is common practice, the Rwandan corporate tax includes carefully tailored tax breaks designed to attract foreign investment.

[56] Ruth Mason explains that pillar two "chiefly benefits rich, high-tax countries." Ruth Mason, *The 2021 Compromise*, 172 Tax Notes Fed. 569, 572 (2021) (detailing the ways in which the global minimum tax addressed intra-European Union squabbles between high- and low-tax states (e.g., Germany vs. Ireland)).

[57] A rate of 15 percent seems to have been chosen to placate OECD member Ireland. Long famous for its 12.5 percent corporate tax rate, Ireland successfully held the line despite demands from African states for a significantly higher figure. A Biden Administration insider explains that "[a]lthough the Administration believed a higher rate was preferable from a revenue perspective, and many other countries, especially developing and emerging countries in Africa and South America desired the same, proposing a Pillar Two rate much higher than the Irish corporate rate of 12.5% would have been a major risk. Most analysts considered the EU to be essential for moving Pillar Two forward given that it comprises one-sixth of the world's GDP." Rebecca Kysar, *The Global Tax Deal and The New International Economic Governance*, 74 Tax L. Rev. 171, 207 (2024).

[58] *See* Afton Titus, *Global Minimum Corporate Tax: A Death Knell For African Country Tax Policies?*, 50 Intertax 414 (2022) (describing the impact of the global minimum tax on Rwanda's corporate tax incentive structure).

Like Subpart F before it, minimum taxes allow wealthy states to expand their claims as residence jurisdictions to include those foregone Rwandan revenues.

A global minimum tax deserving of the title—perhaps the withholding tax sketched out above—would have collected those taxes on behalf of Rwanda. That Rwanda had made reasoned and reasonable policy choices not to collect those taxes would not matter to the OECD. Instead, its pillar two invites wealthy residence countries to earmark those revenues for "once-in-a-generation" investments back at home.

Conclusion

Corporate tax abuse means coding. Techniques like the double Irish Dutch sandwich—with help from the OECD's treaties and more recent innovations like check-the-box—rely on sophisticated planning rather than secrecy. Displacement of the United Nations has allowed the United States extraordinary freedom to reimagine global tax rules over the past six decades. The United States has repeatedly deployed that power, alternately favoring private actors and its bottom line.

As this chapter underscores, such choices have consistently favored the wealthy states that dominate the OECD. The next chapter offers more evidence of the continuing impact of Global Jim Crow, this time in the form of coconut trees. It reveals how policymakers have sustained that lopsided Global Jim Crow system in the face of growing criticism. Simply put, the exclusive structure of the OECD has made global tax policy a safe space for xenophobia and racism.

5

Contesting Global Jim Crow

Palm Trees

Palm trees have become the most important meme in international taxation. Quite by chance, I consider myself something of an expert on them. That goes double for the coconut palms that grew everywhere on the islands where I spent my childhood.

For those familiar only with coconuts from a produce aisle, the explanation for their ubiquity in archipelagos like mine may prove surprising. Particularly before being stripped of their thick outer husk—leaving only the hairy inner shell—coconuts float. This helps coconut trees flourish in a place with a surface area of about twenty times more water than land. Buoyant coconuts wash out to sea and then up on white sand beaches, sprouting and beginning the cycle all over again.

Not long ago, a caricature of coconut palms—bearing little resemblance to the arresting image featured on this book's cover, a painting by a childhood friend—found their way into a publication by the OECD. The colorful publication promoted the pillars that—conveniently overlooking the OECD's sudden rise and its transformative embrace of Global Jim Crow—it falsely presented as the most significant reform of international tax rules in a century. The OECD proposal purported to respond to the challenges presented by the digital economy to "bring the international tax rules into the 21st century."[1] In truth, the OECD's pillars represented an extension of the pattern described in the last chapter—not unique to the digital economy, unless that includes Chrysler cars and Bausch & Lomb contact lenses—of simultaneously enabling corporate tax abuse and expanding taxation by its members while limiting it for others.

This chapter traces how those coconuts drifted into that brochure. It also shows why they unceremoniously vanished from it a year later, with the

[1] OECD, OECD/G20 Base Erosion and Profit Shifting Project: Two-Pillar Solution to Address the Tax Challenges Arising from the Digitalisation of the Economy 3 (2021), https://perma.cc/68NS-R3N7.

Racial Capitalism and International Tax Law. Steven A. Dean, Oxford University Press. © Steven A. Dean 2025.
DOI: 10.1093/9780197526002.003.0006

entire brochure quietly disappearing soon after. Beginning in 2000, the anti-Black racism that had quietly helped fuel the OECD's rise to power played a more conspicuous role in global tax policymaking. Given how much the world has changed since 1960, it comes as no surprise that such bias has been contested.

Thanks to the insular structure of global tax governance, global tax governance has remained stubbornly insular. The United States remains at its core, but is not the same country that brought Global Jim Crow to life. When an OECD spokesman called a group of Black and brown countries "gangsters" in the New York Times and demanded that they be sanctioned to safeguard its members' privileged status, outspoken critics emerged within the United States. Unrepentant, twenty years later, the OECD published its brochure.

The Source of Discontent

As the twentieth century drew to a close, a sense of foreboding gathered around the global tax system.[2] The income tax, once robust, appeared fragile. After decades of embracing treaties and other policies permitting corporate coding and individual evasion, rich states came to believe they had somehow lost the knack of collecting taxes.

Amid considerable uncertainty, the world looked to the OECD for solutions. Unaccustomed to scrutiny—and apparently unprepared to accept any blame for its failures—the OECD lashed out. It rounded up a group of outsiders and castigated them for a reality that Switzerland, the Netherlands, and Ireland—all founding members of the OECD—had helped to create.

A group of non-member countries found themselves cast as villains and threatened with "economic sanctions, a ban on banking transactions and a cutoff of development aid."[3] Thanks to Global Jim Crow, difference could be portrayed as deviance. Because of a flawed algorithm, a lack of sophistication came to signify aggression.

[2] *See, e.g.*, Reuven S. Avi-Yonah, *Globalization, Tax Competition, and the Fiscal Crisis of the Welfare State*, 113 Harv. L. Rev. 1573, 1576 (2000) (arguing that "the individual and corporate income taxes, which traditionally have generated the largest share of revenue for modern welfare states" faced meaningful threats from tax competition); Michael J. Graetz, *Taxing International Income: Inadequate Principles, Outdated Concepts, and Unsatisfactory Policies*, 26 Brook. J. Int'l L. 1357, 1397 (2001).

[3] *See* Barry James, *Tax Havens Face OECD Threat of Sanctions*, N.Y. Times (June 14, 2000), https://www.nytimes.com/2000/06/14/news/tax-havens-face-oecd-threat-of-sanctions.html.

Racial Bias and Blame

For non-US readers, understanding the OECD spokesman's comment about gangsters requires context. In American criminal law, prosecutors often rely on "gang allegations. . . to win over juries and convict criminal Defendants even where actual evidence of guilt is lacking."[4] Here, seeming to embrace the adage that the best defense is a good offense, the OECD once again invoked a compelling threat to win over a wary public. The international tax system it had long ago commandeered might be failing, but it could not be blamed.

The concept of a gang in the United States has become heavily racialized. Take, for example, the Racketeer Influenced and Corrupt Organization (RICO) Act. Despite its role in high-profile cases involving Iran-Contra and the Gambino crime family, "the criminal groups that the government has prosecuted as gangs under RICO are primarily affiliated with one or more racial minority groups."[5]

An episode of *Law and Order: LA*—focused on "a middle class gang that resorts to violence to keep citizens off the beach that borders their property"[6]—offers an illustration. That fictional gang drew on the very real Lunada Bay Boys. The Lunada Bay Boys consisted of wealthy residents of an attractive surfing locale long accused of violence and intimidation designed to exclude outsiders.[7] They fit the profile of a street gang perfectly.[8] However, law enforcement did not treat them as one. Because its members were wealthy and white, they operated with impunity for decades.[9]

[4] Fareed Nassor Hayat, *Preserving Due Process: Require the Frye and Daubert Expert Standards in State Gang Cases*, 51 N.M. L. Rev. 196, 232 (2021).

[5] Jordan Blair Woods, *Systemic Racial Bias and RICO's Application to Criminal Street and Prison Gangs*, 17 Mich. J. Race & L. 303, 315 (2012) (showing that 86 percent of prosecutions involved gangs that were affiliated with a minority group).

[6] *Law & Order: LA: Harbor City*, IMDB, https://www.imdb.com/title/tt1720510/.

[7] *See* Roy Carroll, *California's Surf Wars: Wave 'Warlords' Go to Extreme Lengths to Defend Their Turf*, The Guardian (May 18, 2015), https://www.theguardian.com/travel/2015/may/18/california-surf-wars-lunada-bay-localism-surfing; *see also* Robin Abcarian, *Column: Is the Reign of the Surf Thugs at Lunada Bay Finally Coming to an End? Looks Like it*, L.A. Times (Apr. 23, 2023), https://www.latimes.com/opinion/story/2023-04-23/lunada-bay-boys-surf-california-palos-verdes-estates-coastal-act [https://perma.cc/SSY6-CY3E] (Locals insisted that they excluded outsiders so they would have "driftwood on the beach rather than Kentucky Fried Chicken boxes").

[8] U.S. Federal law does not attempt to define a "criminal street gang." Instead, it offers a list of characteristics. That formal definition does not mention race, instead envisioning "an ongoing group, club, organization, or association of 5 or more persons (A) that has as 1 of its primary purposes the commission of 1 or more of the criminal offenses described in subsection (c); (B) the members of which engage, or have engaged within the past 5 years, in a continuing series of offenses described in subsection (c); and (C) the activities of which affect interstate or foreign commerce." 18 U.S.C. § 521 (1994).

[9] *See* Abcarian, *supra* note 7 ("Until recently, the Bay Boys seemed almost immune from repercussions, as local police and city officials gave little more than lip service to the sacred principle

Punishing Liberia

The tax law has its own Lunada Bay Boys. What the Tax Justice Network calls the "Axis of Tax Avoidance"[10] consists of the United Kingdom, Luxembourg, the Netherlands, and Switzerland. Although responsible for the lion's share of corporate tax abuse, none of them appeared on the OECD's blacklist. The OECD generated a series of factors that were applied to identify tax havens.[11] That algorithm falsely identified Liberia as a gangster. It spared the Axis of Tax Avoidance.[12]

The sanctions that the OECD envisioned being imposed by its members never did fall on Liberia. That was not a result of a change of heart but rather because its algorithm attracted the attention of the Congressional Black Caucus, an influential group of US legislators. Soon after the Black Caucus protested, the OECD effort to impose sanctions collapsed.

Three possible explanations for the unraveling of the OECD effort have been offered. One lies in the results of the 2000 election.[13] Another credits the advocacy of conservative think tanks like the Heritage Foundation and the Center for Freedom and Prosperity.[14] A third cites the intervention of the US Congressional Black Caucus.[15]

enshrined in the California Coastal Act: Our beaches and waves belong to everyone, not just the entitled white few.").

[10] *What is the Axis of Tax Avoidance?*, Tax Justice Network, https://taxjustice.net/faq/what-is-the-axis-of-tax-avoidance/.

[11] The OECD introduced slightly different, more subjective criteria in 1998, but by 2000 had revised them. OECD, Towards Global Tax Co-Operation: Progress in Identifying and Eliminating Harmful Tax Practices 10 n.4 (2000), https://www.oecd-ilibrary.org/towards-global-tax-co-operation_5lmqcr2klgvf.pdf ("1) there is no or nominal tax on the relevant income (from geographically mobile financial and other service activities); 2) there is no effective exchange of information with respect to the regime; 3) the jurisdiction's regimes lack transparency e.g. the details of the regime or its application are not apparent, or there is inadequate regulatory supervision or financial disclosure; and 4) the jurisdiction facilitates the establishment of foreign-owned entities without the need for a local substantive presence or prohibits these entities from having any commercial impact on the local economy.").

[12] *See id.* at 9 (applying "four . . . factors, similar to the tax haven criteria" for OECD member states).

[13] Sunita Jogarajan & Miranda Stewart, *Harmful Tax Competition: Defeat or Victory?*, 22 Austl. Tax F. 3, 13 (2007) ("[I]t is important to acknowledge a simpler explanation for failure of the project—that it was caused by the withdrawal of support by the US government after the election of President George Bush in 2001.").

[14] J.C. Sharman, Havens in a Storm: The Struggle for Global Tax Regulation 102 (2006) (Sharman sees the Center for Freedom and Prosperity as the key actor, with help from the Heritage Foundation).

[15] Steven A. Dean & Attiya Waris, *Ten Truths About Tax Havens: Inclusion and the "Liberia" Problem*, 70 Emory L.J. 1659, 1670-76 (2021).

The first explanation relies on the questionable premise that Democrats—the party that signed off on both treaties and check-the-box—always support higher taxes while Republicans oppose them.[16] The transition to the George W. Bush administration in 2001 came in the year following the publication of the blacklist. And the new president would deliver memorable tax reductions, popularly referred to as "the Bush tax cuts." However neatly the withdrawal of US support fits that narrative, the switch from Democrat to Republican on its own did not end US support for the OECD effort. After taking control, the Bush administration remained "genuinely undecided" on the OECD effort.[17]

Still, the election did have an impact. The departure of Treasury Secretary Lawrence Summers and the arrival of Treasury Secretary Paul O'Neill would prove crucial. Summers, the head of Treasury under Clinton, had been "the strongest proponent" of the OECD blacklist's law and order approach.[18] It would eventually be O'Neill, Bush's replacement for Summers, who came out forcefully against the initiative.[19] By removing Summers, the election paved the way for change.

The idea that right-wing think tanks like the Center for Freedom and Prosperity played a key role in prompting the switch owes much to boasts by those same organizations. The most comprehensive study of the OECD effort and its collapse, conducted by J. C. Sharman, concedes that "[l]ike many other lobby groups, the CFP tends to exaggerate its size and importance."[20] Nevertheless, Sharman endorses the CFP's view of its influence, even crediting the CFP with having duped members of the Congressional Black Caucus into teaming up with a longtime adversary, the Heritage Foundation, and "adopt[ing] a position" not "in line with their 'objective' interests."[21]

In the absence of other evidence, both explanations might seem plausible. Given the right conditions, a presidential election and a right-wing lobbying campaign could have ended US support for the OECD's effort. Had Gore won, the outcome might indeed have been very different. Without the

[16] As Chapter 4 highlights, the Clinton administration created the check-the-box election. That chapter also describes the support Surrey and the Kennedy Administration offered for treaties.

[17] Sharman, *supra* note 14, at 67.

[18] *Id.* at 36.

[19] Paul O'Neill, *Confronting OECD's 'Harmful' Tax Approach*, Wash. Times, May 11, 2001, at A17, http://www.uniset.ca/microstates/oneill.pdf [https://perma.cc/R5VK-7282].

[20] Sharman, *supra* note 14, at 67.

[21] *Id.* at 68.

determined opposition of anti-tax think tanks, sanctions could well have been imposed.

Right-wing think tanks can be relied on to oppose any effort to increase taxes or tax enforcement. However, they do not always persuade Republican presidents to embrace their views. That the Bush administration initially continued support for the OECD effort suggests a more complex sequence of events.

The Congressional Black Caucus

Ultimately, opposition from the left would do what the election of a Republican president had not. Through months of campaigning and governing, Bush had shown no inclination to withdraw US support from the OECD initiative. The Bush administration's support for the OECD effort crumbled only after the Congressional Black Caucus sent a letter to O'Neill.[22] The timing of that intervention suggests that it, rather than the election, provided the necessary spark. With Summers gone and conservative advocates attacking the OECD, adding a new, unexpected voice to the chorus of criticism tipped the balance.

The key question then becomes why Democratic legislators generally inclined to support higher taxes urged a Republican president to abandon an enforcement effort. The explanation usually offered for their intervention presumes that—consistent with the Dunning School's persistent narrative—they did so either in error or weakness. At a superficial level, that might seem more plausible than liberal Democrats proving relatively open to persuasion on this issue, particularly as compared to a Republican administration that would soon author iconic tax cuts.

Having been persuaded, the Black Caucus became excellent advocates. They managed to win over a Bush administration that had ignored the pleas of longtime allies like the Heritage Foundation. Focusing on two members reveals a perfectly rational explanation for a collaboration between the Congressional Black Caucus and its natural adversaries.

Opponents of the OECD campaign might have won over any member of the Caucus. Handed a copy of the *New York Times*, any Black legislator would have already been wary of a blacklist dominated by Black and brown

[22] Cordia Scott, *Black Caucus Says OECD Tax Move Unfairly Blasts Developing Nations*, 22 Tax Notes Int'l 1600, 1600–01 (2001).

countries. The quotation from the OECD spokesman calling them gangsters would have made it difficult to miss the bias distorting its conclusions.[23] And if neither clue proved sufficient, the article also included an ominous warning—not attributed to the OECD spokesman—that the "noose is tightening."

Representative Charles Rangel, a congressman from Harlem, was one of two pivotal members of the Congressional Black Caucus who signed a letter opposing the OECD effort. By 2001, Rangel had been in Congress for decades. He would eventually serve as the ranking Democratic member of House Ways and Means, the committee charged with writing tax laws. He developed unique expertise at the intersection of racism and international tax law.

In 1984, Rangel was arrested for protesting outside the South African Consulate. A few years later, he created "the Rangel Amendment" discussed below. The provision denied the generous tax credits chronicled in Chapter 2 for income taxes paid by US multinationals to South Africa.

The second key Black Caucus member hailed from the US Virgin Islands. Congressional Delegate Donna Christian-Christensen wrote to O'Neill on her own, days before the letter Rangel and others joined was sent.[24] She complained that the OECD "initiative threaten[ed] to undermine the fragile economies of some of our closest neighbors and allies, as well as my own Congressional district, the U.S. Virgin Islands."[25]

The OECD's threats directly targeted her objective interests (and those of her district). Nevertheless, on her own, Christian-Christensen might not have succeeded in persuading the Bush administration to change course. But most of the Black Caucus lending their weight to her effort achieved what neither the election nor the CFP could. Christian-Christensen's district—along with Liberia and the others—would be spared the OECD's sanctions.

Neither letter directly addressed the question of race. Nor did they highlight the bias of the OECD's algorithm. However, Christian-Christensen, Rangel, and the other signatories notched a significant victory by successfully challenging Global Jim Crow with their second letter. They persuaded O'Neill to put down the OECD's noose.

[23] *See* James, *supra* note 3.

[24] A research assistant, Kalina Hannsz, surprised me with that earlier letter, puncturing the Dunning School-inflected narrative of incompetence embraced by Sharman and others.

[25] Letter from Donna M. Christensen, Delegate, U.S. House of Representatives, to Hon. Paul H. O'Neill, Secretary, U.S. Department of Treasury, Tax Notes Today, Mar. 12, 2001, https://www.taxnotes.com/research/federal/other-documents/treasury-tax-correspondence/christensen-asks-oneill-to-reject-harmful-oecd-tax-initiative/10c08.

Protest and Backlash

In the new Bush administration, Rangel and Christian-Christensen found a sympathetic ear.[26] But others were scornful. Decades before, the Rangel Amendment—the "bloody" Rangel Amendment to some critics[27]—had similarly become an object of ridicule. Rangel was vilified by the Washington Post for punishing US corporations operating in Apartheid-era South Africa. The paper denounced Rangel's "unhappy confusion about fighting apartheid."[28] Rangel's effort—dismissed as "foolish"—helped prompt Mobil to divest from South Africa.[29]

In 2001, Rangel's opposition to the OECD blacklist elicited similar contempt from the media.[30] Lee Sheppard is a journalist well known for her dry wit. She is no shill for the OECD, caricaturing it as "a decadent, ineffectual, hypocritical, imperialist, mercantilist European talk shop."[31] But, echoing the Post's sentiments, Lee dismissed Rangel's criticism of the OECD's blacklist as "imaginative" and dismissed a majority of the Congressional Black Caucus as "a boatload of no-name legislators."[32]

After the Black Caucus intervened, the OECD's members refrained from carrying out its threats against Liberia or Christian-Christensen's district. Treasury Secretary O'Neill played a key role in sparing them. O'Neill

[26] Bush's condemnation of a powerful Senator for making favorable remarks about "the pro-segregation 1948 presidential campaign of Strom Thurmond, for example . . . help[ed] lead to his removal as majority leader." Perry Bacon Jr., *Have Republicans Given Up on Winning Black Voters?*, FiveThirtyEight (Dec. 11, 2018, 6:42 AM), https://fivethirtyeight.com/features/have-republicans-given-up-on-winning-black-voters/.

[27] Charles B. Rangel, And I Haven't Had a Bad Day Since: From the Streets of Harlem to the Halls of Congress 52–53 (2007).

[28] *The Rangel Amendment*, Wash. Post, Jan. 3, 1988, at B6 (concluding that the Rangel Amendment meant "yield[ing] to a generalized despair and militancy").

[29] Nancy H. Kreisler, *Mobil is Quitting South Africa, Blaming 'Foolish' Laws in U.S.*, N.Y. Times, Apr. 29, 1989, at 1 (quoting Rangel as saying he saw "the Mobil withdrawal as particularly significant because of Mobil's leading role as a corporate apologist for continued U.S. investment in South Africa").

[30] Lee A. Sheppard, *It's the Bank Secrecy, Stupid*, 22 Tax Notes Int'l 2018, 2019 (2001) (deriding the letter as "imaginative"); Anand Giridharadas, *Saved Havens: The Treasury Coddles Tax Cheats*, The New Republic, Sept. 3, 2001, at 23 ("Most strikingly, on March 14, after laborious persuasion, 26 members of the Congressional Black Caucus—including staunch liberals like Charles Rangel and Maxine Waters—were enlisted, because of their affinity for the Caribbean, to sign a letter drafted by the CFP condemning the OECD. . . . Rosa Parks would be so proud.").

[31] Sheppard, *supra* note 30, at 2018.

[32] *Id.* at 2018–19. A decade later, Rangel and another member of his band of no-name legislators—Barack Obama—bested the OECD again. The 2010 U.S. Foreign Account Tax Compliance Act, better known as FATCA, allowed the United States to collect tax on the offshore income of individuals. The OECD had urged bilateral agreements between states—essentially mini-tax treaties—dismissing unilateral measures as ineffective, where FATCA directly targeted banks, forcing them to provide that information. While far from perfect, FATCA proved as impactful as the Rangel Amendment once had.

proved to be somewhat unconventional. He toured Africa with Bono before being forced out in 2002 for being outspoken.[33] Well after the election, but less than two months after Delegate Christian-Christensen wrote that first letter to him, O'Neill published an opinion piece announcing the change. "Recently, I have had cause to re-evaluate the United States' participation in the Organization for Economic Cooperation and Development working group that targets 'harmful tax practices.'"[34]

Unfortunately, as Black taxpayers learned while challenging racist Jim Crow tax laws like the Kentucky statute described in the introduction, such victories can prove hollow. The power of both Jim Crow and Global Jim Crow lies not in the actions of any one individual but in the array of robust structures that sustains them. An apparently chastened OECD never mentioned gangsters again. However, its sanctions would resurface under the banner of the European Union. Home to most of the tax law's Lunada Bay Boys, it picked up where the OECD left off. Safely beyond the reach of the Congressional Black Caucus, the "European Union has chosen to reproduce outdated and biased patterns of assessment" with the "EU blacklist."[35]

Treasure Islands

Rangel and Christian-Christensen succeeded in disrupting the OECD initiative. Their success also suggests how anti-Black bias may have helped the OECD rise to power and to wield it. Neither the OECD's gangster comment nor its coconut trees represent the first time that misleading, racially charged words or imagery were used to capture the public's imagination in global tax policy.

[33] Robert D. Hershey Jr., *Paul O'Neill, Treasury Secretary Who Clashed with Bush, Is Dead at 84*, N.Y. Times, Apr. 20, 2020, at D6 ("Mr. O'Neill lasted less than two years in the job; his outspoken independence was seen as political disloyalty, and President George W. Bush fired him in December 2002. . . . [H]e was 'fearless' in pressing ideas based on facts and evidence.").

[34] Paul O'Neill, *supra* note 19, at A17 ("The United States does not support efforts to dictate to any country what its own tax rates or tax system should be, and will not participate in any initiative to harmonize world tax systems.").

[35] The European Union would eventually embrace a similarly troubling effort to blacklist and punish non-member states. Stefanie Geringer, *Dissemination of Tax Good Governance Standards by the European Union and the OECD: A Comparative Analysis of Changes in Treatment and Tone*, 77 Bull. Int'l Tax 148, 155 (2023) ("while the OECD has at least been gradually adapting its approach to include non-OECD countries and jurisdictions (especially emerging and developing countries) in the process of defining and enforcing standards, the European Union has chosen to reproduce outdated and biased patterns of assessment without restriction, especially in the context of the EU blacklist").

Decades before, the Wall Street Journal, for example, published a story about Subpart F. As described in the previous chapter, Subpart F targeted European corporate tax abuse. Kennedy and his team focused on Switzerland. The article did not. Instead, it focused on downtown Nassau: "On picturesque Rawson Square here native women sit under gaily colored parasols plaiting and selling handbags, hats and other accessories."[36]

Kennedy initially called out Switzerland but also used the phrase "'tax haven' device" to describe the double Irish Dutch sandwiches of the day. The phrase conflated individual tax evasion and corporate tax abuse, bringing to mind the majority-Black jurisdictions that had drawn attention in the late 1950s as places where wealthy individuals could hide money.[37] The Wall Street Journal article might more accurately have begun with a visit to Zurich's Confiserie Sprüngli or led with the licensing of patents or the shifting of management fees. That Wall Street Journal article is still preserved among Surrey's papers.[38]

Half a century later, the titles of books[39] and peer-reviewed academic articles[40] about tax havens and illustrations used in journals like Foreign Affairs all point at "Treasure Islands." The OECD's recent marketing brochure wordlessly does the same. It suggests that all the public needed to know about its pillar two proposal could be summarized in a single graphic.

[36] Lee Silberman, *Fading Tax Haven? Proposal in Congress Could Hobble American Ventures in Bahamas*, WALL ST. J., Mar. 29, 1962, at 1. Rawson Square lies at the center of downtown Nassau, centrally located among courthouses, shops, and cruise ship terminals. Named after Governor Rawson, an Eton-educated colonial official who ruled over the Bahamas in the nineteenth century, that Rawson Square and its "native women" would serve as a symbol of tax avoidance by US multinationals might genuinely have surprised Surrey, Kennedy's Assistant Secretary of the Treasury for Tax Policy. But, for the media, it is not surprising that the use of the term tax haven meant a jurisdiction that over the 1950s had captured the public imagination.

[37] *See* Vanessa Ogle, *'Funk Money': The End of Empires, The Expansion of Tax Havens, and Decolonization as an Economic and Financial Event*, 249 PAST & PRESENT 213, 227 (2020) ("British decolonization and the departure of funds from parts of the empire helped to propel the growth of one of the most important tax havens over the coming decades in the Caribbean. While the Bahamas had first attracted tax dodgers in the 1930s as a result of increased taxation in the United States (as part of the New Deal) and newly introduced income taxes in Europe, it was after the Second World War and in the second half of the 1950s that the Bahamas experienced a true expansion of business."). Ogle describes the racialized fears driving capital out of a newly decolonized Africa. *Id.* at 214.

[38] Whether Surrey reacted with satisfaction or surprise when he read the Wall Street Journal article, it sits preserved among his personal papers. Archived alongside Chrysler's Geneva organizational chart, both are in the Harvard Law Library's Historical & Special Collection. In addition to serving in the Kennedy administration, Surrey was a revered Harvard Law School professor.

[39] *See, e.g.*, NICHOLAS SHAXSON, TREASURE ISLANDS: UNCOVERING THE DAMAGE OF OFFSHORE BANKING AND TAX HAVENS (2012) (while the title suggests a focus on tropical islands, Shaxson's book describes a reality in which the City of London and Delaware features prominently).

[40] *See, e.g.*, James R. Hines Jr., *Treasure Islands*, 24 J. ECON. PERSPS. 103 (2010).

A combination of images presented a world where a multinational operates across three jurisdictions. The OECD represented the first, the headquarters jurisdiction, as a bland glass office building. The second, where business activities occur, would likewise be reduced to a similarly unremarkable building. The OECD did not use the term tax haven for the third. It did not need to.

Instead, the brochure offered a colorful, sun-drenched, cash-laden island as the final point of its triangle. To be certain not to be misunderstood—the sun sometimes shines in Ireland, after all—the OECD added palm trees. Even generic palm trees being insufficiently specific, the image made certain to include several prominent coconuts (entirely improbable grocery store coconuts, of course).

I critiqued the OECD's brochure.[41] The OECD first quietly removed the original image. Without apology or explanation, they replaced the island with a third glass office tower.[42] They eventually abandoned the brochure entirely. Thanks to the journal editors who published my critical piece, you can still view the original.[43]

Misdirected Blame for Corporate Tax Abuse

Like its flawed algorithm, the OECD's coconut trees could easily be dismissed as an aberration. That they were surreptitiously replaced before the entire brochure was withdrawn suggests a cover-up. But the entire episode could just as easily reveal a guilelessness about racial politics. Given the context Global Jim Crow offers—with the OECD created as an alternate, all-white

[41] *See generally* Steven A. Dean, *Filing While Black: The Casual Racism of the Tax Law*, 2022 Utah L. Rev 801 (2022).

[42] The OECD's failure to take accountability for its errors makes it easy for even the most insightful scholars to repeat those mistakes by highlighting Caribbean jurisdictions in their discussion of corporate tax abuse. For example, in his 2023 book *Crack-Up Capitalism,* Quinn Slobodian refers to "the tax havens where transnational corporations secrete away their earnings." Quinn Slobodian, Crack-Up Capitalism: Market Radicals and the Dream of a World Without Democracy 3 (2023). Early in the book, Slobodian highlights the fact that "[s]ome Caribbean islands count more registered companies than residents" only mentioning on page 234 that "the United States" has "edged out Switzerland, Singapore, and the Cayman Islands . . . as the best place in the world to illegally hide or launder assets." *Id.*

[43] The editors created an archival link that preserved the 2021 version. To see the original version of the brochure, the version that the OECD promoted heavily in connection with its proposed reform, you can use this link: https://perma.cc/68NS-R3N7. OECD, *supra* note 1 I owe a special thanks as well to Professor Young Ran (Christine) Kim for inviting me to participate in the symposium #IncludeTheirStories: Rethinking, Reimagining, and Reshaping Legal Education.

institution at the climax of "the Year of Africa"—and its more recent history of threatening Black and brown jurisdictions, those coconuts tell a straightforward story.

Presidents from Kennedy to Biden have exploited the false belief that a handful of majority-Black countries represents the primary threat to the integrity of tax laws around the globe: "rogue jurisdictions that steal wealth from the coffers of the global community, especially more developed nations."[44] In 2000, the OECD did the same. Such efforts to stir public "[o]utrage over tax havens"[45] rely on the compound lie that companies hide their income in majority-Black places like the Cayman Islands and Bermuda.[46]

The double Irish Dutch sandwich might be named after two OECD members closely tied to corporate tax abuse but in remarks embracing Trump's global minimum tax Biden mentioned neither. In an open letter to Biden, I noted the racism inherent in identifying the only two majority-Black jurisdictions[47] his experts included on their list of "Seven Big Havens . . . Bermuda, the Caymans, Ireland, Luxembourg, the Netherlands, Singapore, and Switzerland."[48] In a speech later that month he added Switzerland while again identifying the two majority-Black jurisdictions.[49] Biden still could not bring himself to name Ireland although it fell third alphabetically on his administration's list; it would have been natural to include it after Bermuda and the Cayman Islands.

In 2021, when Treasury Secretary Janet Yellen made the case for President Biden's anti-tax haven effort, her efforts elicited predictably misleading press coverage. One article in *The Week* explained that the Biden administration

[44] Martin W. Sybblis, *Equality Offshore*, 63 B.C. L. Rev. 2667, 2684–85 (2022) ("As is apparent in the narrative of the Biden Administration and G7 countries, OFCs are viewed as rogue jurisdictions that steal wealth from the coffers of the global community, especially more developed nations.").

[45] Nicholas Shaxson, *How to Crack down on Tax Havens: Start with the Banks*, 97 Foreign Aff. 94, 97 (2018).

[46] *See, e.g.*, Joseph R. Biden Jr., President of the United States, Remarks by President Biden on the American Jobs Plan (Apr. 7, 2021), https://bidenwhitehouse.archives.gov/briefing-room/speeches-remarks/2021/04/07/remarks-by-president-biden-on-the-american-jobs-plan-2/ (falsely stating that multinationals "hide their income in places like the Cayman Islands and Bermuda, in tax havens").

[47] Steven A. Dean, *A Plea to President Biden to Stop Perpetuating Racist Tax Policy*, The Nation (Apr. 13, 2021), https://www.thenation.com/article/economy/biden-tax-policy/.

[48] *See* Press Release, U.S. Department of the Treasury, Testimony of Kimberly A. Clausing, Deputy Assistant Secretary, Tax Analysis, Before the Senate Committee on Finance (Mar. 25, 2021), https://home.treasury.gov/news/press-releases/jy0079 [hereinafter Testimony].

[49] *See* Joseph R. Biden Jr., President of the United States, Remarks by President Biden in Address to a Joint Session of Congress (Apr. 28, 2021), https://bidenwhitehouse.archives.gov/briefing-room/speeches-remarks/2021/04/28/remarks-as-prepared-for-delivery-by-president-biden-address-to-a-joint-session-of-congress/.

planned on "blowing up the model of tax havens around the world."[50] It concluded that such violence need not be purely metaphorical as the United States could "threaten them with military force."[51] In reality, Yellen threatened Ireland with nothing more than pastries[52] but the illustration accompanying the article does feature an ominous image of Yellen looming over a map of Bermuda.

Bureaucratic Racism in Global Tax Policy

Global Jim Crow tells a story that begins in earnest in 1960. The arrival of the OECD created an enduring global tax governance structure that shielded multinationals from taxation while steering what revenues remained towards wealthy states and away from poor ones. Excluding majority-Black states helped entrench that disparate treatment by ensuring that racial bias would remain a part of global tax policy discourse.

In 2000, a truly global governance structure would have recognized that an algorithm that identified the Liberian government as a threat to anyone other than its people could not be trusted. But for the serendipitous intervention of the Congressional Black Caucus after the OECD targeted a Congressmember's district for sanctions, the OECD's exclusivity would have plunged an African country mired in a brutal civil war further into despair. In 2021, a more representative organization would have known what a coconut looks like (and it would have known better than embellishing an illustration with one).

Generations ago, anti-Black racism fundamentally altered the trajectory of global taxation. Intentionally parochial, the OECD has proven in countless ways that it cannot serve the interests of those it does not answer to. It must not be trusted to design a global tax architecture that will shape the fate

[50] Ryan Cooper, *Janet Yellen's Proposal to Revolutionize Corporate Taxation*, The Week (Apr. 6, 2021), https://theweek.com/articles/975735/janet-yellens-proposal-revolutionize-corporate-taxation.

[51] *Id.*

[52] As it turned out, Yellen deployed pastries rather than missiles to bring Ireland to heel. Alan Rappeport, *Pastries and Persuasion: How a Global Tax Deal Got Done*, N.Y. Times (Oct. 27, 2021), https://www.nytimes.com/2021/10/27/us/politics/global-minimum-tax-deal.html ("Over a two-hour breakfast of tea and pastries at the Hotel Amigo in Brussels in July, Treasury Secretary Janet L. Yellen tried to persuade Paschal Donohoe, the Irish finance minister, to abandon Ireland's rock bottom corporate tax rate and join the global deal the Biden administration was racing to clinch.").

of non-member nations for decades to come, particularly when those rules are so complex that few can claim to truly understand them.

A decade ago, when a majority of the world's population had no voice in the design of global tax rules, the most contentious scholarly debates in the field hinged on which form of economic efficiency—capital import, export, and ownership neutrality being the three inscrutable possibilities—could best describe and inform international tax policymaking.[53] The continuing power of race in global taxation owes much to that technical inaccessibility. No lawmaker has ever won an election on a platform focused on elevating capital ownership neutrality over capital export neutrality. Creating an all-white alternative to the United Nations for tax governance attracted little attention because it can be difficult to understand the significance of choices like source versus residence taxation. Straw vendors and coconuts matter precisely because so little of the substance of Subpart F and global minimum taxes can be readily understood by non-experts.

America-First Tax Policies

In her 2019 book, *Open: The Progressive Case for Free Trade, Immigration, and Global Capital*, Kim Clausing decries the "America First" mentality that indulges in "[b]laming foreigners" while yearning for "a return to the halcyon days of yore: a time when the American Dream was alive and well, economic growth benefited all, and children grew up to earn more than their parents."[54] In testimony Clausing offered on behalf of the Biden administration about corporate tax abuse, she insisted on the one hand that "[i]mmigration is a vital source of job creation and innovation in the U.S. economy" while on the other invoking the threat of "foreign tax havens" to advocate for enhanced residence taxation.[55] Clausing had previously gone further, explicitly

[53] *See* David A. Weisbach, *The Use of Neutralities in International Tax Policy*, 68 NAT'L TAX J. 635, 636 (2015) (surveying the international tax literature and concluding that its apparent focus on economic efficiency and neutrality is merely "loose talk, and that the best studies of international taxation do not actually use neutralities.").

[54] KIMBERLY CLAUSING, OPEN: THE PROGRESSIVE CASE FOR FREE TRADE, IMMIGRATION, AND GLOBAL CAPITAL 4–5 (2019).

[55] Testimony, *supra* note 48. The word "foreign" or a variation thereof appeared seventeen times in the press release.

presenting global minimum taxes as an opportunity "policymakers looking for a better way to put 'America first'" should embrace.[56]

What policymakers say in private matters as much as their public comments. As described in Chapter 4, while speaking to a gathering of sophisticated practitioners in 2022, a former Biden administration official congratulated himself on his efforts fighting "the jungle" on behalf of the United States and the OECD. He also made it clear that he knew better than to use such language. Before directing those remarks at one of the few groups capable of fully appreciating the technical aspects of the OECD's pillars he asked first whether any reporters were in the room and then that nobody tweet his comments.

In truth, the global tax governance structure created in 1960 has never stopped fighting the jungle. The system of Global Jim Crow, embraced in response to the threat posed by sovereign African states, continues to undermine their fiscal well-being. Yet in 2000, when finally confronted with the dysfunctional reality it had helped bring about, the OECD threatened sanctions against a list of a few dozen overwhelmingly Black and brown jurisdictions it complained posed an existential threat to its wealthy and influential members.[57]

When the Congressional Black Caucus challenged the structural racism of Global Jim Crow, their opposition was misunderstood. Anand Giridharadas described them as having been "enlisted, because of their affinity for the Caribbean" to condemn the OECD effort.[58] Ironically, he seethed: "Rosa Parks would be so proud."[59]

The passage of time has made their rejection of the OECD's 2000 effort more legible. Today, ample evidence highlights the widespread danger algorithms pose to marginalized groups. Indeed, the discovery of racial bias in algorithms used by US and Dutch tax officials has left no doubt that algorithms can pose a threat in all areas of our lives, even in tax.[60]

[56] Kimberly Clausing, *Fixing our 'America Last' Tax Policy,* THE HILL (Apr. 11, 2019), https://thehill.com/opinion/finance/438274-fixing-our-america-last-tax-policy/.

[57] *See* OECD, *supra* note 11, at 17.

[58] Giridharadas, *supra* note 30.

[59] *Id.*

[60] In 2023, researchers at Stanford revealed Black taxpayers were audited far more often than others. *See generally* Hadi Elzayn et al., *Measuring and Mitigating Racial Disparities in Tax Audits,* 140 Q.J. ECON. 113 (2025); KATHLEEN BRYANT & CHYE-CHING HUANG, NEW EVIDENCE ON RACIAL DISPARITIES IN IRS AUDIT SELECTION CALLS FOR IMMEDIATE ACTION (2023). Several years before, the Dutch Tax Benefits Scandal left a trail of families and lives destroyed by a biased algorithm. Melissa Heikkilä, *Dutch Scandal Serves as a Warning for Europe over Risks of Using Algorithms*, POLITICO (Mar. 29, 2022), https://www.politico.eu/article/dutch-scandal-serves-as-a-warning-for-europe-over-risks-of-using-algorithms/; AMNESTY INT'L, XENOPHOBIC MACHINES: DISCRIMINATION

With the benefit of hindsight, dismissing the Congressional Black Caucus's perspective as naive cosmopolitanism becomes more difficult. In 2001, it derailed an effort that smacked of racial profiling. Then, tax experts found it "entertaining to consider . . . why the larger nations did not use their militaries to enforce their will on smaller nations."[61] Now, even though the threat of military violence remains plausible to some observers, it has nevertheless become acceptable to acknowledge that "[t]ax haven debates, especially in the United States, have always been racialized, both incidentally and deliberately."[62] Two decades ago, Congressional Black Caucus members were dismissed as dangerous fools, even by progressives.

But for the creation of an all-white global tax governance structure decades before, the inclusion of Liberia on the blacklist would have been more likely to set off internal alarm bells. A more inclusive global governance structure would have recognized that, other than white sand beaches lined with coconut trees, the only characteristic that might make Liberia seem a tax haven was its Black population. Liberia had served as a flag of convenience for shipping, but that should have been irrelevant.[63]

International tax conversations remain stubbornly parochial. Even those with every reason to understand the truth repeat the OECD's falsehoods. In 2010, a decade after the OECD's blacklist, a prominent scholar, James Hines, included Liberia on a list of tax havens.[64] A year earlier, he had coauthored a study demonstrating how unlikely a tax haven Liberia represented.[65]

THROUGH UNREGULATED USE OF ALGORITHMS IN THE DUTCH CHILDCARE BENEFITS SCANDAL (2021), https://www.amnesty.org/en/wp-content/uploads/2021/10/EUR3546862021ENGLISH.pdf.

[61] Martin A. Sullivan, *Lessons from the Last War on Tax Havens*, 116 TAX NOTES 327, 334 (2007).

[62] Joseph Thorndike, *In the 1930s, The Bahamas Became a Tax Problem for Treasury*, FORBES, (Jun. 24, 2021, 4:29 PM), https://www.forbes.com/sites/taxnotes/2021/06/24/in-the-1930s-the-bahamas-became-a-tax-problem-for-treasury/.

[63] After I presented a draft of the book at the inaugural Critical Approaches to Taxation and Society Network conference in Sweden, an audience member who had worked at the OECD assured me that the OECD had no racial animus, but had simply targeted vulnerable states that happened to be Black. He insisted that Liberia had been targeted because it served as a flag of convenience for ship registration. I am not sure why he believed any of that to be reassuring.

[64] *See* Hines Jr., *supra* note 40, at 104 tbl.1 (listing Liberia).

[65] The year before, Hines had collaborated on an attempt to determine what factors could be reliably associated with tax haven status, generating a profile that looked nothing like Liberia. *See* Dhammika Dharmapala & James R. Hines Jr., *Which Countries Become Tax Havens?*, 93 J. PUB. ECON. 1058, 1061 n.18 (2009) (concluding that the prototypical tax haven was a politically stable former British colony). Notably, Hines's 2010 list included all four members of the Axis of Tax Avoidance.

The clash between the Black Caucus and the OECD represents the first notable effort to challenge the tax policymaking apparatus at the heart of Global Jim Crow. Perversely, because of Global Jim Crow, its lessons have been widely misunderstood. The OECD attempted to impose sanctions on states it described in the media as gangsters only to back down after being confronted by the Congressional Black Caucus. However, the Black Caucus—not the OECD—would face ridicule from all sides.

Its coconut trees and its blacklist should make the OECD hard to take seriously. However, its willingness to exploit bias has helped rather than hurt its status as the dominant force in international tax. As discussed in Chapter 7, the United Nations hopes to displace it. Unfortunately, questioning the United Nations' competence will be all too easy.

Decades ago, the motivations of the Black Caucus were belittled. But their intervention represented a long-overdue response to decades of exclusion and bias. Today, the effort spearheaded by the same Black states Global Jim Crow disenfranchised looks quite different when viewed as a remedy for ongoing discrimination.

Conclusion

That an organization created to police a post-colonial world—protecting property rights to ensure that "the free flow of capital and goods disciplined the behavior of postcolonial states"[66]—would threaten to punish a group of Black and brown states for "behaving like gangsters"[67] should not be surprising. The same is true of journalists lambasting the Black Caucus for challenging such behavior. However disappointing, even the proclivity of self-styled progressive experts to embrace the fearmongering in tax that they might reject elsewhere makes a certain amount of sense.

Even more worrisome than what they say in public, experts still describe global tax policy behind closed doors as a clash of cultures. Thanks to its stunted governance structure, the international tax policy landscape has changed little since 1960, trapped in a cycle of capture and coding. The

[66] Quinn Slobodian, Globalists: The End of Empire and the Birth of Neoliberalism 220 (2018). The OECD's treaties responded to a desire that "after empire, nations must remain embedded in an international institutional order that safeguarded capital and protected its right to move throughout the world." *Id.* at 9.

[67] James, *supra* note 3 (quoting an OECD spokesman who asked: "Why give aid to people who are behaving like gangsters?").

OECD's coconuts highlight a troubling contemporary reality: an exclusive organization continues to shape rules that help determine which states can afford schools and hospitals. The organization rose to power as an all-white alternative to the United Nations, just as the emergence of African states changed the face of international law. It still has never had a majority-Black member in its more than half century of existence but remains a World Tax Organization in all but name. Jim Crow may have ended in the United States, but in the exclusive spaces in which decisions are made, global tax policy remains stuck in the past.

6

Global Jim Crow's Pyrrhic Victory

Why Nations Fail

In their book, *Why Nations Fail: The Origins of Power, Prosperity, and Poverty*, Nobel laureates in economics Daron Acemoglu and James Robinson offer a theory on why some countries grow rich while others do not. They reject popular explanations based on geography, culture, or ignorance. They conclude that prosperity flows not from a "historically predetermined process but as the contingent outcome of several pivotal institutional developments during critical junctures."[1] Global Jim Crow represents just such a happenstance. Wealthy states seized an opportunity to preserve their privilege at great cost to newly sovereign states in Africa and, as this chapter illustrates, to themselves.

Acemoglu and Robinson take pains to debunk racist explanations for the failure of nations to thrive. They explain that living in warm climates does not make people too lazy to prosper. They insist that belief in the supernatural does not offer a reliable indication that a nation will languish.

Instead, the authors explain that when circumstances permit it, decisionmakers will prioritize their own privilege over the well-being of others, even their own compatriots. They tell the story of a sixteenth-century Englishman who presented Queen Elizabeth I with "a machine that would free people from endless hand-knitting."[2] She rejected it, fearing it would "create unemployment and political instability and threaten royal power."[3] The invention fared no better in France or with Elizabeth's successor.

[1] Daron Acemoglu and James A. Robinson, Why Nations Fail: The Origins of Power, Prosperity, and Poverty 433 (2012). The authors reject an array of theories based on geography (living in nice climates tends to make people lazy), culture (Africans cling to superstitions and resist technology), and ignorance (rulers need smarter economists to tell them how to become rich). They instead suggest rulers simply tend to preserve their privilege even if that requires foregoing opportunities for prosperity.
[2] *Id.* at 182.
[3] *Id* at 183.

Racial Capitalism and International Tax Law. Steven A. Dean, Oxford University Press. © Steven A. Dean 2025.
DOI: 10.1093/9780197526002.003.0007

For those on its winning end, Jim Crow represented a system of privilege. Abandoning its racial hierarchy would indeed, as Acemoglu and Robinson put it, "reshape political power" making white Americans "political losers."[4] Dudziak explains how Cold War pressures altered the calculus of Jim Crow, unacceptably inflating its costs for the Kennedy administration.[5] Unfortunately, pressure from the Soviet Union did not entirely expunge it. Global Jim Crow offers stark evidence of that.

Coase's Farmers and Ranchers

Ronald Coase's hypothetical cattle ranchers and farmers in the American West offer a way to understand the costs of Global Jim Crow for its apparent beneficiaries. Coase used that example to highlight the many obstacles to collaboration among groups with clashing objectives.[6] His farmers care only about their fields and his ranchers for their cattle. In a perfect world, he speculates, they would nevertheless strike bargains that would leave all better off. Even without common goals, each could collaborate to build fences to keep fields and livestock safely apart without requiring interference from meddlesome bureaucrats.

In reality, Coase concedes such cooperation does not always happen. Prosaic obstacles often prevent actors from helping themselves, requiring external intervention. Of course, such transaction costs represent only one obstacle to the creative problem-solving Coase envisions. Sometimes, a stubborn blindness to opportunity borne of privilege can prove a more enduring problem.

In tax, Global Jim Crow has proven to be just such a barrier to change. As described in the first chapter, it supplanted a political body with a "forum

[4] *Id.*

[5] Dudziak begins her book with the story of Jimmy Wilson, a Black handyman in Alabama, who was sentenced to death for "stealing less than two dollars in change" in a story that would garner international attention as "Wilson's case was thought to epitomize the harsh consequences of American racism." MARY L. DUDZIAK, COLD WAR CIVIL RIGHTS: RACE AND THE IMAGE OF AMERICAN DEMOCRACY 1–2 (2011).

[6] R. H. Coase, *The Problem of Social Cost*, 3 J. L. & ECON 1, 15 (1960) ("In order to carry out a market transaction it is necessary to discover who it is that one wishes to deal with, to inform people that one wishes to deal and on what terms, to conduct negotiations leading up to a bargain, to draw up the contract, to undertake the inspection needed to make sure that the terms of the contract are being observed, and so on. These operations are often extremely costly, sufficiently costly at any rate to prevent many transactions that would be carried out in a world in which the pricing system worked without cost.").

and knowledge hub for data, analysis and best practices in public policy."[7] The OECD spent decades pursuing ever-more-sophisticated rules. The resulting clarity revealed a startling—if unsurprising—inequality.

But for Global Jim Crow, the United Nations might have succeeded in forging consensus, nurturing cooperation between disparate states. Instead, a different goal has guided the OECD's work, an imperative that can be traced back to the nineteenth century. Harmonization represents the central objective of global tax policy, animating today's global minimum taxes and embedded in its treaties. Experts like Seligman brought it from the nineteenth century to the twentieth. Global Jim Crow ensured that it survived into the twenty-first, becoming central to the worldview of the OECD as it revived the League's civilizing mission and its moribund handiwork.

Even where falling transaction costs opened the door to Pareto efficient bargains—deals that might benefit both sides—a commitment to harmonization ensured none would be struck. As though Coase's ranchers stormed the statehouse and took control of the levers of power, the OECD's members resolved to remake the world in their image. The OECD's limited membership allowed it to believe that homogeneity represented a panacea. The cautionary tale of—as Acemoglu and Robinson suggest—missed opportunity that follows highlights the fact that the damage done by Global Jim Crow has not been confined to the Global South.

Tax Harmonization

Global tax policy has no rule of recognition, no principle capable of judging the worth of Subpart F or a global minimum tax. In its place, experts have relied on concepts like harmonization, ensuring that difference would be perceived as a threat rather than an opportunity. Emphasizing uniformity over cooperation, the international tax regime has squandered opportunities to reduce cross-border tax conflict. Thousands of harmonizing treaties dominate the global tax policy landscape, closing the door to alternative forms of cooperation.[8]

[7] *The OECD: Better Policies for Better Lives*, OECD, https://www.oecd.org/en/about.html. The OECD prides itself on its expertise and objectivity.

[8] The dominance of the OECD and its experts recalls the evolution of software development. *See generally* Eric S. Raymond, The Cathedral and the Bazaar: Musings on Linux and Open Source by an Accidental Revolutionary (Tim O'Reilly ed., rev. ed. 2001). Eric Raymond uses a cathedral metaphor to describe the pre-open source method of developing complex software.

Although ranchers might daydream of a world without farmers, even they would not really want to live in one. In global tax policy, states could fill complementary—rather than reciprocal—roles to make all parties better off. Particularly when international tax conflicts involve profoundly different states, such asymmetric cooperation might be the only means of forging compromise.

The very heterogeneity of the international tax landscape urges a turn away from uniformity.[9] Economists have demonstrated that "the efficiency of tax harmonization is far from clear-cut."[10] Legal scholars have also noted the risks posed by assuming that there are no meaningful differences among nations.[11]

Creating pathways to acknowledge and account for the differences among states could elevate cooperation over harmonization.[12] Yet, as described

Raymond explains how inexpensive, internet-based communication facilitated the emergence of a collaborative alternative to the conventional "cathedral" approach to software development pursuant to which a small group of experts, which he refers to as "wizards," create a complex piece of software. *Id.* at 21–22. International tax law has its "four economists" of international tax and their cathedral: the network of bilateral double-tax treaties that has served as the backbone of the modern international tax regime for decades. *See id.* Raymond notes that open-source software has provided a counterpoint to the influence of the "geographically compact communities," such as Bell Labs, that once dominated the field. *Id.* at 51. The same fall in transaction costs could have paved the way for the development of innovative alternatives but Global Jim Crow preserved the cathedral.

[9] *See* Julie Roin, *Competition and Evasion: Another Perspective on International Tax Competition*, 89 GEO. L.J. 543, 561 (2000) ("In sum, advocates of tax harmonization overstate their case by implicitly assuming the fungibility of governments and jurisdictions. Countries are not like bushels of corn, indistinguishable from one another. Instead, they vary along many different dimensions. . . ."). Even at the most basic level, the characteristics of states are not uniform. *See, e.g.*, Diane M. Ring, *What's at Stake in the Sovereignty Debate: International Tax and the Nation-State*, 49 VA. J. INT'L L. 155, 161 (2008) ("[S]tates vary widely in the degree to which they possess and demonstrate the elements of sovereignty. . . .").

[10] Carl Gaigne & Stephane Riou, *Globalization, Asymmetric Tax Competition, and Fiscal Equalization*, 9 J. PUB. ECON. THEORY 901, 902 (2007) (arguing that while tax competition may "distort the spatial allocation of capital," tax "harmonization may not be desirable"). When economic differences between nations are taken into account, harmonization can be affirmatively harmful. *See* Richard E. Baldwin & Paul Krugman, *Agglomeration, Integration and Tax Harmonisation*, 48 EUR. ECON. REV. 1, 21 (2004) ("In our model, simple tax harmonisation—defined as adoption of a common tax rate—always harms at least one nation and the seemingly sensible policy of adopting a rate that is between the two initial rates turns out to harm both nations.").

[11] *See generally* Adam H. Rosenzweig, *Why Are There Tax Havens*, 52 WM. & MARY L. REV. 923 (2010) (explaining that by failing to distinguish among jurisdictions across relevant criteria the international tax regime could inhibit cooperation).

[12] *See generally id.* (criticizing the failure of the international tax regime to recognize the significance of differences among nations such as their relative marginal returns on capital). There are exceptions, of course. The most significant is the traditional distinction between capital importers and capital exporters. *See* Michael J. Graetz & Michael M. O'Hear, *The "Original Intent" of U.S. International Taxation*, 46 DUKE L.J. 1021, 1033–34 (1997) (noting conflict between capital importers and exporters). Of course, yesterday's capital exporters can become today's capital importers (the United States being a particularly striking example of this). Structural differences among nations—such as size and population—are likely to prove more problematic. By contrast, the fiscal federalism literature focuses on the differences between jurisdictions that exist at the subnational level and "explores, both in normative and positive terms, the roles of the different levels of government and

below, convergence among national tax systems has been an aspiration since before the birth of the modern international tax regime.[13] Thanks to Global Jim Crow, that long-standing bias has been given undue prominence in global tax policy.

Falling Transaction Costs

Working to turn every rancher into a farmer does not demand much mutual understanding. Identifying unconventional bargains between those groups would. Which group might build and maintain a fence needed to keep fields safe from cattle at the lowest cost represents only one of many key questions requiring communication between disparate actors. The tax law requires fences of a different sort.

Asymmetric tax cooperation promises greater rewards than tax harmonization but demands more of those orchestrating it. Fortunately, it has never been easier for dispersed groups to collaborate. The same forces that have helped global commerce to flourish—in particular a fall in transaction costs—have given rise to a world in which

> [n]etworks of government officials—police investigators, financial regulators, even judges and legislators—increasingly exchange information and coordinate activity to combat global crime and address common problems on a global scale.[14]

the ways in which they relate to one another." Wallace E. Oates, *An Essay on Fiscal Federalism*, 37 J. Econ. Literature 1120, 1120 (1999). Although many of the considerations of fiscal federalism are irrelevant to the international context, to the extent that national governments differ in the same way as levels of government, fiscal federalism may suggest that they should not try to fill identical roles.

[13] Even Avi-Yonah's alternative withholding tax scheme to facilitate capital income taxation called on each cooperating jurisdiction to play parallel roles. *See* Reuven S. Avi-Yonah, *Globalization, Tax Competition, and the Fiscal Crisis of the Welfare State*, 113 Harv. L. Rev. 1573, 1672–74 (2000). Harmonization is often either implicitly or explicitly assumed to be a necessary condition for an optimally efficient international tax regime. *See, e.g.*, Mihir A. Desai & James R. Hines Jr., *Evaluating International Tax Reform*, 56 Nat'l Tax J. 487, 499 (2003) ("[G]lobal welfare is maximized by harmonizing the taxation of foreign income among capital-exporting countries. . . ."). Of course, there are exceptions to the harmonization consensus. *See* Michael J. Graetz, *Taxing International Income: Inadequate Principles, Outdated Concepts, and Unsatisfactory Policies*, 26 Brook. J. Int'l L. 1357, 1412–13 (2001) ("Caution, however, is warranted in assuming that conforming our nation's tax system with that of other nations, even developed nations with effective income taxes, will inevitably improve our national welfare."). *See generally* Roin, *supra* note 9, (critiquing arguments in favor of harmonization).

[14] Anne-Marie Slaughter, A New World Order 1 (2004) (Slaughter warns that "These government networks are a key feature of world order in the twenty-first century, but they are underappreciated, undersupported, and underused to address the central problems of global governance.").

Coase would have cheered the resulting opportunities for creative problem-solving. Unfortunately, Global Jim Crow has stifled such change.

As long as national rules develop in response to unique social and administrative pressures, jurisdictions will continue to rely on tax systems that exhibit at least as many differences as similarities.[15] Harmonization represents the tax expert's reflexive response to those pressures, revealing a confidence that nations can avoid international tax conflicts by becoming more like one another.

Pining for homogeneity represents a relatable impulse. Guido Calabresi and Douglas Melamed suggest a different approach. They offer the example of homeowners unhappy about a smoke-belching factory.[16] Understandably, the homeowners sought homogeneity. However, they lacked the power to compel conformity, and transaction costs prevented them from purchasing the factory collectively.

Of course, conformity might not be necessary or even desirable.[17] As Calabresi and Melamed imagine, the relevant actors might collectively be

[15] That diversity may actually make harmonization counterproductive. "[V]arying social traditions, values, and economic conditions . . . may not be well-served by harmonization. . . . Harmonization . . . might increase economic or social costs." Scott H. Jacobs, *Regulatory Co-Operation for an Interdependent World: Issues for Government*, *in* REGULATORY CO-OPERATION FOR AN INTERDEPENDENT WORLD 15, 33 (1994). Although the same diversity exists in all types of regulation to some extent, this dynamic may be especially significant when it comes to taxation for two reasons. First, tax policy implicates a wider array of issues and interests than, for example, the rules governing the issuance of securities and the protection of shareholders. Second, the near absence of frictions preventing taxpayers from capitalizing on any asymmetries that do exist magnifies the significance of even relatively minor variations in tax rules.

[16] *See* Guido Calabresi & A. Douglas Melamed, *Property Rules, Liability Rules, and Inalienability: One View of the Cathedral*, 85 HARV. L. REV. 1089, 1121–23 (1972). The authors consider the efficiency and distributional implications of different methods of preventing a factory using cheap, polluting coal in a wealthy residential neighborhood. They suggest that instead of having a court shut down a factory or forcing it to pay damages to nearby residents, making those residents subsidize the use of cleaner fuel might also enable us to combine those same efficiency goals with other goals that are often described in justice language. For example, assume that the factory in our hypothetical was using cheap coal before any of the wealthy houses were built. In these circumstances, it will not only achieve the desirable efficiency and distributional results mentioned above, but it will also accord with any "justice" significance which is attached to being there first. And this is so whether we view this justice significance as part of a distributional goal, as part of a long-run efficiency goal based on protecting expectancies, or as part of an independent concept of justice.

Id. at 1123.

[17] Ellickson provides a useful illustration of the potential inefficiency of homogeneity by describing the inefficiencies produced by the absence of a "mom-and-pop or convenience-type grocery store" in the Santa Monica Mountains as a result of zoning restrictions. Robert C. Ellickson, *Alternatives to Zoning: Covenants, Nuisance Rules, and Fines as Land Use Controls*, 40 U. CHI. L. REV. 681, 684–85 (1973). Ellickson suggests that a government could produce a more efficient result by making it easy for grocers and their neighbors to reach a private contractual agreement to compensate neighbors for the harms imposed on them by the existence of the grocery store instead of simply banning grocery stores through zoning. *See id.* at 686.

better off if a court intervened to allow the homeowners to pay the factory owner to eliminate noxious emissions. In a perfect world, all such deals—between homeowners and factories and between farmers and ranchers—would be struck, and there would be less need for uniformity. Even without perfection, as transaction costs fall, so does the need for symmetry.

The Costs of Homogeneity

FATCA—the landmark US response to evasion by individuals—could be interpreted as a judgment that transaction costs would stymie any attempt to harness Calabresi and Melamed's pay-the-polluter approach to solve the problem of cross-border tax evasion described in Chapter 1. Given the many hundreds of billions of dollars lost to tax evasion, that suggests strong assumptions about transaction costs.[18] Even if those assumptions had not already been proven wrong in spectacular fashion—as related below—the same would not be true in general.

Transaction costs would undoubtedly be smaller in other contexts. And, of particular importance here, they have been falling for decades. Whether a bargain will be struck depends partly on whether transaction costs exceed potential benefits. But it also requires a willingness to embrace unconventional solutions. Picturing each actor performing the same actions for precisely the same reasons demands little imagination.

Although more difficult, the rewards could be greater and the opportunities for asymmetric collaboration more varied. Particularly, when your own actions and motivations serve as benchmarks, as is always true for the OECD, convergence appears effortless. Asking states to play roles suited to their relative strengths and weaknesses is different.

[18] If tax evaders and their agents share benefits of $100 in the form of unpaid taxes, a cooperative intergovernmental arrangement that allows participating governments to collect and share that $100 would almost certainly leave those governments collectively better off than they would be without an agreement. In the pre-FATCA world, because the actual benefits of cooperation were so large—the estimated US revenue losses attributed to tax evasion are an order of magnitude larger than the GDP of the Cayman Islands—there did seem to be room for mutually beneficial intergovernmental deal to be struck at the expense of tax cheats. *See* Joseph Guttentag & Reuven Avi-Yonah, *Closing the International Tax Gap*, *in* BRIDGING THE TAX GAP: ADDRESSING THE CRISIS IN FEDERAL TAX ADMINISTRATION 99, 101 (Max B. Sawicky ed., 2005) (estimating US losses to tax flight at $50 billion per year).

Playing complementary roles, motivated by different incentives, would obviate the need for a "double coincidence of wants."[19] As Calabresi and Melamed suggest, the results can be particularly satisfying, with specialization benefitting all parties more than homogeneity.[20] Falling transaction costs have increasingly put the benefits of specialization within reach.

SACU and the Benefits of Asymmetric Cooperation

Although unusual, cooperative asymmetric international tax arrangements do exist. Take, for example, the Southern African Customs Union (SACU) that binds South Africa, Botswana, Lesotho, Namibia, and Eswatini. It boasts being the world's oldest such union, tracing its roots to a very different time. SACU took shape in 1903 after the Second Boer War, a brutal campaign that gave Britain control over a newly formed Union of South Africa.

After independence, SACU evolved, facilitating the collection and sharing of tax revenues.[21] The 1969 SACU agreement provided that "any customs, excise, sales and additional duties collected in the common customs area shall be paid quarterly into the Consolidated Revenue Fund of South Africa."[22] South Africa would then pay a portion of those revenues to Botswana, Lesotho, Namibia, and Eswatini according to a formula, with the balance retained.[23] The special role the 1969 agreement assigned to South Africa—in effect acting as a tax administrator for its SACU partners—reflected its dominant economic position within SACU.

[19] Thinking of the limits of barter transactions offers one way to understand the harmonization conundrum. The success of barter transactions is limited by the fact that they require a "double coincidence of wants" to take place. Dictionary of the Social Sciences 33 (Craig Calhoun ed., 2002). For reciprocal harmonization to occur, jurisdictions must have the same coincidence of wants. As a result, the less similar those jurisdictions are, the less likely they are to harmonize.

[20] Ellickson's grocery store example illustrates the potential benefits of specialization. *See* Ellickson, *supra* note 17, at 684–85. On the one hand, a flat ban on grocery stores provides a benefit by ensuring that no individual property owner is able to impose uncompensated costs on its neighbors by opening a grocery store. However, such a ban would also prevent a group of neighbors from affirmatively bargaining to allocate the costs and benefits of opening a grocery store. As a result, even if opening a grocery store would not impose any uncompensated harm on any property owner while producing a net benefit for the community as a whole, the ban would still apply, leaving the entire community less well off.

[21] *See History of SACU*, S. Afr. Customs Union, https://www.sacu.int/about-sacu/history-of-sacu (last accessed Apr. 29, 2025).

[22] 1969 Southern African Customs Union Agreement art. 13 (entered into force Dec. 11, 1969), https://www.sacu.int/uploads/documents/125758223bab6bd920ecdffe36a45553cf257e50.pdf.

[23] *Id.* art. 14. That revenue-sharing formula contained a compensation mechanism to account for the effects a customs union can have on its less developed members. In the case of SACU, South

In 2002, a revised SACU agreement was signed.[24] The 2002 agreement transformed SACU from a hierarchical arrangement with South Africa in control to one in which member states operate on equal administrative footing.[25] But the new SACU continues to "facilitate the equitable sharing of revenue arising from customs, excise and additional duties levied by Member States."[26] SACU remains a profoundly asymmetric arrangement, making no attempt to ignore the differences among members. Under SACU, its least developed member, Lesotho, receives supplemental transfers valued at more than 5 percent of its GDP.[27]

TIEAs and the Constraints of Symmetry

A pre-FATCA effort to acquire extraterritorial tax information to combat offshore tax evasion took a more roundabout approach to asymmetry. The first modern Tax Information Exchange Agreements emerged in the 1980s.[28]

Africa compensated for the fact that it gathered more economic gains due to the SACU arrangement than its partners by distributing a disproportionate amount of SACU tax revenues to Botswana, Lesotho, and Eswatini (and later Namibia). *See* James J. Hentz, South Africa and the Logic of Regional Cooperation 12 (2005).

[24] 2002 Southern African Customs Union Agreement pt. 7, *opened for signature* Oct. 21, 2002 (entered into force July 15, 2004), https://www.sacu.int/uploads/documents/11ed59ad0efe7652a9f7ea25c343815919ed023c.pdf [hereinafter 2002 SACU Agreement].

[25] The 2002 SACU Agreement means that the SACU operates according to a "one-country, one-vote formula and major decisions of the various intergovernmental and regional institutions require consensus." Martina Metzger, Regional Cooperation and Integration in Sub-Saharan Africa 10 (United Nations Conference on Trade and Dev., Discussion Paper No. 189, 2008), https://unctad.org/system/files/official-document/osgdp20084_en.pdf. It created a Council of Ministers that was to "consist of at least one Minister from each Member State and shall be the supreme decision making authority of SACU matters." 2002 SACU Agreement, *supra* note 24, pt. 3, art. 8, ¶ 1. Rather than being paid into the Consolidated Revenue Fund of South Africa, SACU revenues are now paid into a Common Revenue Pool managed by either a member state or a SACU body, appointed at the discretion of the Council of Ministers. *Id.* pt. 6, arts. 32–33.

[26] The 2002 SACU Agreement appears to have preserved the basic elements of the 1969 agreement in substance, if not in form. For instance, South Africa was designated as the administrator of the Common Revenue Pool "for a transitional period." 2002 SACU Agreement, *supra* note 24, pt. 6, art. 33. As an economic matter, the 2002 revisions "provided the BLNS with basically the same implicit revenue transfers as they had been receiving under the old agreement. Its main benefit for South Africa is that it put a cap on the amount of transfers required under the agreement." Frank Flatters & Matthew Stern, SACU Revenue Sharing: Issues and Options 2 (2006), http://qed.econ.queensu.ca/pub/faculty/flatters/writings/ff%26ms_sacursf_2006.pdf. It appears that South Africa continued to play the lead role in administering SACU. *See* Tsidiso Disenyana, *Development Through Trade*, bilaterals.org (Nov. 3, 2008), http://bilaterals.org/spip.php?article13701.

[27] Flatters & Stern, *supra* note 26, at 16.

[28] TIEAs aspire to be a way to bridge the divide between very different types of states. In that sense, they are another effort to break free of the harmonization conundrum. They attempt to accomplish that by narrowing their focus to a single aspect of the traditional international tax ties between

Recognizing that access to extraterritorial tax information could be crucial in combatting evasion, the United States created TIEAs to purchase it.[29] Authorities hoped to use the acquired information to identify hidden investments and income of US taxpayers.[30]

TIEAs are essentially a single article stripped from a conventional double tax treaty. Accordingly, TIEAs employ a formal structure that assigns reciprocal rights and obligations between pairs of states. The 1984 US model agreement offers a helpful illustration. It provides that the "competent authorities of the Contracting States shall exchange information to administer and enforce the domestic laws of the Contracting States concerning taxes."[31] Such language purports to impose identical burdens on—and appears to grant equivalent benefits to—both signatories.

Although reciprocal, the symmetry was superficial because the TIEA was created to operate between states with very different needs. Since one state needed the extraterritorial tax information contemplated by the TIEA while the other did not, no double coincidence of wants existed.[32] If the US model TIEA described above were to enter into force between the United States and a country without an income tax, the United States might receive helpful information about its taxpayers but its TIEA partner would not.[33]

states: information exchange. At some level, the agreements could encourage tax harmonization between a pair of jurisdictions just as double-tax treaties do. For example, access to tax information of the type needed to enforce a comprehensive, modern income tax provides an incentive for the TIEA partner to develop one.

[29] *See* Roin, *supra* note 9, at 545 ("Although there has already been some movement" toward "obtaining better tax information . . . it should become a primary rather than secondary goal of tax reform efforts.").

[30] *See* Bruce Zagaris, *The Procedural Aspects of U.S. Tax Policy Towards Developing Countries: Too Many Sticks and No Carrots?*, 35 Geo. Wash. Int'l L. Rev. 331, 332–34 (2003).

[31] US Model Tax Information Exchange Agreement art. 4, ¶ 1 (July 24, 1984). The U.S. model treaty of that period similarly states that the "competent authorities of the Contracting States shall exchange such information as is necessary for carrying out the provisions of this Convention or of the domestic laws of the Contracting States concerning taxes." US Model Income and Capital Tax Convention art. 26, ¶ 1 (Jun. 16, 1981). The OECD model TIEA of the era used the same neutral formulation, providing that "each Contracting Party shall ensure that its competent authorities for the purposes specified in Article 1 of the Agreement, have the authority to obtain and provide upon request: a) information held by banks." OECD, Agreement on Exchange of Information on Tax Matters art. 5, ¶ 4 (2002), https://www.oecd.org/content/dam/oecd/en/publications/reports/2002/05/agreement-on-exchange-of-information-in-tax-matters_g1gh2b36/9789264034853-en.pdf.

[32] The report of a UN group concluded that because of structural differences in the tax regimes of TIEA partners, the relatively advanced TIEA partner would receive, but would not be required to provide, tax information. Ad Hoc Group of Experts on Int'l Cooperation in Tax Matters, *Tax Treatment of Cross-Border Interest Income and Capital Flights: Recent Developments*, ¶ 52, U.N. Doc. ST/SG/AC.8/2003/L.10 (July 9, 2003) [hereinafter U.N. Tax Experts Report].

[33] *See* Texas Top Cop Shop, Inc. v. Garland, No. 24-40792, 2024 WL 5203138 (5th Cir. Dec. 23, 2024). As described in Chapter 1, although FATCA evolved to include a nominally reciprocal

Both SACU and TIEAs are outliers. Each embraces Coase's vision in different ways by creating frameworks in which states engage in cross-border interactions while filling different roles. They also illustrate an important point of divergence. SACU acknowledges that states differ in meaningful ways. TIEAs do not.

Under the SACU agreement, one participating state serves as a withholding agent for others, transferring tax revenues collected on their behalf. TIEAs, by contrast, only envision administrative assistance—here in the form of extraterritorial tax information—flowing across borders. Both call for states to expend resources in a way that might not generate accompanying benefits. However, only one delivers a Pareto-efficient result. SACU requires states to share the benefits of cooperation along with the burdens.

The False Appeal of Harmonization

The rise of rules cataloged in Chapter 1 owes a debt to their perceived "simplifying effects."[34] Domestically, tax simplification has long been the holy grail of tax policy, constantly pursued but never attained.[35] Tax harmonization may appear its equivalent in the international context, a benign goal of universal appeal. In truth, as discussed below, tax harmonization represents an imperial artifact.

Eliminating differences among national tax systems might seem the only plausible way to eliminate conflicts. But as our farmers and ranchers (and our homeowners and the factory, and, of course, SACU and TIEAs) suggest, other ways do exist. Cooperation does not require symmetry.

In its purest form, tax harmonization might require translating one set of tax laws into each relevant language and having them enacted by each nation's legislature. In reality, such an effort would in some respects go too far. In others, it would not go far enough.

Because the objective of tax harmonization lies in eliminating differences between tax systems from the taxpayer's perspective, formal differences might not matter. Insisting that exact translations of a given statutory

element, even today, it remains unclear whether US tax authorities have legal authority to provide extraterritorial tax information.

[34] *See* Cass R. Sunstein, *Problems with Rules*, 83 Cal. L. Rev. 953, 972 (1995) (Sunstein identifies the "simplifying effects" of rules as one of their key benefits).

[35] Edward J. McCaffery, *The Holy Grail of Tax Simplification*, 1990 Wis. L. Rev. 1267, 1267 (1990) ("People have long sought, or said they have sought, simpler tax laws. Yet, by most measures, tax laws remain extremely complex.").

provision be employed in each jurisdiction would often be pointless. At the same time, given cultural differences across states, merely using identical statutory language offers no guarantee those laws will be interpreted and applied identically.

Substantive tax harmonization would require each nation to create tax regimes identical in at least three respects. First, each nation would need to tax the same assets and activities. In other words, each nation's tax base would need to be the same as every other nation's.[36] Second, the tax rate imposed on those tax bases must be the same in every jurisdiction.[37] Finally, each nation's tax laws would need to be administered in a comparable fashion.[38] Only by achieving a high degree of conformity with respect to each of those three criteria can two or more nations be said to have achieved tax harmonization. At the risk of understatement, that is easier said than done.

Imposing parallel domestic legal and administrative structures represents one path toward harmonization. International agreements provide an alternative mechanism, a shortcut to harmonization. Since states can effectively rewrite their domestic laws through international law, domestic statutory and regulatory differences may be made irrelevant by treaty.

[36] The base on which a tax is imposed refers to the economic event that triggers the tax or the asset on which the tax is levied. The range of tax bases employed by different jurisdictions is wide. Some jurisdictions rely heavily on consumption taxes such as value-added taxes. Others, such as the United States, rely heavily on income taxes. Even among tax bases that are broadly similar, the differences can be significant. For example, a tax on income could be limited to specific categories of income (such as wages) or it could be a comprehensive tax on all forms of economic income. In addition, subtractions from or additions to a given tax base are often introduced to subsidize or discourage particular activities. Those deviations represent policy decisions that depend entirely on the needs and priorities of particular jurisdictions. Tax base harmonization need not be accompanied by tax rate harmonization. Base harmonization alone, however, is no substitute for base and rate harmonization combined. *See, e.g.*, Michael J. Graetz & Alvin C. Warren, *Income Tax Discrimination and the Political and Economic Integration of Europe*, 115 YALE L.J. 1186, 1227–32 (2006) (examining European proposal to harmonize only the base of the corporate tax within the European Union).

[37] The second important dimension along which tax regimes differ is the nominal rate that applies to a given base. In the simplest case, the amount of tax due is determined by multiplying a single rate by the chosen base. That suggests that two tax regimes employing an identical base need only add an identical rate to be perfectly matched. In practice, achieving true parity is difficult even when questions of tax base are put to one side. One reason is that instead of being applied at a single rate, rates often differ according to a taxpayer's status. For example, the United States imposes income tax at rates ranging from 0 percent up to a nominal maximum of 37 percent, rising to 39.6 percent in 2026, varying according to the nature and amount of income earned by a taxpayer and the taxpayer's status. *See* I.R.C. § 1.

[38] The last key difference among tax regimes is a function of the different tools and methods tax authorities use to encourage taxpayers to pay the taxes that they owe. As a practical matter, even if two tax regimes were identical both in terms of base and rates, employing different enforcement mechanisms could produce very different results for taxpayers. For example, if an income tax were imposed on a base that included both wage income and investment income, but wages are subject to information reporting and withholding while investment income is subject to neither reporting nor withholding, the effective tax rate on the latter would be significantly lower.

In addition to directly overriding disparate domestic rules, treaties can indirectly promote uniformity. As described below, double tax treaties create enormous pressure to conform over time. At a minimum, conformity in this context means adopting and retaining income taxes.

The Age of Symmetry

Today, it is easy to see stifling policy innovation on a critical aspect of sovereignty as a bug rather than a feature. But when the tax treaty emerged, symmetry mattered for its own sake. Europe and its African colonies offer a telling example. During the nineteenth century, they could not have been more different. Nevertheless, from a tax standpoint, the two became a well-matched pair.

That was true despite a host of reasons to expect the opposite. Obviously, the relative revenue potential of the metropolitan and colonial tax bases was different.[39] Imposing tax, at all, in the colonies was not necessary. Politics aside, it may have been downright foolish. The metropoles could have eliminated any need for colonial taxes by modestly boosting their own tax receipts.

Symmetry was a preference. Although bound to the same sovereign, popular resistance made deploying tax revenues collected in the metropoles in the colonies impossible.[40] The metropolitan public held a deep skepticism about the financial benefits of colonial investments.[41]

[39] Senegal—a midsized French colony—contributed revenues in 1898 amounting to 0.12 percent of France's revenue. *See* Edwin R.A. Seligman, *The French Colonial System*, *in* ESSAYS IN COLONIAL FINANCE BY MEMBERS OF THE AMERICAN ECONOMIC ASSOCIATION 21, 38 (1900) (estimating Senegal's 1898 revenues at just under 4,000,000 francs); THE INTERNATIONAL YEAR BOOK 321 (Frank Colby & Harry Peck eds., 1899) (estimating France's 1898 revenues at just over 3,400,000,000 francs).

[40] Isidore Loeb, *The German Colonial Fiscal System*, *in* ESSAYS IN COLONIAL FINANCE BY MEMBERS OF THE AMERICAN ECONOMIC ASSOCIATION 40, 42 (1900) ("Particular emphasis was placed [by opponents of colonial expansion] upon the cost of colonial undertakings, and the resulting burden upon the home taxpayer. . . . The government, accordingly, adopted a conservative policy."); Metropolitan electorates "were decidedly uninterested in their colonial estates, and their parliamentary representatives could not be persuaded to allocate sums for the exploitation of these holdings. Thus the colonies had to be self-financing." Peter Kilby, *Manufacturing in Colonial Africa*, *in* 4 COLONIALISM IN AFRICA 1870–1960, at 470, 492 (Peter Duignan & L.H. Gann eds., 1975) (describing the mood of English and French electorates).

[41] CRAWFORD YOUNG, THE AFRICAN COLONIAL STATE IN COMPARATIVE PERSPECTIVE 97 (1994) ("Metropolitan treasuries, citadels of skepticism concerning the material benefits likely to accrue from colonial expansion in Africa, insisted on an iron law of fiscal self-sufficiency of the newly acquired colonial territories."). The depth of the resistance to expending metropolitan funds on the colonies was exemplified in the granting of concessionary charters to private companies for large capital projects. The metropoles sacrificed valuable future rights to revenues and profits rather than contribute capital up front. *See* IEUAN LL. GRIFFITHS, THE AFRICAN INHERITANCE 54 (1995).

Faced with an imperative to generate tax revenue in the colonies to fund their administration and exploitation, metropoles replicated their own tax systems in the colonies. Had they been introduced decades later, those derivative taxes might have been a precursor to independence.[42] However, the truth was that Europe simply refused to use European revenues to finance African expenditures.

The insistence that colonies finance their own administration—the principle of "colonial self-sufficiency"[43]—may explain the impulse to collect taxes in and for jurisdictions that were not sovereign. But that parochial stance does not justify the particular taxes imposed. Not only did colonies, by and large, collect the taxes necessary to defray the costs of their own domination, but they also relied on the same sorts of taxes as their colonial masters.[44]

Edwin Seligman, by now a familiar figure, contributed to the volume *Essays in Colonial Finance* published by the American Economics Association in 1900.[45] In it, he carefully documented the tax systems of the French colonies in Africa. As in the metropoles, customs duties and liquor taxes predominated.

Seligman disdained such taxes.[46] He became an important champion for progressive income taxes replacing the customs duties and other taxes dominant in the nineteenth century. Although he embraced that evolution,

[42] Had the colonies been sovereign, the traditional arguments linking sovereignty and taxation would apply. *See generally* Ring, *supra* note 9. Alternatively, had sovereignty been the long-term goal of the colonial project, it may have been farsighted to lay the fiscal foundation of each future state at the start. Obviously, the colonies were neither independent nor, in this relatively early stage of the colonial project, being groomed for independence. *See* YOUNG, *supra* note 41, at 182–83 (noting that even by the mid-twentieth century most colonial powers saw independence for their African colonies as something likely to occur in the distant future, if at all).

[43] YOUNG, *supra* note 41, at 97 ("The principle of colonial self-sufficiency dates from 1815. . . . Only Italy was a systematic exception to this rule; Eritrea, Somalia, and Libya were costly ventures, requiring metropolitan financial commitments throughout the colonial period."). The reluctance to finance the administration of the colonies varied somewhat over time, with greater emphasis being placed on the need for fiscal autonomy by the early twentieth century. *Id.*

[44] *Compare* Seligman, *supra* note 39, at 38 (showing the majority of Senegal's 1898 revenues came from customs duties and liquor taxes), *with* THE INTERNATIONAL YEAR BOOK, *supra* note 39, at 321 ("Of the indirect taxes, which yielded according to the estimates for 1898, 59 per cent. of the revenue, the most productive were the customs duties, the tax on spirits, the tax on sugar and the registration tax.").

[45] Seligman, a major figure in the history of US tax policy, appears in prior chapters. *See* Reuven S. Avi-Yonah, *All of a Piece Throughout: The Four Ages of U.S. International Taxation*, 25 VA. TAX REV. 313, 318 (2005) ("Edwin Seligman . . . was the guiding spirit behind the 1923 'four economists' report to the League of Nations (1923 Report), which laid the foundations for the international tax regime.").

[46] Seligman worried that colonial policies had "taken away from the colonies the privilege of levying their own tariffs and has imposed upon many of the dependencies a system of taxation more suitable to the interests of the mother country than to those of the colonies themselves." Seligman, *supra* note 39, at 34.

Seligman retained a nineteenth-century faith in harmonization. Tax laws everywhere should, Seligman reasoned, mirror those preferred by the world's metropoles. Such aspirational taxes would, he believed, help remake the colonies in the image of their respective metropoles. For Seligman, the spread of the progressive income tax represented "the great civilizing work" of empire.[47]

Seligman and his adherents believed that "cooperation would first be enacted through treaties, of course, but, in the long term, the convergence of tax systems seemed more crucial" and that down such a path lay "an era of world peace, and of world progress."[48] As he hoped, the bilateral tax treaties he helped design would indeed become an important vector of harmonization. They allow pairs of nations to align aspects of their tax regimes while, over time, taking two broadly parallel tax regimes and refining their similarities.

Paired with the up-front harmonization tax treaties deliver by rewriting domestic tax laws, network effects promote homogeneity across tax regimes over time. Like any barter arrangement, tax treaties are fueled by a double coincidence of wants. Accordingly, to ensure that its residents have access to treaty benefits to shield them from another jurisdiction's income tax, states engage in a sort of arm's race as protection against income taxes imposed elsewhere.[49] Through those two distinct mechanisms, treaties simultaneously invite and deliver harmonization.

The power of treaties is easy to understand in an era of digital communication. "Similar to telecommunication networks—where the value of a telephone . . . increases with every added user" the tax treaty network "provides an inherent incentive for users to join and stay" in order to "benefit from

[47] Madeline Woker, *Edwin Seligman, Initiator of Global Progressive Public Finance*, 13 J. Global History 352, 361 (2018). Woker notes that Seligman not only believed the progressive income tax represented the highest, most advanced form of taxation but that he maintained a wide circle of influence stretching from Europe to Asia and "was able to convince his numerous interlocutors that income tax was 'essentially a modern phenomenon' and that modern taxation was intrinsically linked to democratic government." *Id.* at 373.

[48] *Id.* at 370.

[49] It may be difficult to imagine a nation introducing a comprehensive income tax simply to secure the reduced US tax burdens such a treaty might ultimately produce. It is not quite so farfetched to think that an unwillingness to give up those benefits would inhibit a move away from an income tax. *See* Staff of Joint Comm. on Taxation, 104th Cong., Impact of International Competitiveness of Replacing the Federal Income Tax 111 (Comm. Print 1996) ("If the United States adopts a new tax system that is vastly different . . . [a] treaty country could choose to terminate its present income tax treaty with the United States, if the treaty is no longer relevant because of the incompatibility of the two taxing systems.").

compatibility with other users."[50] As with social media, treaties become more compelling the more they spread, a "self-perpetuating" phenomenon.[51]

Like Seligman, contemporary scholars view double tax treaties as "the main mechanism for . . . harmonization."[52] They embrace the reality that, where treaties override domestic laws, their reciprocal structure ensures that taxpayers receive identical treatment in both jurisdictions. As soon as treaties enter into force, that circumscribed sphere of harmonization snaps into place and network effects begin to operate.

The Limits of Harmonization

The United States has, as one might imagine, few treaties with Africa.[53] Whatever Seligman hoped, homogeneity remains not only an objective of—but often a precondition for—treaties. They do little to promote cooperation between profoundly different states. Such striking gaps in the international tax regime highlight that even while thousands exist, the "utility of tax treaties" remains "limited."[54]

The limits of tax treaties suggest that some problems will not be solved by tax harmonization. But over a century—thanks in part to Global Jim Crow—harmonization's appeal has hardened into an article of faith. Today,

[50] Tsilly Dagan, *Tax Treaties as a Network Product*, 41 Brook. J. Int'l L. 1082, 1082–83 (2016). *See also* Daniel Shaviro, *Some Observations Concerning Multi-Jurisdictional Tax Competition*, *in* Regulatory Competition and Economic Integration: Comparative Perspectives 49, 58 (Daniel C. Esty & Damien Geradin eds., 2001) ("The global setting of these agreements lowered transaction costs for individual countries to agree on specific terms of mutual forbearance. In addition, to businesses that were anxious to avoid double taxation, the global institutions offered a forum at once more favorable than national politics and yet able to be leveraged into such politics through the argument: This is what everyone else is doing; you'd better join the club.").

[51] John F. Avery Jones, *Are Tax Treaties Necessary?*, 53 Tax L. Rev. 1, 3 (1999) (calling tax treaties "self-perpetuating"). Both today's treaties and the early models from which they evolved operate by orchestrating a quid pro quo of reciprocal tax concessions. For such an arrangement to take root, both treaty partners' tax systems must be similar in important respects. Obviously, each nation must impose an income tax. That income tax must also have a broadly similar reach. As a result, the rise of those treaties gave an advantage to nations that fit the dominant mold and provided an incentive to others to conform. This standardization process reaches its height—or perhaps its nadir—in the lengths to which states go to maintain internal laws for the specific purpose of being replaced by treaty provisions. *Id.* (describing pattern of enacting "outrageous . . . provisions of internal law" so that others "will come running to its door asking for a treaty in familiar form").

[52] Shaviro, *supra* note 50, at 58.

[53] *See* Allison D. Christians, *Tax Treaties for Investment and Aid to Sub-Saharan Africa: A Case Study*, 71 Brook. L. Rev. 639, 641 (2005).

[54] Richard A. Gordon, Department of Treasury, Tax Havens and Their Use by United States Taxpayers—An Overview 208 (1981).

policymakers remain committed to harmonization, even when a different kind of cooperation might yield greater dividends.

The early US TIEAs described above failed because they depended on a symmetry that did not exist. They sought to produce a one-way stream of information using a reciprocal structure. Their creation followed the publication of a breathless 1981 report warning that "taxpayers ranging from large multinational companies to small individuals [sic] to criminals are making extensive use of tax havens."[55] In the international tax equivalent of a Catch-22, it urged the creation of "bilateral exchange of information agreements"[56] to address the fact that "[t]he United States does not have tax treaties with the most important tax haven countries (e.g., Bahamas, Bermuda, Cayman Islands, Liechtenstein, Panama)."[57]

No such agreements existed because the Bahamas—like its counterparts—lacked the commonalities with the United States that give treaties purchase. Roughly 1,000 times smaller than the United States by population, that absence of similarities is no accident. Creating and enforcing an income tax for what was then a population of roughly 200,000 people spread across more than 3,000 islands, rocks, and cays would have been difficult even had its government been inclined to adopt one.

TIEAs promise to provide both countries with access to information from the other. But the kind of extraterritorial tax information they contemplate was necessarily much more important to the United States than to its TIEA partners.[58] To bridge the gap by providing an incentive relevant for states with little interest in income tax information, the United States created, appropriately enough, a tax break.[59] The new rule made it easier for the

[55] *See id.* at 3; *see also* Zagaris, *supra* note 30, at 333–34 (discussing influence of the 1981 report).

[56] Gordon, *supra* note 54, at 212.

[57] *Id.* at 208. This, of course, conveniently ignores the fact that US treaties with Switzerland, Ireland, and the Netherlands helped make them tax havens.

[58] In connection with the initiative to create stand-alone tax information exchange agreements with tax havens, a UN report noted that "[i]t is not very significant that under the OECD Model TIEA, a cooperative tax haven jurisdiction . . . can request information from an OECD country . . . because . . . tax haven jurisdictions generally impose no or low income taxes" and "would not be requesting any such information from the OECD source country." UN Tax Experts Report, *supra* note 32, ¶ 52.

[59] *See* I.R.C. § 274(h)(6); H.R. Rep. No. 98-266, at 28–29 (1983), *reprinted in* 1983 U.S.C.C.A.N. 643, 669–70 ("The committee believes that the favorable convention treatment should be available only to those countries which are willing to assist the United States in enforcing its tax laws. Accordingly, the convention deduction is made available only for conventions in a country that enters into an exchange of information agreement with the United States."). Section 274(h)(6) was added in Internal Revenue Amendments, Pub. L. No. 98-67, § 222, 97 Stat. 369, 395 (1983) (codified at I.R.C. § 274).

Bahamas and other TIEA partner states to host tax-deductible conventions for US taxpayers.[60]

Decades later, the OECD also pursued TIEAs. It first issued, and then abandoned, its threat of sanctions.[61] The OECD then signaled that states could earn their way off the blacklist by pledging to enter into TIEAs.[62]

Tax Simplification

The pursuit of tax harmonization in a heterogeneous world raises an important question.[63] Asking governments to agree to a single, uniform approach for almost any purpose is difficult.[64] Because taxation lies so close to the core of a nation's sovereignty, it is not surprising that attempts to foster

[60] *See* I.R.C. § 274(h)(6) (treating eligible Caribbean countries as part of the North American area and therefore eligible to host tax deductible conventions). The incentive persuaded states to enter into TIEAs but their impact remained minimal. Barbados was the first to enter into a TIEA with the United States. Cynthia Blum, *Sharing Bank Deposit Information with Other Countries: Should Tax Compliance or Privacy Claims Prevail?*, 6 FLA. TAX REV. 579, 600 n.69 (2004). Over the next few years, some other countries followed suit. *Id.*

[61] *See* OECD, HARMFUL TAX COMPETITION: AN EMERGING GLOBAL ISSUE 37 (1998), https://www.oecd-ilibrary.org/harmful-tax-competition_5lmqcr2klm5g.pdf?itemId=%2Fcontent%2Fpublication%2F9789264162945-en&mimeType=pdf (suggesting the possibility of "co-ordinated" "defensive measures").

[62] Michael J. McIntyre, *How to End the Charade of Information Exchange*, 125 TAX NOTES 695, 695 (2009) ("Tax haven countries that agree to this ineffective TIEA are provided with an undeserved patina of respectability. They have been eager to sign up, and most have done so."); Lee A. Sheppard, *Don't Ask, Don't Tell, Part 4: Ineffectual Information Sharing*, 122 TAX NOTES 1411, 1412 (2009) ("Overall, the agreement is more a public relations document than a tool of tax administration. It allows banking havens to make a show of cooperation while going about their essential business of selling tax evasion services to residents of rich countries.").

[63] Even if each nation were writing on a blank slate, creating an identical base, rate structure, and administrative regime in every one would be a Herculean task. In reality, nations would be starting from very different points. Obviously, the formal rules that make up their tax regimes differ. *See generally* Diane M. Ring, *One Nation Among Many: Policy Implications of Cross-Border Tax Arbitrage*, 44 B.C. L. REV. 79 (2002). Perhaps more significantly, the broader tax cultures in which those rules operate are not only distinct but are also deeply entrenched. Michael A. Livingston, *From Milan to Mumbai, Changing in Tel Aviv: Reflections on Progressive Taxation and "Progressive" Politics in a Globalized but Still Local World*, 54 AM. J. COMP. L. 555, 560 (2006) ("Tax culture . . . may be defined to refer to the body of beliefs and practices that are shared by tax practitioners and policy-makers in a given society and thus provide the background or context in which substantive tax decisions are made."). From a more practical perspective, enormous disparities exist in the administration of different national tax systems. *See generally* Richard M. Bird & Eric M. Zolt, *Technology and Taxation in Developing Countries: From Hand to Mouse*, 61 N. TAX J. 791 (2008). In combination, those differences create an environment in which global tax uniformity seems highly unlikely.

[64] *See* Ring, *supra* note 63, at 81 ("Despite many common features in our trading partners' tax systems, the multitude of factors that produce tax law, including social policy, administrative constraints, and political compromise render conflicting rules a likely possibility.").

international tax harmonization have yielded more frustration than cooperation.[65] Does marching in lockstep with others on taxation benefit anyone?

Tax simplification offers potential clues. Complexity is said to impose three distinct costs on taxpayers.[66] Rule complexity refers to the costs taxpayers incur to understand the obligations tax rules impose on them.[67] Compliance complexity represents taxpayers' exertions to ensure that they meet those obligations.[68] The third type of complexity is transactional complexity, so called because it reflects the expenses taxpayers incur by engaging in strategies conducted in pursuit of tax benefits.[69]

In combination, those costs represent a drain on society. Each dollar spent by taxpayers to understand and comply with their tax obligations or to plan and execute tax-saving strategies represents a dollar that will not be spent or invested productively. Even if a given expenditure yields a positive return for the taxpayer in question, it represents a net loss for society.

Tax harmonization targets similarly wasteful expenditures triggered by the interactions of disparate tax systems. That limiting complexity reduces costs is just another way of saying that tax simplification cuts the costs of collecting the revenues society needs to function. Harmonization does the same, but the analogy is imperfect.

While simplification represents complexity's opposite, harmonization represents only one route to eliminating the costs of conflict. Specialization could do the same. One set of tax rules will inevitably be cheaper to master than two. As SACU suggests, that goes double for a single tax administration.

Transaction Costs

Eliminating disparities between jurisdictions represents only one way to limit costs. Leaning into difference can reduce waste from abusive transactions and lower compliance costs.[70] No harmonization required.

[65] "No significant issue in international tax can be discussed without raising the question of sovereignty." *See* Ring, *supra* note 9, at 156.

[66] *See* David F. Bradford, Untangling the Income Tax 266–67 (1986).

[67] *Id.*

[68] *Id.*

[69] *Id.* At the extreme, taxpayers invest in aggressive tax shelters, investing in complex strategies and perhaps spending $2 on rule, compliance, and transactional complexity for every $3 they save in tax. On a more modest scale, tax laws afford taxpayers many opportunities to modify their behavior in more subtle ways, incurring similar costs to reduce their tax liability.

[70] The value of free trade is premised on the notion of comparative advantage. Rather than eliminating differences between jurisdictions, comparative advantage exploits them. Simply

In a world of high transaction costs, harmonization enjoys a structural advantage. Specialization requires coordination. Harmonization limits the need for costly negotiations.[71] Providing a standardized approach to resolving conflicts, treaties "lowered transaction costs for individual countries to agree on specific terms of mutual forbearance" at a time when that mattered a great deal.[72]

Much has changed over the last hundred years. Interjurisdictional transaction costs, not least the costs of acquiring and processing information, have fallen dramatically since Seligman and his peers envisioned the modern international tax regime. Particularly, since the dawn of Global Jim Crow, the changes that have fueled globalization and heightened the need for international tax cooperation have steadily pushed those costs lower.

Improvements in information technology—a process accentuated most recently by the rise of artificial intelligence—have made it far less costly to coordinate. In *A New World Order*, Anne Marie Slaughter considers the implications of the fact that, to an extent impossible in Seligman's day, "government networks are a key feature of world order in the twenty-first century."[73] The vastly increased bandwidth of the connections among states, she suggests, has lowered the obstacles to new forms of global cooperation.

Actors at all levels of government collaborate in ways that would have been impossible a century ago. Those lower costs open the door to strategies that would have once been prohibitively expensive.[74] A century ago, asymmetric cooperation would have been difficult with intergovernmental transaction costs significantly higher. Today, opportunities to engage in it abound if you remain open to it.

by opening their borders to trade, governments find the market's "invisible hand" encouraging businesses to produce goods or services that reflect the relative strengths of each jurisdiction. Specialization in taxation would ask considerably more of governments. Fortunately, they have never been in a better position to meet that burden.

[71] The most familiar example of this comes in the real property context. Zoning rules work to keep incompatible uses separated so that there is no need for residents to strike their own deals to ensure compatibility.

[72] *See* Shaviro, *supra* note 50, at 58.

[73] SLAUGHTER, *supra* note 14, at 1.

[74] One could argue that this is true of the emergence of cap-and-trade regimes such as those created by the Kyoto Protocol. *See* Kyoto Protocol to the United Nations Framework Convention on Climate Change, Dec. 10, 1997, 2303 U.N.T.S. 162. It would be difficult to imagine the Protocol having been developed before the advent of cheap global communications. This sort of cooperation happens domestically within the United States through programs like the Multistate Tax Commission's Joint Audit Program.

Slaughter marvels at government officials effortlessly interacting on a wide range of issues. If not for Global Jim Crow's embrace of harmonization, the same changes that have led to the blossoming of those transnational networks could have nurtured the emergence of an entirely new kind of tax cooperation. But lower transaction costs alone are not enough.

States hoping to develop such strategies—like the Coasian farmer and rancher agreeing in principle that a fence should be built to protect crops from cows—must also determine who should fill specific roles and how to ensure that each party meets its obligations. In the international tax context, as elsewhere, such efforts may also implicate classic bargaining problems (such as bilateral monopolies, holdouts, and free riders).[75] For example, if taxpayers can readily substitute another jurisdiction in their tax evasion schemes, building a fence between any pair of jurisdictions would be futile.[76] Even a single holdout might quickly eliminate any surplus such a bargain might otherwise generate.

The Persistence of Harmonization

Long after transaction costs ceased to justify it, experts remain committed to Seligman's vision of harmonization and to his treaties. Global Jim Crow represents a key part of the problem, a historical contingency that set the world on a course that caused widespread harm while doing grave damage to a continent. The swift rise of the OECD and its treaties entrenched Seligman's dream of a world made safe through tax harmonization.

After initially failing to flourish, the embrace of treaties under Global Jim Crow nurtured homogeneity and stability, just as Seligman hoped. But Global Jim Crow left little room in the international tax regime for countries unwilling or unable to share in that vision. Inevitably, as an exclusive membership organization made up of the world's wealthiest countries, the OECD could not understand the challenges faced by marginalized states. By 2000, frustrated by the limitations of harmonization, it doubled down.

[75] RICHARD A. POSNER, ECONOMIC ANALYSIS OF LAW 60–63 (3rd ed. 1986) (discussing bilateral monopoly, holdouts, and free riders in the nuisance context).

[76] That would be true if tax havens were perfect substitutes. But "[t]ax havens are not undifferentiated units offering perfectly substitutable services, nor is price the most important point of competition between them." J.C. SHARMAN, HAVENS IN A STORM: THE STRUGGLE FOR GLOBAL TAX REGULATION 107 (2006).

In the eyes of the OECD, Liberia's differences loomed ominously. A fundamentally different OECD—perhaps featuring Eswatini as a member—would have seen Liberia more clearly. Such an organization might even have drawn on the experiences of SACU to imagine a response to vulnerable states other than a blacklist, perhaps understanding that asymmetry might represent an opportunity rather than a threat.

Comparative Tax Advantage

In 2007, the Director of the OECD's Center for Tax Policy and Administration testified in Congress about the organization's efforts to combat tax evasion. He left little doubt of the organization's commitment to harmonization and reiterated that Liberia's failure to embrace its demands for conformity made it "uncooperative."[77]

He had no idea that a market for extraterritorial tax information was about to become a reality. A former Swiss banker had just contacted the US Justice Department with an offer to sell tax information to the United States.[78] Hoping to strike a deal—specifically by landing a mammoth whistleblower payout—Bradley Berkenfeld hired a law firm to approach US officials. The information Berkenfeld promised would reveal that a Swiss bank, UBS, had willfully abused its qualified intermediary agreement with the Internal Revenue Service. Just as President Kennedy recognized a half-century earlier, Switzerland lay at the center of the storm.

In his May 3 testimony—apparently ignorant of Berkenfeld's April 19 proposal—the OECD official warned Congress that, unless states like Liberia embraced its harmonization efforts, "offshore tax evasion will continue to grow and undermine the integrity of national tax systems."[79] Berkenfeld's attorneys suggested something very different. In exchange for a statutorily set percentage of the tax revenues it would help recover, Berkenfeld would provide the information decades of OECD harmonization had not.

After a flurry of calls, the United States received a summary of the information Berkenfeld possessed. They learned of the participation by "one of the

[77] *Offshore Tax Evasion: Stashing Cash Overseas: Hearing Before the S. Comm. on Finance*, 110th Cong. 6 (2007) (testimony of Jeffrey Owens, Director, OECD Center for Tax Policy and Administration) [hereinafter Testimony of Jeffrey Owens].

[78] David S. Hilzenrath, *Swiss Banker Turned Whistleblower Ended Up with a Prison Sentence*, National Whistleblower Center (May 16, 2010), https://www.whistleblowers.org/news/swiss-banker-turned-whistleblower-ended-up-with-a-prison-sentence-2/.

[79] Testimony of Jeffrey Owens, *supra* note 77, at 15.

world's most powerful financial institutions in a far-reaching fraud against the U.S. government."[80] The information threatened to "topple Switzerland from its vaunted position as secret banker to the world."[81]

The United States initially declined to strike a deal with Berkenfeld. By the following summer, he "pleaded guilty . . . to conspiring with an American billionaire real estate developer . . . to help the developer evade paying $7.2 million in taxes by assisting in concealing $200 million of assets in Switzerland and Liechtenstein."[82] The United States ultimately paid Berkenfeld more than $100 million, but it also fined him $30,000 and made him a felon for facilitating the very evasion he brought to light.

The Berkenfeld episode suggests that Seligman's time has passed, even if his handiwork remains at the heart of the global tax system. Acquiring extraterritorial tax information no longer depends on harmonization, tax treaties, or TIEAs. Holdouts might once have been a problem, but when any one of thousands of individuals can approach authorities with such revelations, no state possesses that kind of market power.

The US Congressional Black Caucus

Years before, in 2001, the US Congressional Black Caucus implicitly questioned the OECD's insistence on harmonization. A majority of its members defied the OECD, upending its effort to impose sanctions on Liberia, the Bahamas, and other predominantly Black and brown jurisdictions. By 2008, one of the most prominent of what a leading tax journalist had dismissed as a "boatload of no-name legislators"[83] had become the Chair of the House Ways and Means Committee, leading the effort to shape the nation's tax laws.

As detailed in Chapter 5, Charles Rangel had been pilloried decades before while helping end Apartheid by withdrawing US tax credits. The same credits Seligman had derided as a present of revenues were being claimed

[80] Hilzenrath, *supra* note 78.

[81] *Id.*

[82] Press Release, U.S. Department of Justice, Banker Pleads Guilty to Helping American Real Estate Developer Evade Income Tax on $200 Million (June 19, 2008), https://www.justice.gov/archive/tax/txdv08550.htm.

[83] Lee A. Sheppard, *It's the Bank Secrecy, Stupid*, 22 Tax Notes Int'l 2018, 2018 (2001) (dismissing the intervention of a majority of the Congressional Black Caucus).

by multinationals operating in Apartheid-era South Africa. His success with Apartheid showed that Rangel understood both the intricacies of international tax law and the power of unconventional solutions.

By helping create FATCA, Rangel built the fence the OECD insisted was impossible. He did not target states or bankers but banks. By doing so, he finally unlocked the potential of a world very different from the one in which the tax treaty was created, when "airplanes were first becoming a regular means of travel, and when the 'wireless' was a relatively new instrument of communication."[84] And just as Rangel forced Mobil Oil to divest from South Africa, he forced banks to cooperate.

FATCA embraced asymmetry by demanding that banks everywhere provide information about US taxpayers. Or else. This sounds ominous, but it was not the banks that suffered. FATCA represented an enormous burden, but since their rivals bore the same costs, banks faced little difficulty passing along the costs to their customers.[85]

The Panama Papers

Berkenfeld's bombshell would not be the last. The revelations of the Panama Papers in 2016 left no doubt that if there had ever been a time when Liberia's differences had posed the threat the OECD imagined, that time had passed. Harmonization had always represented only one possible approach to ending conflict, and—it now appeared—the one least likely. This time, a single anonymous tipster supplied terabytes of data to journalists.[86]

Hundreds of reporters pulled on threads exposed by that trove to unravel the secrets of 140 politicians, among others.[87] The impact was immediate.

[84] Graetz, *supra* note 13, at 1359.

[85] Arguably, the customers that suffered the most were US expatriates. By threatening the institutions that served them, the United States left many of its own citizens without access to banking services. FATCA could have eased that burden by dedicating some portion of the tax revenues it generated to shielding expatriates from FATCA's fallout. But it did not. As a result, ordinary American citizens overseas suddenly faced the challenge of facing life overseas without a bank account. *See generally* Shu-Yi Oei, *The Offshore Tax Enforcement Dragnet*, 67 Emory L.J. 655 (2018).

[86] Lily H. Newman, *The Panama Papers Are 2.6 Terabytes of Leaked Data. How Big Is That Really?*, Slate (April 4, 2016), https://slate.com/technology/2016/04/contextualizing-the-2-6-terabytes-of-leaked-panama-papers-data.html.

[87] Carmen Molina Acosta, *Where are the Key Panama Papers Figures, Seven Years Later?*, Int'l Consortium of Investigative Journalists (Apr. 3, 2023), https://www.icij.org/investigations/panama-papers/where-are-they-now-2023/.

Iceland's Prime Minister Sigmundur Davíð Gunnlaugsson resigned.[88] Pakistan's Prime Minister Nawaz Sharif "was disqualified from the prime ministership, sentenced to 10 years in prison, fined $10.6 million and banned from holding public office for life."[89]

Had US authorities chosen to acquire extraterritorial tax information from banks or bankers in 2000, they could have. Soon after the OECD's expert testified in Congress in 2007, insisting that Liberia's intransigence demanded punishment, they finally did. FATCA showed that the United States had the power—even in a world in which Liberia and the Bahamas had the temerity to exist—to fence its own taxpayers in.

The New International Economic Order

The great irony of harmonization lies in the way demanding symmetry entrenches inequality. Had global tax policy evolved in the direction of SACU, Liberia might actually look just a little more like Luxembourg, one of the four members of the Axis of Tax Avoidance.[90] Wealthy states helping poorer states collect their taxes—or vice versa—could have done just that.

An alternate Subpart F or global minimum tax—with the US or the OECD playing the role of South Africa in SACU—might have returned revenues that rightly belonged to Liberia or Rwanda. Pairing those repatriated taxes along with additional development support, as SACU did, would have closed the gap between states. But the harmonization imperative demanded otherwise. Even had the OECD chosen a different approach in 2000, Liberia was already lost to war and strife.

The self-inflicted wound the OECD suffered by waiting so long to fence its taxpayers in suggests that its commitment to harmonization was sincere

[88] Gunnlaugsson resigned not because of accusations of tax evasion, but because of a conflict of interest. He had not disclosed an interest as a creditor in collapsed Icelandic banks. Gunnlaugsson had described creditors as "vultures" while he himself indirectly was one and was involved in negotiations over the future of the banks. *Panama Papers: Iceland PM Sigmundur Gunnlaugsson Steps Down*, BBC (Apr. 6, 2016), https://www.bbc.com/news/world-europe-35966412.

[89] Molina Acosta, *supra* note 87.

[90] Liberia's story is different than many other African states. Gardiner provides a thoughtful and thorough exploration of Liberia's economic history as a small sovereign African nation during the colonial era and in particular its complex relationship with the United States. For example, she details the US role in the rise of the Liberian shipping registry. LEIGH A. GARDNER, SOVEREIGNTY WITHOUT POWER: LIBERIA IN THE AGE OF EMPIRES, 1822–1980, AT 253-54 (2022) (noting a favorable US State Department Review of the 1948 law establishing the registry which "pointed out flaws and inconsistencies in the text but was otherwise uncritical of the concept").

(unless it was deeply cynical). It simply could not envision such a bargain until the data it hungered for literally called the United States and demanded to be purchased. Clinging to outdated methods while shielding global tax policy from pressures for reform produced suboptimal results for everyone, including the OECD's members.

For non-members, the results proved decidedly worse. In the 1970s, with Global Jim Crow entrenched—and with the generosity that marked an earlier era of global tax policy faded from memory—tension over growing economic disparities between Global North haves and Global South have-nots boiled over. At the United Nations, frustration set "the stage for a strangely secluded and artificial version of the broader struggle for independence" in which developing state "leaders . . . voic[ed] discontent with their position in the world economy."[91]

Objections to "former colonial powers' control over the international economy" accompanied demands for a renegotiation of the terms on which private investment occurred.[92] Thanks to Global Jim Crow, tax remained safely siloed from those conversations.[93] In 1974, the UN General Assembly embraced its Declaration of a New International Economic Order (NIEO) and a Charter of Economic Rights and Duties of States. The Global South rejected the harmonization that Global Jim Crow made a hallmark of international tax policy, insisting that "wherever feasible," international economic cooperation should deliver "preferential and non-reciprocal treatment for developing countries."[94]

[91] Vanessa Ogle, *State Rights Against Private Capital: The "New International Economic Order" and the Struggle over Aid, Trade, and Foreign Investment, 1962–1981*, 5 HUMANITY 211, 213–15 (2014).

[92] *Id.* at 218.

[93] With the transition of global tax policymaking from the United Nations to the OECD, even the idea of tax policies favoring poor countries—such as what the British dismissively termed the old Cuban taxation gambit—seemed to have been lost. That global tax policy had been remade to do the reverse—delivering regressive redistribution from poor countries to rich—went unrecognized. *See* ADOM GETACHEW, WORLDMAKING AFTER EMPIRE: THE RISE AND FALL OF SELF-DETERMINATION 165 (2019) ("In 'the absence of a world government' that could institute international taxation, the NIEO relied on these indirect mechanisms to create a welfare world in which international trade was structured by interdependence rather than dependence.").

[94] G.A. Res. 3201 (S-VI), ¶ 4(n) Declaration on the Establishment of a New International Economic Order (May 1, 1974) ("The new international economic order should be founded on full respect for the following principles . . . (n) Preferential and non-reciprocal treatment for developing countries, wherever feasible, in all fields of international economic co-operation wherever possible"); G.A. Res. 3281 (XXIX), art.19 Charter of Economic Rights and Duties of States (Dec. 12, 1974) ("With a view to accelerating the economic growth of developing countries and bridging the economic gap between developed and developing countries, developed countries should grant generalized preferential, non-reciprocal and non-discriminatory treatment to developing countries in those fields of international economic co-operation where it may be feasible.").

For a time, the NIEO "posed a credible threat to business as usual for Western governments and multinationals."[95] But, thanks to Global Jim Crow, OECD control over global tax policy remained secure. The NIEO yielded to the bruising realities of the economic upheaval and growing power imbalances of the 1970s. Of course, even had the NIEO succeeded at the United Nations, the OECD's treaties would have continued to flourish.

Whatever the NIEO's ambitions, the OECD and its treaties remained insulated from the UN General Assembly. In the following years, neoliberalism's rise would serve as "the death knell for state-based economic rights claims as formulated by the NIEO."[96] Global tax policy should have sat at the center of the NIEO movement. But—thanks to Global Jim Crow's successful effort to displace the United Nations with the OECD—international tax rules remained safely separate.

Stanley Surrey's ersatz 1978 UN tax treaty—actually prepared by his Harvard students—hints at what might have been. Had that treaty been prepared not under the supervision of the man who viewed tax sparing as a perversion but by Pierre Benoit, the Haitian economist Surrey held such contempt for, or by the architects of the NIEO, it would undoubtedly have been different. But before the "NIEO help[ed] to put . . . rights into conversation with . . . economic development"[97] Global Jim Crow had already isolated global tax policy.

The NIEO declaration mentions raw materials and trade. It demands assistance to developing countries and insists on "[t]he right of every country to adopt the economic and social system that it deems the most appropriate for its own development and not to be subjected to discrimination of any kind as a result."[98] But, in silent testimony to the power of Global Jim Crow, nowhere does the declaration mention source taxation.

The Logic of Improvement

Tax harmonization rejects the lessons of SACU. Seligman's conviction that peace and prosperity would naturally follow the spread of US tax policy overseas and Surrey's uncharitable view of the United Nations recall what

[95] Ogle, *supra* note 91, at 211.
[96] *Id.* at 212.
[97] *Id.*
[98] G.A. Res. 3201 (S-VI), *supra* note 93, ¶ 4(d).

Ntina Tzouvala calls the "logic of improvement." Tzouvala distinguishes that perspective—reflecting a "progressivist, linear outlook on human history, and an unconditional privileging of the historically specific legal and political infrastructure of European capitalism"—from the "logic of biology" which views international law through the lens of "racial, gendered and sexual imaginaries of immutable difference and hierarchy."[99]

As they imposed their notions of civilization abroad, it would be almost reassuring to imagine Surrey and Seligman safely in the embrace of the logic of improvement and beyond the influence of the logic of biology. But Tzouvala emphasizes the fragility of the distinction. She warns that "the inclusion brought about through conformity to the imperatives of 'civilisation' will always be fragile and prone to collapse into the logic of biology."[100]

Which would explain how the OECD found itself embracing threats and palm tree memes. However well-intentioned they may have been, efforts to improve other states by remaking them in Europe's image led to talk of gangsters and a noose. Just as the League had done a century before, in 2000 and again in 2021, the OECD telegraphed its skepticism of Black governance.[101]

The NIEO demanded not merely freedom from interference but also increased economic support. Had Global Jim Crow not triggered the historical contingency that caused a rupture between global tax policy and discussions of rights—one that scholars like Attiya Waris would later work to heal—tax harmonization might have yielded to new cooperation models half a century ago.[102] The boon that the United States delivered to Europe—but that Surrey stubbornly refused to grant Pakistan—might have been granted

[99] Ntina Tzouvala, Capitalism as Civilisation: A History of International Law 2, 4 (2020).

[100] *Id.* at 220.

[101] In the early twentieth century, Liberia and Ethiopia became the subject of efforts by the League of Nations that highlighted the danger Tzouvala describes. They aimed "to transform states that could not yet implement international norms into ones that could" but at the same time "they emphasized and reproduced racial difference as an intransigent and insurmountable challenge to the aim of emancipation and conceived of white rule in Africa as a permanent feature of the international order. Black sovereignty appeared increasingly as a contradiction in terms." *See* Getachew, *supra* note 93, at 55.

[102] Waris, a UN Independent Expert on foreign debt and human rights, has long been at the vanguard of efforts to reframe global tax policy conversations to incorporate human rights concepts. Most recently she has spearheaded a UN challenge to the OECD's pillars. *See* Letter from the OECD to the United Nations Human Rights Council, Information Received Concerning the OECD and Its Member States' Failure to Reform the Global Taxation System in Line with Their International Human Rights Obligation, OL OTH 145/2023 (Dec. 22, 2023), https://spcommreports.ohchr.org/TMResultsBase/DownLoadPublicCommunicationFile?gId=28676.

again. Instead, thanks to Global Jim Crow, as the United Nations pursued economic justice for the Global South, Surrey became its apparent champion on taxation.

Conclusion

Tax harmonization began as a political imperative of the colonial era. Before Europe's colonies enjoyed the pretense of sovereignty, they inherited its taxes. First Seligman then Surrey embraced harmonization's logic.

Opportunities to embrace new approaches that might yield better results for states of all kinds came and went. The old Cuban tax gambit, tax sparing, and the NIEO would all threaten the privilege of powerful states. The result ensured the continuation of policies tracing their origins to nineteenth-century colonialism.

The shibboleth of tax harmonization made it easy to ignore the possibility that a changing world had made heterogeneity less threatening. For a brief moment in 2007, the future and the past converged in the US Capitol. In a flash, Victorian prudishness gave way to brash dealmaking.

7
Beyond Global Jim Crow

September 11, 2001

The OECD's targeting Liberia for sanctions caught my attention for reasons that have nothing to do with tax and everything to do with a former client. My colleagues and I met Joseph outside a federal building in Lower Manhattan early on September 11, 2001. We went inside to find the room where an immigration officer would weigh the Liberian's asylum application.

When we exited the building an hour later, a roiling black cloud loomed over us. The hearing had, of course, not taken place. We had begun the day confident we would carve a place for Joseph in our world of gleaming glass towers. Instead, we glimpsed the violence and chaos he fought to leave behind.

Over the preceding months, Joseph had described the turmoil he had fled. When the OECD blacklisted Liberia, President Charles Taylor—a former rebel—was embroiled in his second civil war.[1] No multinational would be tempted to create a subsidiary in Charles Taylor's Liberia, and only a foolhardy American or European would entrust him with their wealth.

Yet the OECD called on its members to punish Liberia and dozens of other Black and brown states. As detailed in Chapter 5, the OECD called Liberia a gangster and complained that it had sabotaged its members' fiscal systems. In time, despite all its flaws, that 2000 report and its blacklist would become one of the OECD's greatest successes.[2]

Before we returned safely to our midtown skyscraper, that unsettling morning revealed the despair Global Jim Crow offers much of the world.

[1] President Taylor had campaigned on the slogan "He killed my Ma, he killed my Ma, but I'm going to vote for him anyway." Jon Lee Anderson, *Charles Taylor and the Killing Tree*, THE NEW YORKER (Apr. 26, 2012), https://www.newyorker.com/news/news-desk/charles-taylor-and-the-killing-tree.

[2] OECD, TOWARDS GLOBAL TAX CO-OPERATION: PROGRESS IN IDENTIFYING AND ELIMINATING HARMFUL TAX PRACTICES 17 (2000), https://www.oecd.org/content/dam/oecd/en/publications/reports/2001/04/towards-global-tax-co-operation_g1ghgcc1/9789264184541-en.pdf (listing a group of overwhelmingly Black and brown countries as tax havens and blaming them for all the ills of the global tax system the OECD had overseen for decades).

Racial Capitalism and International Tax Law. Steven A. Dean, Oxford University Press.
DOI: 10.1093/9780197526002.003.0008

Beyond the OECD's towers, would-be migrants are far more likely to find suffering than piles of cash. Thanks in no small part to decades of exclusive global tax governance, Joseph's world and ours remained not only separate but profoundly unequal. No amount of restitution will undo all the harm caused by more than a half-century of inequality. But dismantling the structure that has preserved Global Jim Crow for more than half a century represents a necessary first step.

Accountability in Global Tax Policy

In 2023, more than twenty years after the OECD abandoned its sanctions, the Africa Group notched a second victory against Global Jim Crow.[3] At Nigeria's urging, the UN General Assembly overwhelmingly voted to create a global tax policy architecture distinct from the OECD. The road to that General Assembly vote began with the blacklist and the backlash it prompted. The OECD had urged its members to take action, but because of the intervention of the US Congressional Black Caucus, its punishments would not become a reality until the European Union intervened a decade later.

The immediate trigger for the Africa Group's effort came two decades after 9/11. This time, rather than aiming at Liberia, the OECD targeted Nigeria.[4] The OECD's pillars—and in particular pillar one's moratorium on the digital services taxes that Nigeria and many other states had implemented—offered a stark illustration of the systemic inequality Global Jim Crow had produced. It prioritized the interests of billionaires at the expense of billions of people.[5]

[3] Emma Agyemang, *Developing Countries Secure Bigger International Tax Role for UN*, Fin. Times (Nov. 22, 2023), https://www.ft.com/content/5a7353e8-6aec-4896-b6e5-fa88033c399a ("Countries at the UN have voted for it to take a greater role in international tax matters, in a move that threatens the ascendancy of the OECD, the body that has led these discussions for decades.").

[4] *See* OECD, OECD/G20 Base Erosion and Profit Shifting Project: Two-Pillar Solution to Address the Tax Challenges Arising from the Digitalisation of the Economy 15 (2021) [https://perma.cc/68NS-R3N7].

[5] *See* Okanga Ogbu Okanga & Kim Brooks, *Lower-Income Countries' Ongoing Quest for International Tax Justice: A Case Study of the OECD's Tax Allocation Proposal*, 66 Can. Bus. L.J. 291, 293 (2022) ("[W]hy are some countries—lower-income countries especially—still unhappy and some ready to leave the table, even after a 'consensus' has been found? Because the deal is unfair. Because it forces lower-income countries—the likes of Nigeria and Kenya—to give up taxing rights to a degree that they consider unfair. We agree with them."); Yariv Brauner, *Agreement? What Agreement? The 8 October 2021, OECD Statement in Perspective*, 50 Intertax 2, 5 (2022) (concluding that "the developing world was again left behind" by BEPS 2.0); Luke Holland, *OECD Tax Reforms Risk Violating Human Rights Law, UN Experts Warn in Special Intervention*, Tax Just. Network (Jan. 11, 2024), https://taxjustice.net/press/oecd-tax-reforms-risk-violating-human-rights-law-un-experts-warn-in-special-intervention/.

However, Nigeria was not just reacting to the substance of the pillars. It might not have been spurred into action if not for another provocation. Global Jim Crow's inequality had never before elicited such a reaction. From the perspective of source countries, pillar one looked little different than the OEEC's permanent establishment threshold or the US Subpart F regime, rewriting tax rules again to favor insiders and punish outsiders.

The Africa Group's unprecedented reaction had as much to do with process as substance. In response to criticism, a deeply flawed governance structure had been modified to be marginally less exclusive than the OECD's ordinary operations. Ironically, that glimmer of inclusivity helped stir Nigeria and the rest of the Africa Group into action.

An Inclusive Political Framework

In 2015, frustrated by the OECD's long-standing complicity in Global Jim Crow, activists pressed the United Nations to reclaim a more prominent role in global tax policymaking, pushing for "an inclusive political framework where all countries could participate in tax negotiations on an equal footing (one country, one vote)."[6] The OECD only answers to its wealthy members, so such pleas left it unmoved. Its opposition doomed that 2015 reform effort.

However, questions about the OECD's exclusivity lingered. The OECD fatefully conceded that non-member states should no longer be entirely left out of its process. In response, the OECD created what it called the Inclusive Framework. The Inclusive Framework offered a limited role for non-member participation in a member-driven process, revealing in exquisite detail what the OECD envisioned as inclusion.[7]

The OECD's Inclusive Framework recalled the Black Codes embraced in the American South after the Civil War more than the promise of full participation envisioned by the Fifteenth Amendment. The Inclusive Framework offered non-members an observer status with no agenda-setting power and virtually no ability to influence outcomes. Unsurprisingly, the Inclusive Framework provoked the OECD's critics more than it mollified them.

[6] Oxfam International, Pulling the Plug: How to Stop Corporate Tax Dodging in Europe and Beyond 6 (2015), https://oxfamilibrary.openrepository.com/bitstream/10546/346860/1/bn-pulling-plug-corporate-tax-EU-190315-en.pdf.

[7] *See* Rasmus C. Christensen et al., *At the Table, Off the Menu? Assessing the Participation of Lower-Income Countries in Global Tax Negotiations* (Int'l Ctr. for Tax & Dev., Working Paper No. 115, 2020), https://opendocs.ids.ac.uk/ndownloader/files/48077767.

Ultimately, its gesture toward democracy delivered more rules highlighting the OECD's lack of accountability. Its Inclusive Framework would be marred by a pattern of strong-arm tactics designed to secure cooperation by non-members with "coercion-based pathways" fueled by EU sanctions driving "the proliferation of BEPS Inclusive Framework membership."[8] Once states joined, participation seemed almost intentionally made burdensome, deploying the contemporary equivalents of the literacy tests and poll taxes that prevented Black Americans from voting during Jim Crow.

Meetings that could have been held anywhere took place at the OECD's headquarters in Paris. Many could not afford the high costs of attendance. Those that could found that carefully choreographed consultation meetings offered no meaningful opportunities for non-member states to revisit decisions made in advance by members.

Despite such shortcomings (and its cartoon coconuts), the OECD insisted that its 2021 proposal represented a collective effort, approved by acclamation by its coercion-tainted Inclusive Framework. The OECD weighed support for the OECD proposal and found that nearly all of the more than 100 members of the Inclusive Framework had embraced it. However, even the OECD acknowledged that not every member did. Nigeria refused to play along. Along with Kenya, Sri Lanka, and Pakistan, Nigeria rejected the OECD's pillars.[9]

The OECD persevered, presenting its pillars as a reform the world welcomed. The 2023 UN General Assembly vote offered a powerful rejoinder to the OECD's claims of inclusivity. As it must, the OECD speaks for its members, not for the world. It is no slight to say that its Inclusive Framework serves as a vehicle for members' interests rather than non-members' aspirations. For the OECD to have done otherwise would betray both the letter and the spirit of its 1960 charter.

For their part, in voting against Nigeria's counterproposal at the United Nations, the OECD members sent an equally clear message. They endorsed

[8] Shu-Yi Oei, *World Tax Policy in the World Tax Polity? An Event History Analysis of OECD/G20 BEPS Inclusive Framework Membership*, 47 Yale J. Int'l L. 199, 203 (2022) ("Inclusion in the contemporaneous European Union tax haven listing process . . . and on a related watch list (commonly referred to as the EU greylist)—which were designed to shame countries with harmful tax regimes into correcting problematic features, under threat of sanctions—was significantly correlated with an increased hazard of joining the Inclusive Framework.").

[9] Mary Izuaka, *Why Nigeria Didn't Sign OECD Minimum Corporate Tax Deal – FIRS*, Premium Times (Nov. 30, 2021), https://www.premiumtimesng.com/news/more-news/498198-why-nigeria-didnt-sign-oecd-minimum-corporate-tax-deal-firs.html (citing "serious concerns that the pillars did not address negative revenue outcome for Nigeria and other developing countries").

their continued monopoly over global tax policymaking more than six decades after the Year of Africa, rejecting an African-led push for a more democratic alternative. An overwhelming majority of the world's population—if not GDP—threw their lot in with Nigeria. Global Jim Crow was not on the ballot, but by voting to approve a global tax convention, the UN General Assembly decisively rejected more than half a century of exclusion.

Against that backdrop of contestation, the splintering of the neoliberal consensus promised by President Trump's brash disregard for decades of solidarity with its OECD counterparts may present an opportunity. The pattern of US leadership and OECD ratification described in Chapter 4 undoubtedly holds less appeal for many than it once did. The United States may refuse to see that a global tax system that silences and impoverishes the Global South might not serve its own long-term interests. However, other states might decide that the time has come to choose a different path, unilaterally or collectively embracing one of the remedial options described below.

Jim Crow Stone

In 2021, the same year the OECD published its brochure, Dunoon, Scotland unveiled a brightly painted homage to one of the country's most beloved residents, appropriately designated Puffin Rock.[10] Until then, the landmark had been known as Jim Crow Stone, "[p]ainted black, with a large red mouth."[11] Although Jim Crow Stone had long been controversial, "[p]revious attempts to paint over the rock had been met with resistance, with some people taking it upon themselves to return it to its previous form whenever it was graffitied."[12]

Anti-Black racism can hardly be said to be a uniquely American phenomenon. However, as with Jim Crow Stone, American culture and history tend to shape its expression. Before the rise of Global Jim Crow and before that dreadful image could be painted on a boulder in Scotland, Jim Crow emerged in the United States, a minstrel character performing racist

[10] Gregor Young, *Dunoon's 'Jim Crow' Rock Gets a Fresh Coat of Paint with Puffin Redesign*, THE NATIONAL (Sept. 16, 2021), https://www.thenational.scot/news/19585517.dunoons-jim-crow-rock-gets-fresh-coat-paint-puffin-redesign/.

[11] Polly Bartlett, *Controversial 'Jim Crow Stone' Transformed into Proud Puffin Rock*, STV (Oct. 18, 2021), https://news.stv.tv/west-central/controversial-jim-crow-stone-transformed-into-proud-puffin-rock.

[12] *Id.*

stereotypes in blackface. It would eventually become a derogatory term for Black Americans, cruelly suggesting that offensive jokes told at their expense defined their humanity.

Violence and segregation represent the face of Jim Crow. An unequal allocation of resources formed its hidden heart. Tax laws produced widespread deprivation. Taxation would help make the separate lives of Black and white Americans, from the perspective of the Supreme Court, appear inherently equal.

As detailed in the Introduction, Camille Walsh traces the road from *Plessy v. Ferguson* to *Brown v. Board of Education* through contests over taxes. Even successful challenges had little impact on Black Americans' access to their own tax revenues. "[I]n the end the power to control taxation and distribute those resources proved to be the most effective tool for segregationists"[13] by granting them the power to guarantee that—whatever the constitution demanded—inequality would remain a persistent fact of Jim Crow life.

Black workers and property owners routinely paid taxes that funded white schools. Legal challenges to tax laws that denied equal access to education succeeded again and again but failed each time to secure the sought-after funding. A win in court might be met with delay, entirely new racist laws, or ignored. As a result, "though courts may have technically declared separate taxation principles invalid in many cases, the customary practice of racially labeling tax monies and diverting the bulk of tax funds overwhelmingly to all-white schools continued well into the twentieth century. . . ."[14] While not inherently so, tax law helped ensure that segregated schools in the United States would be universally unequal.

President Biden's 2021 boast that he would force a pair of majority-Black jurisdictions to pay for a once-in-a-generation investment in America's future bore only a passing resemblance to reality. But it nevertheless spoke to an important truth. Upending the logic of colonial self-sufficiency, Global Jim Crow has forced countries like Rwanda to finance spending in the OECD.

The UN General Assembly's vote may represent the beginning of the end of Global Jim Crow. However, the US experience with Jim Crow suggests little reason for optimism in the near term. A global tax convention might accomplish what neither three constitutional amendments nor waves of federal troops managed in the years following the Civil War. Votes in the General

[13] Camille Walsh, Racial Taxation: Schools, Segregation, and Taxpayer Citizenship, 1869–1973, at 53 (2018).
[14] *Id.* at 33.

Assembly might prove more effective than US court verdicts in ensuring that rights translate into resources. However, the families that sued for adequate schools for their children time and again might not be confident in such a happy outcome.

Statism, Cosmopolitanism, and Tax Subsidies

Countless would-be Josephs—confronted with ever-more-restrictive immigration laws and militarized borders—can attest that Global Jim Crow boasts its own forms of segregation and violence.[15] But tax law fuels Global Jim Crow. International tax rules once treated poor countries with generosity. But that generosity did not survive the decolonization of the African continent.

In 2018, shortly after enacting the world's first global minimum tax, President Trump derided Africa as a collection of "shithole countries."[16] He relied on their relative poverty and lack of access to education to explain why he preferred immigrants from countries like Norway. As was true for Black Americans under Jim Crow, Global Jim Crow ensures that tax revenues find their way to residence countries in Europe and North America and away from Africa—and poor countries everywhere—with the resulting inequality perversely serving as its own justification.

Both Jim Crow and its cross-border counterpart could be read to suggest that tax rules always favor those with wealth. The present of revenue from the United States to Europe in the wake of World War I that Chapter 2 documents unequivocally shows that notion to be false. Obviously, countries can be parochial even without much at stake. The decades France quixotically resisted adopting Greenwich Mean Time leave no doubt of that. Cosmopolitan international cooperation can never be taken for granted, even when nothing more than pride lies in the balance. However, states can

[15] Although the book focuses on domestic issues, in the tenth anniversary edition of *The New Jim Crow*, Michelle Alexander identifies those immigration restrictions as a key aspect of today's Jim Crow. *See* Michelle Alexander, The New Jim Crow: Mass Incarceration in the Age of Colorblindness xxxix (10th Anniversary ed. 2020) (drawing parallels between "mass incarceration" and "mass deportation").

[16] Alan Fram & Jonathan Lemire, *Trump: Why Allow Immigrants From 'Shithole Countries'?*, The Associated Press (Jan. 12, 2018), https://apnews.com/article/immigration-north-america-donald-trump-ap-top-news-international-news-fdda2ff0b877416c8ae1c1a77a3cc425. In rejecting a bipartisan immigration deal, then-President Trump "questioned . . . why the U.S. would accept more immigrants from Haiti and 'shithole countries' in Africa rather than places like Norway." *Id.*

also do the opposite. Sometimes, they do embrace costly concessions to bolster cross-border commerce.

As described in Chapter 2, in the wake of decolonization, the original system of international mail that allowed states selling stamps to keep whatever they collected created an imbalance. Far more mail entered than left newly independent states, so allowing the sending states to go on keeping all amounts paid for postage would have left poor states selling relatively little postage and delivering disproportionately more mail. To keep mail flowing, states pocketing more than their share agreed to pay "terminal dues" to those receiving too little. Wealthy states could have balked—pulling out of the UN's Universal Postal Union as President Trump threatened to in 2019[17]—but instead embraced cosmopolitan cooperation.

More than half a century of Global Jim Crow makes it easy to believe that statism always prevails in the international tax context. The history of global tax policy reveals a different reality. The last century can be divided into roughly equal periods of cosmopolitan and statist approaches, with 1960, the Year of Africa, as the pivot point.

As World War I drew to a close, the United States recognized that Europe would soon need revenues to rebuild and pay its war debts. A skeptical US public made the prospect of direct involvement in that rebuilding effort unlikely. Even traditional subsidies would have been challenging politically. So US legislators offered Europe a tax subsidy. Long before the term "tax expenditure" would be popularized to describe the use of hidden spending to achieve what would be challenging to accomplish with ordinary spending, a tax credit subsidized US businesses and investors operating in postwar Europe.

Contrasted with the period of Global Jim Crow that would follow, such generosity can be difficult to believe. Cosmopolitanism suggests "that principles of distributive justice should be applied universally: to all human beings across the entire globe."[18] Most tax experts today would reject such an expansive vision out of hand, insisting that "[o]utside the framework of the state, in

[17] The postage stamp faced a crisis when President Trump threatened to withdraw from the Universal Postal Union—"a United Nations body that has regulated international mail service for more than a century"—over a dispute related to its favorable treatment of developing countries (including China). Nick Cumming-Bruce, *U.S. Will Remain in Postal Treaty After Emergency Talks*, N.Y. Times (Sept. 25, 2019), https://www.nytimes.com/2019/09/25/business/universal-postal-union-withdraw.html.

[18] Tsilly Dagan, International Tax Policy: Between Competition and Cooperation 190 (2017).

the absence of such unique relations and, in particular, of the state's coercive power, justice does not impose distributive duties. . . ."[19]

Statists argue that whatever obligations we owe to those at home should not apply to allies—much less adversaries—abroad. From critics like Seligman, the cosmopolitan credit faced skepticism. After the US adopted it, he and a handful of experts at the League of Nations endorsed the double tax treaties that would eventually form the backbone of Global Jim Crow. But that statist impulse only blossomed into enduring inequality and exclusion decades later.

Shielding Multinationals from Taxation

In addition to being stingy with poor countries, treaties help to reduce multinationals' overall tax burdens. Credits require proof of payment of an overseas tax to qualify for a tax break. Before treaties, multinationals had to do what global minimum taxes purport to require. They had to pay tax somewhere to claim a credit. As President Kennedy warned, treaties empower multinationals to engage in coding to avoid paying taxes anywhere.[20] In a sense, global minimum taxes recreate a pre-treaty world with one key difference. They give residence countries the primary tax claim.

Anti-Black racism can inspire choices that can be difficult to understand. Heather McGhee offers it as an explanation for policy decisions that harm everyone.[21] Ira Katznelson tells the story of decades of generous support for programs benefiting working-class white Americans curdling when such programs could no longer legally exclude Black Americans.[22] Katznelson argues that this made public support for generosity impossible, even though most beneficiaries would continue to be white.

[19] *Id.* at 191.

[20] *See* Bret Wells & Cym Lowell, *Tax Base Erosion and Homeless Income: Collection at Source is the Linchpin*, 65 Tax L. Rev. 535, 578 (2012).

[21] In the waning days of Jim Crow, when American cities and towns faced court orders to integrate their swimming pools, many simply chose to have no pools at all. In a spiteful display of power, white Americans simply refused to share, preferring deprivation for all to integrating public pools. Heather McGhee, The Sum of Us: What Racism Costs Everyone and How We Can Prosper Together 25 (2022) ("In Montgomery, Alabama, the Oak Park pool was the grandest one for miles. . . . The [city] council decided to drain the pool rather than share it with their black neighbors. . . . [W]hite children cried as city contractors poured dirt into the pool, paved it over, and seeded it with grass. . . .").

[22] Ira Katznelson, When Affirmative Action Was White: An Untold History of Racial Inequality in Twentieth-Century America (2005).

Despite headwinds from experts and multinationals, the tax credit remained the cornerstone of US international taxation for half a century. Indeed, the credit's supremacy lasted until its largesse had to be shared with newly independent nations in Africa. When the OECD's charter was signed, Jim Crow's days were numbered. But thanks to the OECD and its treaties, the era of Global Jim Crow had just begun.

Global Taxation at a Crossroads

During the colonial era, metropolitan powers faced few obstacles to keeping tax burdens—and spending on services—low in the colonies. As empire's fortunes faded and new African governments embraced their power to spend on education and other priorities, the cosmopolitan approach to international tax cooperation lost its appeal. Source taxation fell from favor once majority-Black states gained access to it.

At that moment—with African states emerging and the United Nations working toward the entrenchment of source taxation principles—the OECD was born. Simultaneously stripping newly independent states of their ability to shape international tax policy and access to urgently needed resources, the OECD launched the era of Global Jim Crow by reviving the fortunes of Seligman's dormant treaties. An all-white OECD would displace an inclusive United Nations without objection from the Soviets. Relatively robust source taxation—and the prospect of enhanced source taxation—gave way to new forms of residence taxation paired with decades of corporate tax abuse. Rather than fading into history, Jim Crow went global.

Racial Bias in Domestic Tax Policy

The unraveling of a half-century of cosmopolitanism occurred without fanfare. The transformation occurred so quietly that even most experts insist it never happened. The remaking would be so complete that the first chapter of modern global history would not be so much misunderstood as entirely forgotten.[23] Embracing an approach now dismissed as impossibly naive,

[23] *See, e.g.*, Thomas Rixen, *From Double Tax Avoidance to Tax Competition: Explaining the Institutional Trajectory of International Tax Governance*, Rev. Int'l. Pol. Econ. 197, 197 (2011) ("This is the story of the global tax regime, which carries the seeds of its own undermining, but

for four decades, US international tax policy treated our most implacable enemies more generously than it would newly independent African states.

Seligman's embrace of imperialism and Surrey's contempt for the United Nations quietly made Global Jim Crow possible. Mirroring the reality that Dorothy Brown highlights in her book, *The Whiteness of Wealth: How the Tax System Impoverishes Black Americans—And How We Can Fix It*, racism permeated international tax policy without ever openly declaring itself. Brown demonstrates how race and privilege shaped US tax policy. Brown shows how the US tax code "came to harm black families and their ability to build intergenerational wealth" and, in doing so, reveals "much about American tax policy, its history, and its intentions."[24] Brown does not focus on international tax policy, but her insights apply equally.

Among the features of US tax law Brown highlights as impacting Black Americans, the most surprising may be the "marriage bonus."[25] Because of the interaction of progressive rates and joint filing for married couples, Brown explains, the federal government offers a wedding present to many couples in the form of a smaller tax bill. Joint filing for married couples effectively allows a primary earner (most often the husband) to elect to have part of their income taxed at the lower rates applicable to a spouse with no earnings. (If this sounds familiar, it may be that the principle is no different than Bausch & Lomb's effort to have part of its income taxed at Ireland's low rate.)

The result is a tax system offering some married couples a tax break. Not all married couples that benefit from the marriage bonus get one quite as big as one notable couple. Brown recounts how the wealthy, white Seaborns helped create the marriage bonus by fighting all the way to the Supreme Court. The Seaborns succeeded in producing lasting change where challenges to Jim Crow laws by Black taxpayers had failed. Thanks to a combination of privilege, good lawyering, and a favorable response from legislators, they saved a fortune.

Their victory would prove a significant loss for Brown's parents and many others. Congress's embracing the marriage bonus also created a "marriage penalty."[26] Brown's parents, as in most Black families, both worked. When

nonetheless persists to this day. When it was created in the 1920s and 1930s the sole purpose of the international tax regime was to mitigate international double taxation so that governments could benefit from international economic liberalization.").

[24] Dorothy A. Brown, The Whiteness of Wealth: How the Tax System Impoverishes Black Americans—And How We Can Fix It 30 (2021).
[25] *Id.* at 51.
[26] *Id.* at 44.

they married in 1956, Jim Crow's labor market discrimination gave them little choice. Both Browns had to enter the workforce to support themselves while raising their daughter. Because they both worked, neither could elect to have part of their incomes taxed at the lower rates applicable to a non-working spouse. Unlike the wealthy Seaborns, the Browns paid more tax when they got married rather than less.

Brown notes that the racial divide between those who received the marriage bonus and those who paid the marriage penalty did not grow from any single action by policymakers.

> Like most tax policies, it was the result of decisions made by many different actors, over many years. But when those actors—members of Congress, judges and clerks, lobbyists, and more—sit down to craft or modify tax law, they bring their conscious and unconscious biases to the table. And our most foundational tax laws were created at a time when racial bias wasn't just common—it was the norm and quite legal.[27]

No one choice gave rise to Global Jim Crow. No one person demanded the disenfranchisement of a continent. But Seligman, Surrey, and countless other experts and policymakers each played a role. And, of course, Global Jim Crow—like the marriage penalty—originated in a world of legal and ubiquitous racism.

The League of Nations embraced racial hierarchy.[28] On the surface, its treaties merely favored wealthy states at the expense of poor ones. Like its Mandate System, they delivered the substance of empire in a new form.

One could interpret American experts' and policymakers' support for the OECD and its treaties as pure statism. Concern for Citibank and General Motors, after all, more than anti-French bias led to the creation of one of the first US treaties.[29] Creating an exclusive forum for international economic

[27] *Id.* at 12.

[28] *See* Adom Getachew, Worldmaking After Empire: The Rise and Fall of Self-Determination 55 (2019) (describing the ways that through the League "Ethiopia and Liberia were not excluded from, but instead unequally integrated into, international society.").

[29] Madeline Woker, *Global Taxation Is a Mess. Here's How to Start Fixing It*, The Nation (Dec. 20, 2019), https://www.thenation.com/article/archive/france-tax-wine-tariff/ (explaining that the US–France treaty arose at a time when "the United States had a keen interest in using its new-found economic and political clout to promote rules that would maximize its own taxing rights and the interests of its corporations. . . . In 1933, the Franco-American tax dispute was still unresolved. Americans were pressuring the French into ratifying a treaty that the latter viewed as much too favorable to American interests. The French caved in only under the direct threat of reprisal taxes. . . .").

issues would silence the world's poorest countries. Excluding states far less likely to be concerned about the welfare of General Motors and Citibank than the OECD's wealthy members would help its multinationals. However, that does not preclude bias from playing a role. In truth, it would be remarkable if it played no role at all. When the OECD came into existence, Americans still drank from separate water fountains.

Racial Bias in Global Tax Policy

The story of Global Jim Crow features both too few villains and too many to be genuinely satisfying. Some of the most revered figures in US international tax policy helped breathe life into Global Jim Crow. Surrey's autobiography hints that bias may have influenced policy choices. His own words suggest that Surrey was no more immune to the Dunning School's ideas than any other American.[30]

Surrey developed the precursor of the global minimum tax and personally approved US involvement in the OECD's treaty work.[31] His steep ascent in policy circles began when he came to the attention of then-Senator John F. Kennedy. Surrey's "determined, virtually unassisted and eventually successful opposition to the 'tax-sparing' article in the 1959 tax treaty with Pakistan" caught Kennedy's eye.[32] Just as Seligman once disdained the tax credit's generosity, Surrey saw "mindless perversion" rather than pragmatism in "the idea that the United States should grant a 'foreign tax credit' for a host country tax which was never paid but rather forgiven."[33]

[30] In his autobiography, he questions the competence of a Haitian economist he managed to make a "personal enemy" of. STANLEY S. SURREY, A HALF-CENTURY WITH THE INTERNAL REVENUE CODE: THE MEMOIRS OF STANLEY S. SURREY 290 (Lawrence A. Zelenak & Ajay K. Mehrotra eds., 2022). Surrey was dismissive of the man despite the fact that he was the head of the Fiscal and Financial Branch of its Department of Economic and Social Affairs at the United Nations.

[31] Describing his involvement in the development of both the 1963 OECD model treaty and the UN version developed as an alternative Surrey's memoirs note that "the more astute negotiators from the developing countries saw the problem for them in using the OECD treaty. . . . The OECD Model, with its emphasis on reduction in source taxation . . . would mean for these developing countries a revenue loss without a compensating revenue gain." *Id.* at 284. Surrey acknowledges that "[i]n the Treasury I had agreed that the United States would be party to the development of that treaty." *Id.* He believed the problem did not lie in the unfairness of the treaty he helped create but in the fact that developing country tax representatives were inexperienced. *Id.*

[32] David R. Tillinghast, *The Contributions of Stanley S. Surrey to the International Aspects of Taxation*, 38 NAT'L TAX J. 267, 268 (1985).

[33] *Id.*

When Kennedy became president, he remembered Surrey. In what would "as far as international policy was concerned . . . be another of those fateful intersections"[34] Kennedy hired him.[35] Surrey was as knowledgeable as anyone on questions of global tax policy. He must have understood the threat that treaties—including the Swiss treaty that helped inspire his Subpart F—posed to US tax revenues. He recognized what treaties meant for developing countries but blamed poor countries for their poor treatment.[36] But none of that persuaded him to reject treaties.

Structural Change in Global Tax Policy

Global Jim Crow continues to punish vulnerable states and favor multinationals. The UN. General Assembly vote to create a global tax convention signals the potential for structural change that could challenge the OECD's policymaking dominance. But—when even self-styled progressive policymakers openly advocate for "America-first" tax policies[37]—the return of cosmopolitan global tax policy seems a long way off.

With the interruption of Reconstruction by white violence and fraud, it took a full century after the end of the Civil War for the United States to deliver on the promise of voting rights for Black Americans. More than half a century after that, Americans continue to experience profound differences in education and health based on the color of their skin.[38] Even if a return to

[34] *Id.* at 269.

[35] What might have happened had Boris Bittker been selected instead? Bittker, Surrey's rival, publicly challenged anti-Black bias. In 1973, Bittker published a book weighing the damage of a century of Jim Crow and calling for Black reparations. Toni Morrison, then working as an editor, published the first edition of the book and a later edition features a quote from Morrison declaring that Bittker's "work is more than significant—it is vital." *See* Boris I. Bittker, The Case for Black Reparations (2d ed. 2003). Reflecting on a question from a Black student at Yale Law School about reparations that Bittker mused that "our system of law is shaped by political and economic power and that it serves those who possess that power, not those who live their lives outside the mainstream of American society." *Id.* at 4.

[36] *See* Surrey, *supra* note 30, at 284 (insisting that the problem did not lie in the unfairness of the treaty but in the fact that developing country tax representatives "being new to international tax negotiations . . . lacked the experience and insight necessary to reshape the OECD Model in a direction to benefit them").

[37] *See* Kimberly Clausing, *Fixing our 'America Last' Tax Policy*, The Hill (Apr. 11, 2019), https://thehill.com/opinion/finance/438274-fixing-our-america-last-tax-policy/ ("On inauguration day, Trump promised the American people he would put 'America first.' . . . But policymakers looking for a better way to put 'America first' might usefully start with the tax code.").

[38] *See, e.g.*, Ibram X. Kendi, *What the Racial Data Show*, The Atlantic (Apr. 6, 2020), https://www.theatlantic.com/ideas/archive/2020/04/coronavirus-exposing-our-racial-divides/609526/ (highlighting the different COVID health outcomes experienced by different US racial and ethnic groups).

the United Nations accomplishes what Reconstruction did not—providing Nigeria with the simple dignity of a meaningful vote on the future of global tax policy—that would not be nearly enough to reverse the damage of decades of Global Jim Crow.

Creating a global tax policymaking structure that speaks for everyone would be no easier. Three alternative pathways suggest how it might deliver justice to those most impacted by Global Jim Crow. Reparations could replace the revenues lost by states to the rise of the OECD and its impact on source taxation. Prospectively enshrining the principle of enhanced source taxation—a modern version of "the old Cuban tax gambit"—would provide under-resourced states with access to critical revenues in the years to come. Finally, ending the era of the double tax treaty could return the world to the more innocent era that came before the OECD.

Reparations

A modest reparations framework might identify the historical revenues collected under Subpart F or one of its many variants and allocable to a particular source jurisdiction. Paying out those amounts would hardly put adversely impacted states in the position they would have been in had the OECD members not conspired to displace the United Nations. It would certainly not undo all that followed when a newly independent Ghana, for example, lost access to desperately needed tax revenues. However, such an approach would quantify one aspect of Global Jim Crow and deliver a small measure of justice.

Enhanced Source Taxation

A prospective solution delivering enhanced source taxation—terminal dues of a sort—could take different forms. The formula proposed in the United Nations in the 1950s represents one possibility. A new pro-source alternative like the digital services tax—or a variant of its UN-sponsored counterpart[39]—would be another.

[39] U.N. Tax Committee, *Tax Consequences of Digitalized Economy*, U.N., https://financing.desa.un.org/what-we-do/ECOSOC/tax-committee/thematic-areas/tax-consequences-digitalized-economy.

Any source-friendly arrangement would strengthen the capacity of poor states to pursue human rights and sustainable development goals. Karen Brown once suggested an "exemption from U.S. tax for specified income from African sources."[40] A Southern African Customs Union (SACU)-inspired withholding arrangement by residence states on behalf of source states could accomplish much the same ends. But none of those options would offer compensation for decades of Global Jim Crow.

Phasing Out the Tax Treaty

A third alternative imagines a world without double tax treaties. Their rise coincided with the start of an enduring decline in corporate tax revenues.[41] Perhaps without them the fortunes of the corporate tax would begin to recover. Whatever advantages those treaties do provide could be preserved by restricting their benefits to individual taxpayers of modest means (and perhaps to fledgling businesses).

Surrey fought tax breaks of all kinds. His tax expenditure budget hoped to eradicate them from the US Internal Revenue Code. So it is no surprise that he said no to the lost revenues from tax sparing. But, uncharacteristically, he said yes to treaties.

Belatedly heeding the warning offered by Chrysler's Swiss precursor of the double Irish Dutch sandwich would disproportionately benefit the poor countries that rely heavily on corporate tax revenues. Such a change would offer neither compensation for past harms nor a prospective thumb on the scale for poor countries. It would merely roll back decades of tax policies prioritizing residence jurisdictions.

Global Reconstruction

In *The Whiteness of Wealth*, Brown offers specific tax reforms targeting racial wealth disparities. Given the vast gulf between white and Black investment

[40] *See* Karen B. Brown, *Missing Africa: Should U.S. International Tax Rules Accommodate Investment in Developing Countries*, 23 U. Pa. J. Int'l Econ. L. 45, 48 (2002).

[41] *See* Press Release, U.S. Dep't of the Treasury, Testimony of Kimberly A. Clausing, Deputy Assistant Secretary, Tax Analysis, Before the Senate Committee on Finance (Mar. 25, 2021), https://home.treasury.gov/news/press-releases/jy0079 ("corporate taxes as a percentage of GDP have been trending downwards in the United States since the 1950s").

income, Brown suggests eliminating the tax code's generous treatment of capital gains. Such a change would ensure that Black wage income would not be taxed more heavily than overwhelmingly white investment income. In a new book, Brown explores possible paths toward reparations.

Delivering either at the federal level would require legislative—and quite possibly constitutional—action difficult to imagine in today's polarized political environment. None of the three global tax policy reforms described above would be any easier to achieve. Even the most ambitious vision of reconstituted United Nations tax governance would struggle to realize such ambitions.

In Seligman's time, favoring Europe with source-friendly tax credits proved controversial. Imagining a global tax governance architecture sufficiently robust to embrace a full-throated cosmopolitan vision seems virtually impossible today. It would be naive to imagine that the OECD and the multinationals its policies have long shielded will embrace such a shift. The United States could unilaterally embrace a cosmopolitan vision of international taxation as it did a century ago. But it appears unlikely that it will.

Fortunately, the future of global tax policy no longer hinges on decisions made by today's Surreys and Seligmans. Despite widespread skepticism within the United States, some cities and institutions have already paid reparations while others have announced an intention to do so.[42] Whatever happens at the United Nations—and to the OECD—the countries that once joined forces with the United States to create Global Jim Crow could now act independently. Certainly, no country needs to adhere to the principles of Global Jim Crow out of solidarity with a United States uninterested in preserving its long-standing relationships.

As the Trump administration moves away from multilateralism, potentially signaling the end of the World Trade Organization,[43] what might that mean for the future of the unofficial World Tax Organization? OECD members in Europe and elsewhere may unilaterally pursue a different approach vis-à-vis countries of the Global South. Or the European Union

[42] *See* Adeel Hassan, *Where Reparations Stand in the U.S.*, N.Y. Times (Jul. 1, 2023), https://www.nytimes.com/2023/07/01/us/black-americans-reparations.html ("Georgetown said that it would raise about $400,000 a year to benefit descendants of the 272 enslaved people who were sold to aid the college nearly 200 years ago. A few cities and towns have taken action. In 2021, the Chicago suburb of Evanston, Ill., became the first to pass a measure, providing up to $25,000 to direct descendants of its Black residents who were harmed by discriminatory housing policies between 1919 and 1969.").

[43] Keith Bradsher, *'The W.T.O. Is Toast.' What Happens to Global Trade Now*, N.Y. Times (Feb. 14, 2025), https://www.nytimes.com/2025/02/14/business/trump-tariffs-world-trade-organization.html.

could collectively carve a new role for itself in the global arena by embracing a more cosmopolitan approach toward the Global South, much as the United States once did for Europe.

Any individual OECD member could calculate how much its treaties and enhanced residence taxes have taken from other, less fortunate states. They could merely document and acknowledge the theft. Or they could work to make their victims whole. States could withdraw from or renegotiate treaties according to a strongly pro-source vision.[44] Likewise, their domestic laws could be rewritten to favor source prospectively. Any state can choose to unlearn the lessons of Global Jim Crow.

Jim Crow may lie safely in our rearview mirror, but America-first policies and racist memes have not lost their appeal. A century ago, the United States prioritized the revenue needs of former enemies and allies. Today, it leads the charge *against* democratic global tax policymaking.[45] Other states face the choice of rejecting Global Jim Crow or clinging to it.

Conclusion

Nigeria's success in the General Assembly represents a critical victory. But history offers no shortage of warnings that such victories do not always deliver fundamental change. Reconstruction ran aground amid Northern apathy despite the ratification of the Thirteenth, Fourteenth, and Fifteenth Amendments. In *The New Jim Crow*, Michelle Alexander shows how, in an

[44] A 2015 tax treaty between Kenya and the Netherlands fell apart due "to the unlikelihood that the DTA would be ratified by Kenya." *Netherlands MOF Announces Withdrawal of Bill Ratifying DTA With Kenya*, Bloomberg Tax (May 25, 2022), https://www.bloomberglaw.com/product/tax/bloombergtaxnews/daily-tax-report-international/XEFJLJFG000000. Kenyan civil groups argued that the agreement had been used to facilitate tax avoidance, depriving Kenya of much-needed tax revenue. *See* Larissa Hoaglund, *Netherlands Withdraws Bill to Ratify Tax Treaty with Kenya*, Tax Notes (May 20, 2022), https://www.taxnotes.com/tax-notes-today-global/treaties/netherlands-withdraws-bill-ratify-tax-treaty-kenya/2022/05/20/7dht4; Annagabriella Colón, *Civil Groups File Petition to Annul 10 Kenyan Tax Treaties*, Tax Notes (Sept. 28, 2020), https://www.taxnotes.com/tax-notes-today-global/treaties/civil-groups-file-petition-annul-10-kenyan-tax-treaties/2020/09/28/2d02g. This decision reflects how states can take independent action to address inequitable tax arrangements and promote a more source-friendly tax policy.

[45] It is not surprising that the Trump administration has resisted the UN process, but it has also refused to participate in the OECD process, drawing praise from Republicans and conservative organizations like the Cato Institute and eliciting pledges from top OECD officials to continue their work on the pillars. Tim Shaw, *OECD to 'Keep Working' With US Despite Trump's Rejection of Tax Deal*, Thomson Reuters (Jan. 23, 2025), https://tax.thomsonreuters.com/news/oecd-to-keep-working-with-us-despite-trumps-rejection-of-tax-deal/.

age of color-blindness, Black Americans have been silenced through mass incarceration and related state laws that, once again, deprive millions of the right to vote.

The United Nations has demanded change before. As recounted in Chapter 6, in 1974, the General Assembly approved a Declaration for the Establishment of a New International Economic Order (NIEO).[46] It represented a forceful challenge to "the vestiges of alien and colonial domination, foreign occupation, racial discrimination, apartheid and neo-colonialism"[47] demanding "[p]referential and non-reciprocal treatment for developing countries"[48] but in the face of skepticism from wealthy states it had little practical impact. Although it continues to serve as a rallying cry against the economic inequality that defines the postcolonial era, the neoliberal Washington Consensus would overshadow it.[49]

Those suffering the deprivation of Global Jim Crow may appreciate the vindication offered by a UN resolution. But—like a court's judgment or a constitutional amendment—it represents no substitute for adequate schools. A practical man, Joseph would no doubt be wary of such promises. The answer to Global Jim Crow lies in preventing wealthy countries from creating and enforcing unjust tax rules like Subpart F and global minimum taxes. It seems unlikely that the United Nations would ever be able to enforce such a prohibition.

Still, the new beginning the NIEO demanded could be launched with a global tax convention.[50] Or it could come from individual states choosing a different path. It must not end with nothing more than a moral victory. Any state could embrace the NIEO's demands by enacting pro-source tax policies

[46] G.A. Res. 3201 (S-VI), Declaration on the Establishment of a New International Economic Order (May 1, 1974).

[47] *Id.* at ¶ 1 (emphasis omitted).

[48] *Id.* at ¶ 4(n).

[49] The NIEO's call for equality eventually would be drowned out by the oil and debt crises of the 1980s. It would ultimately be overshadowed by the Washington Consensus, a suite of policies promoted by multilateral institutions like the International Monetary Fund and the World Bank and by the United States. In contrast to the NIEO's call for "[f]ull and effective participation on the basis of equality of all countries in solving of world economic problems in the common interest of all countries . . . devoting particular attention to the adoption of special measures in favour of the least developed, land-locked and island developing countries," the Washington Consensus emphasized market solutions. *Id.* at ¶ 4(c).

[50] Thanks to Global Jim Crow's disenfranchisement and the misconception that global tax policy could not generate gifts of revenue without the existence of a world government, tax remained safely shielded from the NIEO's demands. *See* Getachew, *supra* note 28, at 165 ("In 'the absence of a world government' that could institute international taxation, the NIEO relied on these indirect mechanisms to create a welfare world in which international trade was structured by interdependence rather than dependence.").

or, at a minimum, rejecting facially neutral rules biased in favor of residence. A new UN tax convention could do the same.

While it might do many things, the UN tax convention must do one. Global tax policy needs a rule of recognition to know when an innovation represents a step forward or a step back.[51] Thanks to Global Jim Crow, the world lacked the political leadership the United Nations might have provided and instead relied on ideas borrowed from the past. Notions such as tax harmonization—once embraced as an expression of the virtues of imperialism—became talismans invoked to defend an unjust status quo. The future must deliver real accountability to ensure that billions of people matter more than billionaires.

[51] Ivan Ozai makes this point, emphasizing that "justice requires not only improving inclusivity of less affluent countries in the current tax policy decision-making (political justice) but also establishing a normative framework that provides them with differentiated taxing rights based on their different levels of development (distributive justice)." Ivan Ozai, *Two Accounts of International Tax Justice*, 33 Can. J.L. & Jurisprudence 317, 338 (2020).

Conclusion

Fear of a Black Planet

Black Disenfranchisement

In his book, *The Black Tax*, Andrew Kahrl tells a story about power. He recounts techniques used to weaponize state and local taxes against Black Americans in the century following the Civil War. Most importantly, he explains how "Black disenfranchisement gave local administrators free rein to treat Black people less as constituents to serve and more as subjects to exploit and punish."[1] The creation of the OECD replicated that feat at the global level. And nobody noticed.

Katznelson begins the conclusion of *When Affirmative Action Was White* with a hypothetical. He invites readers to "[i]magine two countries, one the richest in the world, the other amongst its most destitute. Then suppose that a global program of foreign aid transferred well over $100 billion, but to the rich nation, not the poor. This is exactly what happened in the United States as a result of the cumulative impact of the most important domestic policies of the 1930s and 1940s."[2] His illustration, meant to capture the impact of the exclusion of Black Americans from the New Deal in Jim Crow America, offers an eerie echo of an early skeptic of double tax treaties who compared them to "unrestricted grants in aid" from developing countries to developed ones.[3]

[1] Andrew W. Kahrl, The Black Tax: 150 Years of Theft, Exploitation, and Dispossession in America 7 (2024). Kahrl explains that Black Americans suffered at the hands of state and local authorities because "the federal judiciary and Congress were making it impossible for victims of discriminatory taxation at the hands of state and local governments to pursue justice at the federal level." *Id.* at 30–31.

[2] Ira Katznelson, When Affirmative Action Was White: An Untold History of Racial Inequality in Twentieth-Century America 142 (2005).

[3] Charles R. Irish, *International Double Taxation Agreements and Income Taxation at Source*, 23 Int'l & Comp. L.Q. 292, 292 (1974) ("In a developing country, nobody would propose unrestricted grants in aid from his country to a developed one. And yet, the practical effect of the present network of double taxation agreements between developed and developing countries is to shift substantial amounts of income tax revenues to which developing countries have a strong legitimate and equitable claim from their treasuries to those of developed countries.").

Racial Capitalism and International Tax Law. Steven A. Dean, Oxford University Press. © Steven A. Dean 2025.
DOI: 10.1093/9780197526002.003.0009

Acemoglu and Robinson's central insight in *Why Nations Fail* hinges on the power of "pivotal institutional developments during critical junctures" to shape states' fates.[4] Global Jim Crow tells just such a story of disenfranchisement and reverse foreign aid denying scores of newly sovereign countries the opportunity to flourish. Such stories can be, but are not always, stories of racial capitalism.

Racial Capitalism

Racial capitalism highlights how bias can put a thumb on the scale at crucial moments. As with Global Jim Crow, it grants private actors an opportunity to profit at the expense of marginalized communities. The rise of the OECD and its treaties allowed precisely that, shielding multinationals from taxes in the Global South. Discord over concepts like permanent establishment yielded to a new consensus favoring residence over source taxation. That new consensus just happened to prevent newly independent African states "from taxing American enterprises as heavily as they wished."[5]

Thanks to such twists and turns, international economic law has not been reliably cosmopolitan or statist over the past century. Tax exemplifies that inconsistency. For decades, source taxation flourished. Only later did treaties rise. The generosity of the tax credit came effortlessly when neither racism nor corporate interests interfered. When both forces buoyed them, treaties that had languished for decades became a shield multinationals could wield against Black sovereignty.

Had the New International Economic Order (NIEO) promised to pad corporate bottom lines, its fate might have been different. The heavy burden of cosmopolitanism alone might not have doomed it. Had it—like terminal dues—advanced rather than threatened corporate interests, the NIEO might have remade international economic law.

[4] Daron Acemoglu and James A. Robinson, Why Nations Fail: The Origins of Power, Prosperity, and Poverty 433 (2012). The authors reject an array of theories based on geography (living in nice climates tends to make people lazy), culture (Africans cling to superstitions and resist technology), and ignorance (rulers need smarter economists to tell them how to become rich). They instead suggest rulers simply tend to preserve their privilege even if that requires foregoing opportunities for prosperity.

[5] Nikki J. Teo, The United Nations in Global Tax Coordination: Hidden History and Politics 29 (2023) (quoting a League representative describing the Latin American reaction when US experts like Mitchell Caroll pushed for treaties with Latin America in the 1940s).

Viewed from this vantage point, the postage stamp ceases to be a hopeful outlier. Juxtaposed against the demise of the old Cuban tax gambit and the NIEO, it no longer offers much reassurance. Had the United Nations not been displaced, fair play might have prevailed. However, a more just global taxation system would hardly have been inevitable.

In an era in which racial bias remained both legal and pervasive, the United States worried about source taxation. Those fears crystallized at the prospect of Black states' participation in one-country, one-vote global tax policymaking at the United Nations. The backlash might have taken a different shape, but it undoubtedly would have come. The NIEO, in part a rebellion against an already entrenched reality of Global Jim Crow, evoked just such a response from the Global North.

But it remains possible that, if not for the OECD, the old Cuban tax gambit might have been embraced via the United Nations alongside terminal dues at the behest of the Global South on a rising cosmopolitan tide. Instead, powerful private actors exploited bias to boost their profit margins. Multinationals leveraged fear to secure protections from taxation and regulation, illustrating the power of racial capitalism.[6]

Paternalism

Decades later, wealthy states bemoan the devastation caused by the double Irish Dutch sandwich, willfully ignorant of their role in its creation. It is fitting that the League's treaties would serve as the lynchpin of Global Jim Crow. Although the United States never joined, President Woodrow Wilson played a key role in shaping the League of Nations. His "rhetoric on self-determination as the guiding principle of U.S. war aims, politics, and international relations" may have been "understood . . . as a repudiation of empire, especially because their author was the powerful president of a nation forged in an anticolonial revolution."[7] But, for Wilson, "the right to immediate self-determination ended at the color line; only whiteness conferred full rights of self-determination."[8]

[6] The world's first bilateral investment treaty was born on the eve of the Year of Africa. Today, even wealthy states advocate for reform of the investor-state dispute resolution mechanism, chafing at the same regulatory constraints they once eagerly embraced during a long-forgotten racial panic.

[7] Sam Erman, Almost Citizens: Puerto Rico, the U.S. Constitution, and Empire 147 (2018).

[8] *Id.* (considering Wilson's treatment of US territories, particularly Puerto Rico).

Wilson and other key figures, such as Seligman and Surrey, make it easy to imagine how human frailties could warp international economic law. As detailed in the Introduction, Seligman lent his scholarly prestige to the Dunning School. Chapter 3 relates how Surrey made plain his contempt for the Haitian economist leading UN tax efforts (and for his entire Secretariat). Seligman and Surrey may have been equally great, but inevitably, they were uniquely flawed.

That does not suggest that Seligman or Surrey held views less savory than their contemporaries. For all its wealth and privilege, Seligman's family found itself confronted by the ugliness of anti-Semitism.[9] Perhaps because of his own experiences, while many of Seligman's Columbia University colleagues embraced scientific racism, Seligman has acquired a reputation as an "anti-racialist."[10] Despite his ties to the Dunning School, Seligman's record suggests he did not share its conviction that Black people represented a distinct—inferior—species. Seligman wrote sympathetically to W.E.B. Du Bois after a race massacre, hosted Booker T. Washington at his home, and was "the first president of the National League on Urban Conditions Among Negroes."[11]

[9] *See* Luca Fiorito & Tiziana Foresti, *Economists and Eugenics: Progressive Era Racism and Its (Jewish) Discontents*, *in* HAYEK: A COLLABORATIVE BIOGRAPHY PART X: EUGENICS, CULTURAL EVOLUTION, AND THE FATAL CONCEIT 317, 323 (Robert Leeson ed., 2017); Adrian Muster, The First Step to the International Tax Regime in 1923 – Edwin R. A. Seligman, New York, and the League of Nations: Ramblings in New York City and Lake Placid, Streifzüge in Heidelberg, Flâneries à Genève et à Paris 147 (Nov. 30, 2023) (Working Paper, University of Zurich) (Zurich Open Repository and Archive).

[10] Fiorito & Foresti, *supra* note 9, at 323.

[11] Fiorito & Foresti, *supra* note 9, at 327. How could Seligman have been an "anti-racialist" while supervising a core Dunning School work? Rejecting scientific racism is hardly inconsistent with espousing racist convictions. Booker T. Washington viewed slavery as a cleansing fire, regrettable but necessary to free people of African heritage of their ancestral burden of savagery. He believed that his own civilization justified the extravagant cruelty of the enslavement of millions of men, women, and children. Seligman's contradictions reflect the nation's drift toward the "reconciliation" that ultimately made the North—despite its military victory—amenable to the South's vision of Black disenfranchisement and oppression. Blight explains that:

> Three overall visions of Civil War memory collided and combined over time: one, the reconciliationist vision, which took root in the process of dealing with the dead from so many battlefields, prisons, and hospitals and developed in many ways earlier than the history of Reconstruction has allowed us to believe; two, the white supremacist vision, which took many forms early, including terror and violence, locked arms with reconciliationists of many kinds, and by the turn of the century delivered the country a segregated memory of its Civil War on Southern terms; and three, the emancipationist vision, embodied in African Americans' complex remembrance of their own freedom, in the politics of radical Reconstruction, and in conceptions of the war as the reinvention of the republic and the liberation of blacks to citizenship and Constitutional equality.
>
> DAVID W. BLIGHT, RACE AND REUNION: THE CIVIL WAR IN AMERICAN MEMORY 2 (2003).

Notably for his time, Seligman's paternalism allowed for the possibility that Black people might be civilized. But they could not, his behavior implies, be trusted to find their way to that brighter future on their own. Surrey's autobiography suggests he shared a similar outlook. Surrey's own words demonstrate a certainty that even if the Global South could be saved it could not save itself.

Half a century apart, Seligman and Surrey passionately opposed the US tax credit and tax sparing. T.S. Adams represents as close to a champion of cosmopolitanism as we encountered in the preceding chapters. Yet even his credit quietly embraces a softer version of the same paternalism. Only income taxes like those imposed by the United States generate a credit. No other tax system, however legitimate, secures access to the credit's generous subsidy. Surrey rejected tax sparing, but he might have welcomed it as a simple acknowledgment that not all taxes need look just like those preferred in North America and Europe.

Adams may have championed a generous tax credit, but his ideals did not dampen his resolve to fight for US corporate interests. After creating the credit, he served as one of the US experts pressuring France to accept the treaty, elevating US corporate bottom lines over the well-being of a former—and future—wartime ally. That treaty, of course, represented an effort to mollify Citibank and General Motors in the dramatic episode described in Chapter 3. Adams's traveling companion, Mitchell Carroll, quipped "that France 'was trying to collect enough to cover the World War I debt to the United States!' "[12]

The success of Adams and Carroll in securing protections for US corporations against France long proved the exception to the rule. It—along with the Swiss treaty that Kennedy would learn to stop worrying about and perhaps even to love—would represent one of a relative handful in existence before the 1950s. If the determined efforts of such experts fighting for powerful corporate interests but enjoying so little success for so long represents the central mystery of modern global tax history, the dramatic turn in the tax treaty's fortunes only deepens it.

Learning to Stop Worrying and Love the Tax Treaty

Drawn partly by the fear of a Black planet to the Chateau de la Muette in 1956, as described in Chapter 3, North America and Europe fatefully

[12] Madeline Woker, *Global Taxation Is a Mess. Here's How to Start Fixing It*, The Nation (Dec. 20, 2019), https://www.thenation.com/article/archive/france-tax-wine-tariff.

discovered shared purpose in opposing source taxation. Decades of rivalry eclipsed by the danger presented by an increasingly sovereign Africa, whatever misgivings might have dampened their embrace of the permanent establishment threshold would be forgotten. Even when confronted with the consequences of their folly, Cold War imperatives made articulating doubts about tax treaties—as Kennedy briefly did before the Cuban Missile Crisis—risky.

When the United Nations offered to lend technical support to the OECD's forerunner, it could not have appreciated the irony of doing so. Since 2001, it has become increasingly obvious that an excess of expertise has become global tax governance's biggest weakness as well as its greatest strength. Its proposals offer complexity in place of common sense, delivering results that transparently favor insiders.

At long last, states the OECD has disenfranchised have loudly registered their disapproval. The future will be no kinder to the OECD. The United Nations has projected that by 2050, a quarter of the world's population will be African.

At some point, Global Jim Crow may end. What will follow remains unclear. Today, the OECD has an opportunity to reciprocate long-ago UN generosity by welcoming its contributions. The pair of organizations exhibit neatly complementary imperfections that invite collaboration. The OECD's technical sophistication and ruthless efficiency could perfectly balance the UN's ponderously democratic process.

Suppose its members embrace rather than resist the one-country, one-vote future its creation deferred. If they did, the OECD could draw on a deep well of expertise to ensure that the global tax system deserves the title. So far, the OECD has chosen not to do either.[13]

The US experience with Jim Crow—and, dispiritingly, the New Jim Crow—offers reason for both hope and pessimism. Neither federal troops nor constitutional amendments could inoculate minds against the Dunning School's grotesque lies or prevent a century of disenfranchisement. The United States has undoubtedly made great strides since Jim Crow's end. But, as Chapter 7's discussion of Dorothy Brown's work highlights, entrenched racism remains a profound problem in tax as elsewhere.

[13] The organization did once hire me as an expert consultant. But not for its work on global tax policy.

Integrating states long left on the outside of global tax governance would be complicated even if the world were suddenly cleansed of bias and greed. The challenge becomes even more complex as conflicting US drives to boost its tax revenues and shield its multinationals converge in a dismissal of the Global South's priorities. Even during the lost cosmopolitan era of global tax policy, Adams did not stand idly by while France taxed Citibank and General Motors. Today's progressive policymakers openly reject "America Last" thinking.[14] Behind closed doors, its most influential fret about the threat posed by an unspecified jungle.

The demands of the Cold War once loosened Jim Crow's grip. Ironically, they did the opposite for Global Jim Crow, clearing a path for its rise. While Soviet pressure pushed Kennedy on civil rights domestically, Global Jim Crow took shape without similar criticism. In 1963, Kennedy sought a foreign policy victory by calling for affirmative intervention on civil rights after years of relying on reactive public relations efforts. That same year, the first OECD model treaty became a reality with Surrey's support. Ironically, just two years earlier, Kennedy and Surrey had railed against the danger posed by the Swiss treaty in a message to Congress.

Mary Dudziak details the reaction to events in the United States by delegates at the May 1963 meetings in Addis Ababa that gave birth to the African Union. Horrified, the world bore witness to images of firehoses and police dogs being turned on peaceful protesters in Alabama.[15] The following month, Kennedy gave a televised speech calling for civil rights legislation, which was "distributed to all American diplomatic posts with directions from the secretary of state and the president himself regarding how the speech should be used, and why this issue was of such importance."[16]

Unfortunately, the embrace of the OECD's treaties made no such headlines. Nor did the displacement of the United Nations. Rangel would not challenge the OECD's blacklist for many years (and when he did, his efforts would be profoundly misunderstood). The OECD's brochure would not be published until just a few years ago. Its coercive practices would not be documented until 2022.[17]

[14] Kimberly Clausing, *Fixing Our 'America Last' Tax Policy*, THE HILL (Apr. 11, 2019, 9:00 AM), https://thehill.com/opinion/finance/438274-fixing-our-america-last-tax-policy.

[15] MARY L. DUDZIAK, COLD WAR CIVIL RIGHTS: RACE AND THE IMAGE OF AMERICAN DEMOCRACY 171–78 (2011).

[16] *Id.* at 181.

[17] Shu-Yi Oei, *World Tax Policy in the World Tax Polity? An Event History Analysis of OECD/G20 BEPS Inclusive Framework Membership*, 47 YALE J. INT'L L. 199, 216–20 (2022).

Having neutralized any meaningful resistance from the United Nations, the United States quietly extended its tax reach with Subpart F. The Soviets had made their indifference to the tax treatment of multinationals plain. Unlike Jim Crow, Global Jim Crow did not threaten to upset a precarious Cold War balance. The OECD dutifully began its long-standing practice of laundering America-first policies.

In the years to come, it will become increasingly difficult for an organization responsible for the future of global tax policy to avoid scrutiny. The fact that it has never had a majority-Black member will complicate its work. The emergence of organizations like the African Tax Administration Forum and the advocacy of the Africa Group will ensure that alternative perspectives will be available even when the OECD might prefer otherwise. Their insights will challenge the notion that an exclusive organization can work for the benefit of all.

The bias at the heart of Global Jim Crow might one day vanish. But yielding privilege tends to be a messy affair. Shu Yi Oei's coercion-based pathways—described in Chapter 7—feature blacklists and sanctions rather than firehoses and police dogs but are brutal nonetheless. Such heavy-handed tactics may succeed in the short term, but their use broadcasts weakness rather than strength.

The rejection of multilateralism by the United States under the Trump administration creates both risks and opportunities. In acknowledgment of its past, Europe could embrace a cosmopolitan future by welcoming the United Nations' role in global tax policy. Or it could double down its hand-me-down blacklists.

Beyond Bias

As I completed work on this book, my mother inherited a photo album. In it, she found a picture of her with a friend in 1964. Both women beamed while wearing the crisp white uniform of a student nurse. Many decades later, those two friends still visit—and even travel with—one another. But that friend did not attend mom and dad's wedding the year after the photo was taken.

Mom explained that her friend's family, farmers living in rural Ohio, refused to allow her to join the ceremony. It would be impossible to know why, but I choose to believe they did it out of love. Mom remembered that, a century after the end of the Civil War, the family feared violence from the Ku

Klux Klan. Allowing a daughter to attend an entirely legal interracial wedding ceremony could threaten the whole family's safety.

I do not suggest that such behavior deserves to be celebrated. But it can at least be understood. Compassion rather than animus may have motivated any of the men described in the preceding pages. Seligman thought it appropriate that he should be the leader of an organization dedicated to Black uplift. Surrey thought himself the voice the Global South needed.

Ultimately, actions matter more than motivations. Within my own family, my grandfather's death seemed to open the door to a reconciliation. I remember laughing amiably with my grandmother near the end of her life. I do not know whether grief prompted a change of heart or loss freed her from the bonds of someone else's hatred. Or perhaps she simply found a place in her heart for me despite continued misgivings.

A return to the days before Global Jim Crow—when poor countries had enough say in global tax policy to prevent the rise of treaties—would require an equally remarkable reversal by wealthy states. Today, with neoliberalism collapsing in the face of a rising tide of nationalism, such a world seems to be receding into the distance.[18] Nevertheless, our leaders may find the courage to deliver just such an unlikely result. Until then, it must be enough to acknowledge the lasting harm caused by Global Jim Crow.

I still wonder at the unbelievable wildlife featured in the pages of my *Ranger Ricks*. Even compared to the improbable facts about the natural world that I learned from it, the lesson the magazine itself embodies seems hard to credit. Had fear of a Black planet not breathed life into an all-white policymaking forum, the story of terminal dues in Chapter 2 suggests that global tax justice might now be more than a slogan.

Preserving the pro-source orientation of the first decades of global tax policy could have altered the economic trajectory of a continent. But for the rise of the OECD as a World Tax Organization in all but name, an inclusive United Nations would have secured the taxing rights of dozens of newly sovereign states. Fairness would have prevailed.

That cozy alternative history overlooks a critical fact. The narrative of the postage stamp's triumph obscures the reality that both cosmopolitan

[18] *See generally* Gary Gerstle, The Rise and Fall of the Neoliberal Order: America and the World in the Free Market Era (2022). Gerstle argues that dislocations from 9/11 to the Great Recession robbed the United States of an optimism that anchored its embrace of open markets and pushed the world into a new era of global competition.

terminal dues and statist treaties serve corporate interests. In that respect they are not so different.

Long before digital overtook legacy media, limiting the taxing power of source jurisdictions with concepts like the permanent establishment threshold padded corporate bottom lines. The global media giants of the pre-digital era—their dominance fueled by sales of print publications—would have seen no contradiction in favoring both the terminal dues the Global South fought for and the tax treaties it fought against. After all, such a pairing subsidizes sales to the developing world while shielding the ensuing profits from taxation there.

Small Things

Having grown up in a country orders of magnitude smaller than the United States, it seems evident that little does not mean insignificant. Windows, stamps, coconuts, contact lenses, and, of course, balloons all have compelling stories to tell. Seemingly trivial details like the fact that double tax treaties barely existed before the OECD offer easily overlooked but critical clues. Paying attention to them makes it possible to unravel the mystery at the heart of our global tax system's failures.

The story of Global Jim Crow will be hard for many—particularly tax experts—to believe. But it is certainly no less likely than the conventional account. Wei Cui dissects that narrative, dismissing what has been presented as a global consensus cemented during the interwar period as "more reflective of the endeavours of a few individuals than it was of national policies, let alone international negotiations."[19]

If no such international accord had been reached after World War I, then the rise of the OECD to its status as a de facto World Tax Organization requires a different explanation. Global Jim Crow offers one. Having pressed for treaties for decades, Cui's handful of experts suddenly found themselves pushing on an open door.

[19] Wei Cui, *False Idols in the Early History of International Taxation, in* 12 Studies in the History of Tax Law (Peter Harris & Dominic de Cogan eds., forthcoming 2025) ("The idea that nations reached some explicit or implicit international agreement in the early 20th century—used to frame recent policy debates as a matter of countries revisiting that century-old agreement—has little historical basis. The inaccuracy of many oft-repeated claims about international taxation's early history is remarkable in itself. Even more significant is the fact that such claims are often made or implied by those who should know that they are inaccurate.").

The International Chamber of Commerce formally petitioned the OECD's predecessor to take up the cause of the treaty. It did just that and the results came quickly. Dismissed by a UK official as a "gathering of international chatterers for the purpose of chattering"[20] at its inception, experts from this exclusive group of wealthy nations quickly found consensus on issues like permanent establishment.

Identifying the precise role race played in catalyzing that long-elusive agreement will be no easier than imagining how the US civil rights movement might have unfolded had the Soviets taken as little interest in it as they did in global tax justice. But it would be truly remarkable if North American and European businessmen's fears of increased taxation following the arrival of independence for African colonies had no effect at all. Whatever its cause, discerning the impact of the preemptive disenfranchisement of the seventeen African states that earned their sovereignty in the year the OECD charter was signed requires no great effort. It transformed billions of Black people from constituents into subjects.

[20] Martin Hearson, "*A Gathering of International Chatterers for the Purpose of Chattering.*" *The Birth of the OECD's Committee on Fiscal Affairs* (July 4, 2018), https://martinhearson.net/2018/07/04/a-gathering-of-international-chatterers-for-the-purpose-of-chattering-the-birth-of-the-oecds-committee-on-fiscal-affairs.

Index

For the benefit of digital users, indexed terms that span two pages (e.g., 52–53) may, on occasion, appear on only one of those pages.

Abbott, Kenneth W., 31n.59, 31–32n.63, 32n.64, 33n.69
accountability in global tax policy, 143–44
Acemoglu, Daron, 113–14, 113n.1, 115, 163, 163n.4
Adams, T.S., 51, 52, 166
Africa
  colonization of, 56n.46
  decolonization and, 62, 67–68
  global tax policy, in, 19
  single-party rule in, 62n.4
  See also newly independent African states; *specific country*
Africa Group, 143, 169
African Tax Administration Forum, 169
aggressive tax shelters, 131n.69
Agyemang, Emma, 143n.3
Alexander, Michelle, 8, 8n.13, 148n.15, 159
"America First" tax policies, 108–11, 155
American Economics Association, 126
Angelou. Maya, 1
Anghie, Antony, 74n.59
Apple, 81–82, 86, 88–89
"arm's length" standard, 21n.8, 23n.18, 25n.26, 26–27, 27n.37, 29–30n.52, 33–34
asymmetric cooperation, 120–21
Ault, Hugh J., 31–32n.63
Avi-Yonah, Reuven S., 24n.22, 28–29n.47, 29n.49, 30, 30n.54, 38n.93, 41, 82n.13, 90n.45, 91n.51, 117n.13
"Axis of Tax Avoidance," 98, 137

Bahamas
  double tax treaties (DTAs) and, 129
  National Wildlife Federation, 44
  sanctions threatened by OECD on, 135, 137
Bailey, Thomas, 66
Baldwin, Richard E., 116n.10
balloons, 1–2
barter system, 90n.47
Base Erosion and Profit Shifting (BEPS), 81n.6
Bausch & Lomb, 25, 33–34, 81–82, 86
benefits principle, 20–21n.4
Benoit, Pierre, 69n.42
BEPS 1.0, 40
Berkenfeld, Bradley, 134–35, 136
Bermuda as alleged tax haven, 89, 90
beyond Global Jim Crow
  generally, 18–19, 159–61
  accountability in global tax policy, 143–44
  double tax treaties (DTAs), phasing out, 157
  enhanced source taxation, 156–57
  global reconstruction, 157–59
  Inclusive Framework, 144–46
  reparations, 156
  shielding multinationals from taxation, 150–51
  structural change in global tax policy, 155–56
  tax subsidies, 148–50
Biden, Joe
  corporate tax abuse, on, 108–9
  corporate tax rates, on, 93n.57
  tax havens, on, 106–7
  tax policy and, 89, 147
bilateral investment treaties, 164n.6
bilateral tax treaties. *See* double tax treaties (DTAs)
Bittker, Boris, 155n.35
Black Codes, 64, 65, 144
Blight, David W., 165n.11
Bono, 102–3
Botswana, SACU and, 120–21
Bretton Woods Conference, 37
Brooks, Kim, 19n.51, 143n.5
Brown, Dorothy, 152–53, 157–58, 167
Brown, Karen B., 19n.50, 157
Brown v. Board of Education (1954), 7, 7n.12
Bruins, G.W.J., 47, 53–54n.34
Burgess, John W., 15, 15n.33
Bush, George W.
  OECD and, 99, 100
  segregation, on, 102n.26

Calabresi, Guido, 118–19, 118n.16, 120
Canada, OECD and, 9, 69
Carroll, Mitchell, 72n.47, 72n.48, 72n.49, 166
cattle ranchers, transaction costs and, 114
Cayman Islands as alleged tax haven, 89, 90
Center for Freedom and Prosperity, 98, 99
Center for Tax Policy and Administration (OECD), 134
Central Bank of the Bahamas, 79
Charles III, 1, 2, 9
Charter of Economic Rights and Duties of States, 138
check-the-box rules, 18, 83–85, 85n.26, 91
China, Universal Postal Union and, 159n.45
Chorvat, Elizabeth, 21n.6
Christian-Christensen, Donna, 101–3
Christians, Allison, 19n.48
Chrysler, 86–87, 157
Citibank, 71–72, 72n.47, 153–54, 166
civil rights, 168, 172
Civil War, 15, 63
Clausing, Kimberly, 29n.49, 30, 41, 108–9, 155n.37
Clinton, Bill
  generally, 99
  check-the-box rules and, 18, 83–84, 85
  tax policy and, 83n.14
Coase, Ronald, 114, 114n.6, 115, 118, 133
Cold War, 77, 87, 114, 168
Colombia, international mail and, 44–45
colonialism
  Africa, colonization of, 56n.46
  decline of, 55
  Global Jim Crow and, 9
  Jim Crow in US and, 5n.7, 7
  symmetry and, 125–27
Columbia University, 9, 15
Common Reporting Standards (CRS), 38, 40, 42
comparative tax advantage, 131–32n.70, 134–35
"compliance pull," 36
Congressional Black Caucus
  FATCA and, 18, 136, 136n.85
  OECD and, 18, 98, 100–3, 107, 109, 110, 111, 135–36, 143
  tax harmonization and, 135–36
contesting Global Jim Crow
  generally, 18, 95–96
  "America First" tax policies and, 108–11
  Congressional Black Caucus, impact of, 98, 100–3, 107, 109, 110, 111, 143
  corporate tax abuse, misdirected blame for, 105–7
  "gangster" comment and, 97
  income tax and, 96
  racial bias and, 97, 103, 107–8
  right-wing think tanks, impact of, 98, 99–100
  sanctions threatened by OECD, 96, 98
  tax havens, 103–5
  "Treasure Islands" and, 103–5
  2000 US election, impact of, 98–99
corporate transfer pricing, 23–25, 23n.18, 25n.26
Corporate Transparency Act, 42n.105
Corrections Corporation of America, 8n.13
cosmopolitanism, 45, 50–52, 61, 149–50
Coulter, E. Merton, 66n.21
criminal street gangs, 97n.8
cross-border tax subsidy. *See* foreign tax credit
Cuban Missile Crisis, 87, 166–67
"Cuban taxation gambit," 76–77, 79, 138n.93, 141, 156, 164
Cui, Wei, 171, 171n.19

Dagan, Tsilly, 128n.50
Davis, William Watson, 15
Declaration on the Granting of Independence to Colonial Countries and Peoples, 12
decolonization
  Africa and, 62, 67–68
  Ghana, in, 67–68
  global tax policy and, 74
  Kenya, in, 67–68
  Nigeria, in, 67–68
Delaware corporations, check-the-box rules and, 84
digital services taxes, 82–83, 92–93
domestic tax policy, racial bias in, 151–54
Donohoe, Paschal, 107n.52
"double Irish Dutch sandwich," 81–82, 88–89, 94, 104, 106, 157, 164
double taxation, problem of, 47–48
double tax treaties (DTAs). *See also specific country*
  Dunning School and, 15
  foreign tax credit versus, 48–49
  Global Jim Crow and, 164
  League of Nations and, 48–49, 55–56, 58–59, 60–61, 80, 80n.4, 150
  "Mexico draft," 72n.49, 72–73
  multinationals and, 153–54
  newly independent African states and, 76
  OECD and, 11–12, 80
  OECD Model Tax Treaty, 72–74
  phasing out, 157
  proliferation of, 22, 22n.13, 48

reasons for newly independent countries to embrace, 2–4, 3n.2
Seligman on, 51–52, 55
tax avoidance and, 4–5n.6
DTAs. *See* double tax treaties (DTAs)
Du Bois, W.E.B., 15, 66, 67, 165
Dudziak, Mary L., 75n.64, 114, 168
Dunning, William A., 16
Dunning School
double tax treaties (DTAs) and, 15
Jim Crow and, 9, 62, 63, 67–68, 167
Reconstruction and, 16, 17–18, 66–68, 77
tax policy and, 100
threat of Black governance and, 70

Einaudi, Luigi, 47
Elizabeth I, 113
Ellickson, Robert C., 118n.17, 120n.20
Emancipation Proclamation, 63
enhanced residence taxation, 80–81, 82–83
enhanced source taxation, 76–77, 156–57
Equal Protection Clause, 6–7
Eswatini, SACU and, 120–21
Ethiopia
League of Nations and, 140n.101
racist aspersions toward, 69
European Union
EU blacklist, 103, 103n.35
global tax policy and, 158–59
national tax laws in, 31n.62
sanctions threatened by, 103
extraterritorial tax information, 21, 27–28, 30, 34–35, 38, 42

FACTA. *See* Foreign Account Tax Compliance Act (FATCA)
"facts and circumstances" test, 29n.50
farmers, transaction costs and, 114
Fifteenth Amendment, 65, 144, 159
Floyd, George, 60
Foner, Eric, 67
Foreign Account Tax Compliance Act (FATCA)
generally, 80
Congressional Black Caucus and, 18, 136, 136n.85
"dragnet," 90n.48
extraterritorial tax information and, 42
Global Jim Crow and, 91
legitimacy and, 37–38, 37n.90
personal income taxation and, 89–91
qualified intermediaries and, 38
Subpart F compared, 90–91
Swiss banking scandal and, 40
transaction costs and, 119
foreign tax credit. *See also specific country*
generally, 70
challenges of, 50n.18
complexity of, 50
cosmopolitanism and, 50–52
criticism of, 12n.28, 51
double tax treaties (DTAs) versus, 48–49
economic effects of, 53
generosity of, 50–51, 52–53, 71n.46
mechanics of, 49–50
origins of, 12–13
statism and, 52
formulary apportionment, 21, 26n.35, 28–30, 34
Foucault, Michel, 30n.57
Fourteenth Amendment, 6–7, 67–68, 159
Framework Convention on International Tax Cooperation, 42–43
France
check-the-box rules and, 84
digital services tax, 16n.42
double tax treaties (DTAs) and, 70, 74
source taxation and, 71–72
time zones and, 44, 56–57, 148–49
Franck, Thomas, 36–37

Gaigne, Carl, 116n.10
"gangster" comment, 97–98, 103, 142
Gardner, Leigh A., 11n.24, 11n.25, 62n.4, 137n.90
Geertz, Clifford, 18n.47
General Motors, 71–72, 72n.47, 153–54, 166
Germany
check-the-box rules and, 84
foreign tax credit and, 12, 13
Gerstle, Gary, 170n.18
Getachew, Adom, 14–15, 55n.39, 55n.42, 56n.47, 59n.55
Ghana
decolonization in, 67–68
OECD and, 78
tax revenues, loss of, 156
Gideon, Kenneth W., 34n.76
Gingrich, Newt, 83n.14
Giridharadas, Anand, 102n.30, 109
Global Intangible Low-Taxed Income (GILTI), 81, 81n.8, 82–83, 93
Global Jim Crow. *See also specific topic*
beyond Global Jim Crow (*see* beyond Global Jim Crow)
check-the-box rules and, 91
Cold War and, 168

Global Jim Crow (*cont.*)
colonialism and, 9
contesting Global Jim Crow (*see* contesting Global Jim Crow)
cruelty of, 13–16
double tax treaties (DTAs) and, 164
explanation for rise of OECD, as, 171–72
FATCA and, 91
Jim Crow in US compared, 68–69, 78, 163
newly independent African states, disproportionate harm to, 70
OECD and, 10, 11–12, 94, 139, 171–72
origins of (*see* origins of Global Jim Crow)
pyrrhic victory of (*see* pyrrhic victory of Global Jim Crow)
silencing of newly independent African states, 10, 16–19, 70
Subpart F and, 91, 169
US and (*see* United States, Global Jim Crow and)
global minimum tax, 81, 82, 93–94, 103, 137, 160
global reconstruction, 157–59
global tax policy
accountability in, 143–44
Africa in, 19
bureaucratic racism in, 107–8
cosmopolitanism and, 45, 50–52, 61, 149–50
crossroads, at, 151
"Cuban taxation gambit," 76–77, 79, 138n.93, 141, 156, 164
decolonization and, 74
EU and, 158–59
"fairy tale" of, 60–61
idealists and, 45
League of Nations and, 17, 45–46, 70
OECD and, 91–92, 158–59
OECD taking control of from UN, 11–12, 16, 41, 61, 62, 70, 78, 79, 91, 151
permanent establishment and, 48, 48n.11
racial bias in, 154–55
racism in, 61–63
reclaiming by UN, 143, 144, 145–46, 147–48, 159
residence versus source of income, 46, 47–48
statism and, 45, 52, 61, 149, 150
structural change in, 155–56
UN and, 2, 8, 70, 74
undemocratic governance structure of, 62–63
Google, 81–82, 82n.11, 86, 89
Gore, Al, 99–100
Graetz, Michael J., 19n.49, 47n.9, 54n.38, 74n.58, 77n.75, 90n.44, 117n.13
Grant, Ulysses S., 63, 64–65
Greenwich Mean Time, 44, 56–57, 148–49
Grinberg, Itai, 92, 92n.54
Gunnlaugsson, Sigmundur Davíđ, 137n.88, 137

Harding, Warren, 53n.30
"hard" law, 21–22n.9, 23n.15, 31–33, 32n.64, 33n.69
"hard" rules, 31–33
Harlan, John Marshall, 6n.10
Hart, H.L.A., 20–21, 20n.3, 22, 36n.83, 42–43
Hassan, Adel, 158n.42
Hathaway, Oona A., 31n.60
Hearson, Martin, 4–5n.6
Heinz, 86–87
Heritage Foundation, 98, 100
Hershey, Robert D., Jr., 103n.33
Hines, James, 110, 110n.65
homogeneity, costs of, 119–20
hyperglobalization, 13n.31

Immigration and Nationality Act of 1952, 33n.70
Immigration and Naturalization Service, 33n.70
immigration restrictions, 8, 8n.13
Inclusive Framework, 144–46
India
global tax policy and, 77
sovereignty in, 11–12
individual tax evasion, 25–26, 119n.18
Indonesia, sovereignty in, 11–12
Internal Revenue Code, 29n.51, 49, 157
Internal Revenue Service, 84, 134
International Chamber of Commerce, 9n.19, 172
international mail, 45–46, 57–58, 149, 149n.17
International Monetary Fund (IMF)
generally, 69
hyperglobalization and, 13n.31
input legitimacy and, 37
Ireland
alleged tax haven, as, 90–91
corporate tax rate in, 93n.57
corporate transfer pricing and, 23–25
"double Irish Dutch sandwich," 81–82, 88–89, 94, 104, 106, 157, 164
OECD and, 96
Irish, Charles R., 162n.3
IT&T, 86–87
Izuaka, Mary, 145n.9

Jacobs, Scott H., 118n.15
Jim Crow in US
generally, 60, 63
African diplomats and, 75
Black disenfranchisement in, 162–63
colonialism and, 5n.7, 7
Dunning School and, 9, 62, 63, 67–68, 167
Global Jim Crow compared, 68–69, 78, 163
overview of, 5–7
tax law and, 62, 147
Twentieth Century, in, 13–14, 150n.21
Jim Crow Stone, 146–47
Jogarajan, Sunita, 48n.12, 55n.43, 98n.13
Johnson, Andrew, 64
Jones, John F. Avery, 38–39n.95, 128n.51

Kahrl, Andrew W., 162n.1
Katznelson, Ira, 13–15, 150, 162
Kelly, Claire R., 36n.83
Kennedy, John F.
generally, 2–3, 69
civil rights and, 168
Cold War and, 114
double tax treaties (DTAs) and, 166–67
Jim Crow, on, 75
shielding multinationals from taxation, on, 150
Subpart F and, 18, 82, 87
Switzerland DTA and, 86, 87n.33, 87n.36, 87, 104, 134, 166
tax havens, on, 104, 106
tax policy and, 81–82, 86–87, 155
tax sparing and, 154
Kenya
decolonization in, 67–68
digital services taxes, 92–93
double tax treaties (DTAs) and, 159n.44
OECD and, 42, 145
Keynes, John Maynard, 69, 79
King, Martin Luther, Jr., 60, 61, 63, 70
Krugman, Paul, 116n.10
Ku Klux Klan, 64–65, 65n.15, 65n.17, 65n.18, 169–70
Kyoto Protocol to the United Nations Framework Convention on Climate Change, 132n.74
Kysar, Rebecca M., 16n.41, 52n.29, 61n.2, 80n.5

Langston, John Mercer, 65
Latin America
double tax treaties (DTAs) and, 74
source taxation and, 72
League of Nations
double tax treaties (DTAs) and, 48–49, 55–56, 58–59, 60–61, 80, 80n.4, 150
global tax policy and, 17, 45–46, 70
international stability as mission of, 53–54
legacy of tax rules, 89–90
Mandate System, 55, 56–57, 56n.48
racial bias in, 153
Lee, Robert E., 63
legitimacy
"compliance pull" and, 36
input legitimacy, 36–37
output legitimacy, 36–37
rules and, 36–38
standards and, 36–38
Lesotho, SACU and, 120–21
Liberia
alleged tax haven, as, 98, 110
blacklisting of, 142
contesting OECD actions on, 101, 102–3, 107, 110
flawed algorithms identifying, 96, 98, 101, 105–6, 107
League of Nations and, 140n.101
OECD and, 18, 134, 136
racist aspersions toward, 69
sanctions threatened by OECD on, 98, 135, 137
tax harmonization and, 134
tax haven, erroneously identified as, 98
Lincoln, Abraham, 63–64
Loeb, Isidore, 125n.40
"logic of improvement," 139–41
Lokken, Lawrence, 85n.27
Lunada Bay Boys, 97–98
Luxembourg as alleged tax haven, 90–91

marriage bonus, 152–53
marriage penalty, 152–53
Marshall Plan, 13n.30
McGhee, Heather, 14–15, 63n.6, 150
McIntyre, Michael J., 39n.98, 130n.62
Mckeown, Adam, 8
Melamed, Douglas, 118–19, 118n.16, 120
"Mexico draft," 72n.49, 72–73
Mobil Oil, 102, 136
Model Tax Information Exchange Agreement (US), 122n.31
Model Tax Treaty (OECD), 2–3, 3–4n.3, 72–74, 154n.31, 168
Moore, John, 6–7n.11
Morrison, Toni, 155n.35
Mugler, Johanna, 92n.54

multilateralism, 169
multinationals
double tax treaties (DTAs) and, 153–54
racial capitalism and, 164
shielding from taxation, 150–51, 168
source taxation and, 71–73

Namibia, SACU and, 120–21
National Association for the Advancement of Colored People (NAACP), 6–7
Netherlands
alleged tax haven, as, 90–91
"double Irish Dutch sandwich," 81–82, 88–89, 94, 104, 106, 157, 164
double tax treaties (DTAs) and, 159n.44
OECD and, 96
tax benefits scandal, 109–10n.60
New Deal, 13–14
New International Economic Order (NIEO), 61, 137–39, 160–61, 160n.49, 160n.50, 163–64
newly independent African states. *See also specific country*
demise of tax policy in, 91–94
disproportionate harm from Global Jim Crow, 70
double tax treaties (DTAs) and, 76
education in, 11
Euro-American distrust of, 75–76
resources, lack of, 62, 70
silencing of by Global Jim Crow, 10, 16–19, 70
single-party rule in, 62n.4
source taxation and, 70
tax treaties, reasons to embrace, 2–4
Nigeria
decolonization in, 67–68
digital services taxes, 92–93
global tax policy and, 155–56
OECD and, 42, 92–93, 144, 145–46, 159
Nkrumah, Kwame, 74–75, 78
nominal tax rate, 124n.37

Obama, Barack
criminal justice reform and, 8n.13
FATCA and, 102n.32
global minimum tax, on, 81
Oei, Shu-Yi, 145n.8, 169
Ogle, Vanessa, 58n.54, 104n.37
O'Hear, Michael M., 19n.49, 47n.9, 54n.38, 77n.75
Okanga, Okanga Ogbu, 143n.5
O'Neill, Paul, 99, 100, 101, 102–3, 103n.34
Organisation for Economic Co-operation and Development (OECD)
barter system, 90n.47
Base Erosion and Profit Shifting (BEPS), 81n.6
BEPS 1.0, 40
blacklist, 98, 99, 100–1, 102, 110, 111, 142, 143
Center for Tax Policy and Administration, 134
Common Reporting Standards (CRS), 38, 40, 42
Congressional Black Caucus, impact of, 18, 98, 100–3, 107, 109, 110, 111, 135–36, 143
corporate tax abuse, misdirected blame for, 105–7
digital services taxes and, 82–83, 92–93
disenfranchisement by, 167
double tax treaties (DTAs) and, 11–12, 80
establishment of, 9, 69
flawed algorithms identifying, 96, 98, 101, 105–6, 107
"gangster" comment, 97–98, 103, 142
Global Jim Crow and, 10, 11–12, 94, 139, 171–72
global minimum tax and, 81, 82, 93–94
global tax governance and, 107, 109
global tax policy and, 91–92, 158–59
hyperglobalization and, 13n.31
Inclusive Framework, 144–46
increasingly sophisticated rules, 42–43, 114–15
"Mexico draft," 72n.49, 72–73
Model Tax Treaty, 2–3, 3–4n.3, 72–74, 154n.31, 168
opportunity to overcome prior errors, 167
providing neither rules nor standards, 40–41
racial bias in, 97, 103, 107–8
right-wing think tanks, impact of, 98, 99–100
sanctions threatened by, 96, 98, 109, 135, 137
shielding US corporations from taxation and, 70
Subpart F compared, 144
tax harmonization and, 133, 134, 137–38
tax havens and, 98, 98n.11, 103–5
Tax Information Exchange Agreements (TIEAs) and, 130
tax rules, failure to craft, 20–21
"Treasure Islands" and, 103–5
2000 US election, impact of, 98–99
UN, taking control of global tax policy from, 11–12, 16, 41, 61, 62, 70, 78, 79, 91, 151

US and, 9
See also specific country
Organisation for European Economic Co-operation (OEEC), 79, 144
origins of Global Jim Crow, 2, 14–15, 17–18
Ortiz, Paul, 15n.38
Ozai, Ivan, 161n.51

Pahuja, Sundhya, 76n.67
Pakistan
double tax treaties (DTAs) and, 154
global tax policy and, 140–41
OECD and, 145
palm trees, 95–96, 105–6, 140
Panama Papers, 136–37
Paris Time, 44
Parks, Rosa, 109
paternalism, 164–66
permanent establishment, 48, 48n.11, 163, 171
personal income taxation, 89–91
Philippines, sovereignty in, 11–12
Pistor, Katharina, 82
Plessy v. Ferguson (1896), 5–6, 147
postage stamps, 44, 57–58, 149, 149n.17, 170–71
Procter & Gamble, 86–87
pyrrhic victory of Global Jim Crow
generally, 18, 113–14, 141
asymmetric cooperation and, 120–21
comparative tax advantage and, 134–35
homogeneity, costs of, 119–20
"logic of improvement" and, 139–41
symmetry and, 121–23, 125–28
tax harmonization and (*see* tax harmonization)
Tax Information Exchange Agreements (TIEAs) and, 121–23, 121–22n.28, 129–30
tax simplification and, 130–31
transaction costs and, 114–15, 117–19, 131–33

qualified domestic minimum top-up tax (QDMTT), 93
qualified intermediaries, 38–40

racial bias
beyond bias, 169–71
domestic tax policy, in, 151–54
global tax policy, in, 154–55
League of Nations, in, 153
OECD, in, 97, 103, 107–8
racial capitalism, 163–64
Racketeer Influenced and Corrupt Organization (RICO) Act, 97
Radical Reconstruction, 64–65
Rangel, Charles
FATCA and, 90–91, 135–36
OECD and, 101–2, 102n.32, 103, 168
Rangel Amendment, 101, 102
Rawson Square (Bahamas), 104, 104n.36
Raymond, Eric, 115–16n.8
recommendations. *See* beyond Global Jim Crow
Reconstruction
Black Codes and, 64, 65, 144
Dunning School and, 16, 17–18, 66–68, 77
end of, 65
failure of, 65–68, 147–48, 155–56
Johnson and, 64
Lincoln and, 63–64
myths of, 65–68
Radical Reconstruction, 64–65
Seligman and, 69
"Redeemers," 68–69
reparations, 156
residence
enhanced residence taxation, 80–81, 82–83
source of income versus, 46, 47–48
right-wing think tanks, 98, 99–100
Ring, Diane, 21–22n.9, 31n.62, 130n.64
Riou, Stephane, 116n.10
Rixen, Thomas, 4–5n.6
Robinson, James A., 113–14, 113n.1, 115, 163, 163n.4
Rodrik, Dani, 13n.31
Roin, Julie, 116n.9
Rosenberg, Emily, 53n.30, 53n.31
Rosenbloom, H, David, 89n.43
Rosenzweig, Adam H., 116n.11, 116–17n.12
rules
choosing between standards and, 33n.72
costs of, 32–33, 34
extraterritorial tax information and, 30, 34–35
"facts and circumstances" test, 29n.50
formulary apportionment and, 26n.35, 28–30, 34
"hard" rules, 31–33
international taxation, in, 33–35
legitimacy and, 36–38
OECD failure to craft, 20–21
OECD providing neither rules nor standards, 40–41
optimal precision and, 32
qualified intermediaries and, 38–40
rise of, 28–30, 41–42

rules (*cont.*)
secondary rules, 21, 36n.83
standards, efforts to replace, 17, 21–23
standards distinguished, 32
Rwanda
corporate taxes in, 93–94
OECD and, 147

sanctions threatened by OECD, 96, 98, 135, 137
Sarfo, Nana Ama, 11n.26
secondary rules, 21, 36n.83
Seligman, Edwin R.A.
generally, 68, 132, 135
anti-Semitism directed toward, 165
colonialism and, 126n.46
compassion and, 170
double tax treaties (DTAs), on, 51–52, 55, 128, 150, 151
Dunning School and, 9, 15, 15n.33, 16–17, 165
foreign tax credit, on, 12, 12n.28, 150, 158, 166
Global Jim Crow and, 63, 153
global tax policy and, 17, 139–40
imperialism and, 152
paternalism of, 166
racial bias and, 62, 165n.11
Reconstruction and, 69
residence versus source of income, 47
statist, as, 61
symmetry, on, 126–27
tax harmonization and, 115, 133, 141
Senegal, colonial taxes in, 125n.39
September 11 attacks, 142–43
Sharif, Nawaz, 136–37
Sharman, J.C., 99, 133n.76
Sheppard, Lee A., 102, 130n.62
Singapore as alleged tax haven, 90–91
Skrzycki, Cindy, 16, 83n.15
Slaughter, Anne Marie, 117n.14, 132, 133
slavery, 15
Slobodian, Quinn, 56n.44, 105n.42
Smith, John David, 15n.34
Smuts, Jan, 55n.39
Snidal, Duncan, 31n.59, 32n.64, 33n.69
"soft" law, 21–22n.9, 23n.15, 31–33, 32n.64, 33n.69
software development, 115–16n.8
source taxation
enhanced source taxation, 76–77, 156–57
multinationals and, 71–73
newly independent African states and, 70
opposition to, 163
permanent establishment versus, 166–67, 171
UN and, 76
South Africa
Apartheid in, 5, 135–36
Consolidated Revenue Fund, 120
Mobil Oil, divestiture of, 102, 136
Rangel Amendment and, 101, 102
SACU and, 120
Southern African Customs Union (SACU), 25, 120–21, 120–21n.23, 121n.25, 123, 131, 134, 157
Soviet Union
Cold War and, 77, 87, 114
global tax policy and, 77, 169
OECD and, 151
Sri Lanka, OECD and, 145
Stamp, Josiah, 47
standards
"arm's length" standard, 21n.8, 23n.18, 25n.26, 26–27, 27n.37, 29–30n.52, 33–34
choosing between rules and, 33n.72
costs of, 32–33
dominance of, 26–28
extraterritorial tax information and, 27–28
international taxation, in, 33–35
legitimacy and, 36–38
OECD providing neither rules nor standards, 40–41
optimal precision and, 32
qualified intermediaries and, 38–40
rules, efforts to replace with, 17, 21–23
rules distinguished, 32
"soft" standards, 31–33
State Department, 76–77
statism, 45, 52, 61, 149, 150
Stewart, Miranda, 98n.13
structural change in global tax policy, 155–56
Subpart F
generally, 18, 160
alternatives to, 137
corporate tax abuse and, 82, 104
demise of, 85
enhanced residence taxation and, 80–81, 82–83
FATCA compared, 90–91
Global Jim Crow and, 91, 169
global minimum tax and, 93–94
OECD compared, 144
reparations and, 156
tax havens and, 87–88
Summers, Lawrence, 99
Sunstein, Cass R., 22n.10, 34

Surrey, Stanley S.
compassion and, 170
corporate tax abuse, on, 81
double tax treaties (DTA), on, 3–4
foreign tax credit, on, 53n.32
Global Jim Crow and, 153
global minimum tax and, 154
global tax policy and, 140–41, 155
model tax treaty, 139
OECD and, 69–70, 69n.42
OECD Model Tax Treaty and, 154n.31, 168
paternalism of, 166
racial bias and, 154–55, 154n.30, 165
Switzerland DTA and, 86–87, 104, 104n.38
tax breaks, on, 157
tax harmonization and, 141
tax sparing, on, 62n.4, 154, 166
UN and, 139–40, 152
Switzerland
banking scandal, 40
double tax treaty (DTA) with, 18, 82, 86–88, 87n.33, 87n.36, 104, 134, 166
OECD and, 96
Sybblis, Martin W., 106n.44
symmetry, 121–23, 125–28

Táíwò, Olúfémi O., 4n.5
tax avoidance, 4–5n.6
tax base, 124nn.36–38
tax evasion, 25–26, 119n.18
tax harmonization
generally, 20–21, 141
Congressional Black Caucus and, 135–36
false appeal of, 123–25
limits of, 128–30
OECD and, 133, 134, 137–38
persistence of, 133–34
purported benefits of, 115–17
tax havens, 88–89, 103–5
Tax Information Exchange Agreements (TIEAs), 39n.99, 121–23, 121–22n.28, 129–30
Tax Justice Network, 98
tax law during Jim Crow, 62, 147
tax shelters, 131n.69
tax simplification, 130–31
tax sparing, 62n.4, 154, 166
tax subsidies, 148–50
Taylor, Charles, 142, 142n.1
Taylor, Keeanga-Yamahtta, 10n.20, 56n.45, 67n.24
Teo, Nikki, 54, 72n.49, 73n.53, 76
terminal dues, 57–58
Thirteenth Amendment, 63, 67–68, 159
Thurmond, Strom, 102n.26
time zones, 44, 56–57, 148–49
Titus, Afton, 18
transaction costs, 114–15, 117–19, 131–33
transfer pricing, 23–25, 23n.18, 25n.26
"Treasure Islands," 103–5
Truman, Harry, 13n.30
Trump, Donald
Africa, on, 148, 149n.18
global minimum tax and, 81, 103
multilateralism and, 169
OECD and, 146
Universal Postal Union and, 149, 149n.17
World Trade Organization and, 158–59
2000 US election, 98–99
Tzouvala, Ntina, 139–40, 140n.101

UBS, 134
United Kingdom
foreign tax credit in, 51, 51n.21
time zones and, 44
United Nations
Charter of Economic Rights and Duties of States, 138
Declaration on the Granting of Independence to Colonial Countries and Peoples, 12
Department of Economic and Social Affairs, 69n.42
enhanced source taxation and, 156
Fiscal Commission, 76
Framework Convention on International Tax Cooperation, 42–43
global tax policy and, 2, 8, 70, 74
Kyoto Protocol to the United Nations Framework Convention on Climate Change, 132n.74
New International Economic Order (NIEO), 61, 137–39, 160–61, 160n.49, 160n.50, 163–64
OECD taking control of global tax policy from, 11–12, 16, 41, 61, 62, 70, 78, 79, 91, 151
reclaiming global tax policy, 143, 144, 145–46, 147–48, 159
source taxation and, 76
tax convention, possibility of, 43, 145–46, 147–48, 155
United States, Global Jim Crow and
generally, 7–10
check-the-box rules, 18, 83–85, 85n.26, 91

United States, Global Jim Crow and (*cont.*)
  Foreign Account Tax Compliance Act (FATCA) (*see* Foreign Account Tax Compliance Act (FATCA))
  Subpart F (*see* Subpart F)
  tax havens, 88–89
Universal Postal Union, 57, 149, 149n.17, 159n.45

van Apeldoorn, Laurens, 19n.51
voting rights, 155–56

Walsh, Camille, 6n.9, 6–7, 147
Waris, Attiys, 140–41, 140n.102
Warren, Alvin C., Jr., 34n.74
Washington, Booker T., 68, 165, 165n.11
Weisbach, Dvid A., 108n.53
Wilkins, William J., 34n.76
Wilson, Woodrow, 53n.30, 55n.39, 164–65
Woker, Madeline, 72n.47, 72, 73n.52, 127n.47, 153n.29
World Bank, 13n.31, 69
World Tax Organization (unofficial), 158–59, 170
World Trade Organization, 158–59

Yellen, Janet, 106–7, 107n.52
Yin, George K., 84n.24
Young, Crawford, 125n.41, 126n.43

zoning, 132n.71